Strategic Synergy

Strategic Synergy
Second Edition

Edited by
Andrew Campbell and
Kathleen Sommers Luchs

INTERNATIONAL

THOMSON
BUSINESS PRESS

INTERNATIONAL THOMSON BUSINESS PRESS
I(T)P® An International Thomson Publishing Company

London • Bonn • Boston • Johannesburg • Madrid • Melbourne • Mexico City • New York • Paris
Singapore • Tokyo • Toronto • Albany, NY • Belmont, CA • Cincinnati, OH • Detroit, MI

Strategic Synergy

Copyright © 1998 Andrew Campbell and Kathleen Sommers Luchs

I(T)P® A division of International Thomson Publishing Inc.
The ITP logo is a trademark under licence

British Library Cataloguing-in-Publication Data
A catalogue record for this book is available from the British Library

First edition published by Butterworth-Heinemann Ltd 1992
Second edition published by International Thomson Business Press 1998

Typeset by J&L Composition Ltd, Filey, North Yorkshire
Printed in the UK by TJ International, Padstow, Cornwall

ISBN 1–86152–222–3

International Thomson Business Press
Berkshire House
168–173 High Holborn
London WC1V 7AA
UK

http://www.itbp.com

Contents

Introduction

Synergy is a topic that rightfully commands the attention of managers. The synergy equation $2 + 2 = 5$ signifies that a corporate portfolio of businesses is worth more than its businesses would be worth as stand-alone entities and synergy, therefore, provides a rationale for a diversified company. It frequently underpins corporate decisions on diversification and it is often a critical consideration in how diverse businesses should be managed. If managers are to make the most of this vital ingredient in the corporate portfolio, they need to understand the concept and they also need practical approaches to synergy issues. Over the last three decades, managers, consultants and academics have devoted much effort to understanding how the synergy equation works, testing and refining both the theory and practice of synergy. There is a wealth of literature relevant to synergy issues and even the briefest survey of the topic reveals just how broad and complex it is.

First of all, there are different kinds of interrelationships that a corporation can promote across its businesses to gain synergies. A company can integrate backwards or forwards, seeking benefits through controlling its major raw materials or channels of distribution. Another kind of benefit arises from economies of scale, where businesses share production facilities, research and development, or other activities or services, at lower cost than if each individual business engaged in these activities independently.

Or advantages can accrue if skills or know-how can be shared or transferred across businesses, providing new, or better, approaches in manufacturing, marketing, or any other area. Nestlé, for example, aims to capitalize on its skills in product promotion, advertising, and market research by sharing concepts and practices developed in one product or market across its globally spread businesses,[1] and Motorola has drawn on its technological expertise in radio communications and semiconductors in developing its business in cellular telephones.[2] Another kind of synergy is corporate branding, where separate businesses can capitalize on a corporate reputation for quality or on its luxury image. Corporate managers can also aim to co-ordinate the strategies of a group of businesses, aiming at broader advantages than any one business could achieve on its own. The concept of synergy encompasses all of these kinds of horizontal relationships.

The topic of synergy also covers different kinds of situations and circumstances. It is often a critical issue in mergers and acquisitions, since potential synergies frequently provide the rationale for such moves. Corporate decisions on divestments, on refocusing the corporate portfolio, or on restructuring, can be based on a consideration of synergy – or the lack of it. Achieving interrelationships can pose particular problems for multinational companies trying to co-ordinate manufacturing across different countries, or to transfer marketing concepts across different cultures. Often synergy is the aim of corporate alliances and joint ventures, where different organizations aim to learn from one another or to gain benefits from a partnership. The variety of the situations in which synergy is a relevant issue adds to the complexity of the topic.

The concept of synergy also leads into many other areas of management. Synergy requires integration or co-ordination among the different functions and businesses of the corporate portfolio, so organizational structure, co-ordinating mechanisms and corporate systems are all important issues. Achieving synergy means that different parts of the organization co-operate with and learn from one another, and therefore organizational learning, management processes and corporate culture contribute to the understanding of synergy.

The different types of synergy, the variety of situations in which synergy issues arise, and the broad range of subjects relevant to understanding synergy make it a daunting topic. There is substantial literature in each area, and a book on synergy could legitimately focus on any one of them. We have, therefore, sought to make the topic manageable by biasing this book of readings towards issues concerned with skill sharing and know-how transfer. We have not included work that focuses specifically on issues of vertical integration, or on corporate branding, or on economies of scale, nor have we aimed to draw a firm line between these areas. Much of the work on synergy covers some or all of the different types of linkages that are possible across businesses.

In this introduction we provide the reader with an overview of the subject of synergy. In the readings that follow we have been more selective. We have limited the selections to readings that discuss the horizontal relationships across businesses. We make only limited reference to the more general work in the fields of organizational design and behaviour. The book takes a broad scope, covering the different situations in which synergy issues arise. There are articles on acquisitions, diversification strategies, international and multinational companies, and alliances or joint ventures. Whilst we recognize that there are specific issues in managing synergies in each context, we gained insights from the literature in each of these areas.

This book of readings has developed from our own research on synergy at Ashridge Strategic Management Centre. Our field work has focused on how decentralized companies share skills across different businesses, and as part of this project we searched the management literature for work on synergy, testing our own findings against the assumptions and evidence in the literature.

We discovered that synergy became an important concept in corporate strategy over 30 years ago, when many companies embarked on diversification strategies. Igor Ansoff, whose work is included in Part I, first explained to managers during the 1960s how a strategy based on synergy could provide a 'common thread' for a diversifying company, allowing it to exploit its existing strengths in new areas. This basic concept has proved remarkably enduring. In the 1980s, Michael Porter, one of the pre-eminent authorities on strategy, argued that the management of interrelationships between businesses was the essence of corporate level strategy. In his view, without carefully managed interrelationships a diversified company is 'little more than a mutual fund'.[3] Porter encouraged managers to examine the value chains of different businesses to identify similar activities and potential interrelationships that could lead to competitive advantage. Rosabeth Moss Kanter, a Harvard professor and an authority on corporate innovation and change, has also argued that the only justification for a multibusiness company is the achievement of synergies.[4] Her work has focused on the type of corporate culture and values that encourage sharing across businesses.

In the 1990s, scholars have continued to explore the concept of synergy, further refining its theoretical basis and practical applications. The resource-based view of the firm has become increasingly important in the academic literature. In this view, firms are defined as bundles of tangible and intangible resources, including competencies, knowledge and skills.[5] The only viable strategy for a diversified company, according to this thinking, is based on building resources with competitive advantage and exploiting them across businesses. In the managerial literature, the idea that diversified companies must seek to exploit skills and know-how across its businesses also remains an important concept, albeit with a new emphasis. In 1990, Gary Hamel and C.K. Prahalad published a prize-winning article, 'The Core Competence of the Corporation', in which they argued that successful corporations build their strategy on exploiting technological or other competences across different businesses.[6] They urged managers to identify and nurture the critical skills and know-how in their businesses and to explore how these competences could be applied to different end products.[7]

Although the concept of synergy has been a fundamental idea in the academic and managerial literature over the last four decades, we also discovered that there is a worrying gap between theory and evidence where synergy is concerned. While many authorities argue that synergy – or the sharing of skills, activities, resources or competences – is the cornerstone of a successful corporate strategy, in practice there are notable examples of highly successful conglomerate companies that make no attempt to manage synergies among their businesses. In the 1960s companies such as Textron and ITT grew rapidly and profitably by acquiring business in many different industries and sectors, and their success owed little to horizontal relationships among their highly diverse holdings. More recently, companies such as Dover Corporation and KKR, the leveraged buy-out specialist, have successfully pursued no-synergy strategies.

These examples are more than the exceptions that prove the rule. There have been numerous studies on how companies diversify, and on the benefits companies gain from having businesses in related markets or technologies, but clear-cut evidence that synergy strategies result in superior performance remains elusive. Empirical investigations on these issues began with Richard Rumelt's landmark study on the association between diversification strategy and performance of large American corporations.[8] He categorized the diversification strategies of companies according to the extent to which their businesses were related, explaining in his subsequent work that, 'In making judgements as to the relatedness of business units, particular attention was paid to the absence or existence of shared facilities, common selling groups, and other tangible evidence of attempts to exploit common factors of production.'[9] Rumelt's original findings showed that related diversifiers, or companies whose businesses shared some common activity or skills, significantly outperformed companies that had unrelated businesses across different industries, providing powerful empirical evidence for the concept of synergy. This evidence, though, has proved to be ambiguous, with follow-up studies undermining the original message. Studies of companies in particular industries in the UK have shown unrelated diversifiers and single-business firms to be the best performers during certain periods. Also, the data on the relationship between diversification strategy and performance has been shown to be sensitive to market structures, the period studied, firm size and the way in which researchers have defined relatedness in categorizing companies.[10]

Other researchers have investigated the relationship between diversification and performance by looking at the specific issue of mergers and acquisitions, and the returns associated with different acquisition strategies. In a 1990 study, Anju Seth concluded that neither the empirical evidence nor economic theory supports the claim that related acquisitions outperform unrelated acquisitions; different types of mergers create value in different ways.[11]

The extensive but inconclusive literature on diversification and performance undermines the argument that creating interrelationships across businesses is the only approach to corporate strategy. Our own view is that synergy, or horizontal relationships across businesses, is one way of creating value in a corporate portfolio, but different approaches can also be successful. In *Corporate-Level Strategy*, by Michael Goold, Andrew Campbell and Marcus Alexander[12], the authors argue that in companies such as Dover Industries, Emerson Electric and Rio Tinto, it is the vertical relationships between the corporate centre and the businesses which underpin their effective corporate strategies. In these companies, the corporate centre improves the performance of the businesses through its influence on business-level appointments, through the budgetary process, or by providing important services to the businesses. A comprehensive view of corporate strategy includes such vertical relationships, as well as lateral relationships across different units. Synergy is not, therefore, an imperative for every diversified company.

When synergy is an appropriate strategy it can appear to be a Herculean challenge for managers. Whilst synergy has been a basic component in the thinking about diversification for at least four decades, it often seems to promise more than it delivers. When we first began investigating synergy we read widely in the case literature, trying to understand how companies have managed synergies. We discovered that it is much easier to find examples of failure than of success and that even a strong commitment to synergy and an array of co-ordinating mechanisms do not necessarily result in benefits. For example, case work on BOK Chemicals, a disguised European chemical company, explores the efforts of the company trying to exploit the opportunities for synergies in manufacturing, marketing and research among its various businesses. The company identified centres of excellence, set up co-ordinating committees and task forces, invested in cross-cultural training to improve co-operation and understanding, encouraged informal meetings among managers of different businesses, initiated key account projects, developed complex decision matrices and attempted to create co-ordinated strategies. The result was virtual civil war among the different businesses. The creation of a wide range of linkage mechanisms failed to result in any substantial synergies.[13]

A series of cases on Corning Glass Works International[14] also illustrates just how complex it can be to put in place the mechanisms, systems and procedures required to achieve synergy. Corning aimed for closer co-ordination and integration between its domestic organization and its overseas subsidiaries, especially in the areas of technology transfer, manufacturing, marketing and sales. Its solutions included international business managers, world boards, functional analogues (linking managers of the same functions in different locations) and decision grids to help define responsibilities. In 1980 Corning abandoned the matrix structure and the complex linkage mechanisms in which the company had invested almost a decade of organizational effort.

It is not just the case literature that highlights how hard it can be for companies to gain synergy benefits. Broader studies on diversification tell the same story. For example, in 1985 Michael Porter published a study showing the very poor success rate of American corporations in diversifying into new businesses, with the corporations in his sample divesting many of their acquisitions within a few years.[15] Mark Sirower's recent study of acquisitions, *The Synergy Trap*, examines how difficult it is for companies to gain benefits from synergy which match the acquisition premium they often pay.[16] Yet even as we accumulated more and more evidence on the high failure rate from our search in the management literature we found that this dismal record by no means led to rejection of the concept but to just the opposite: management authorities such as Michael Porter and Rosabeth Moss Kanter strongly reaffirm the importance of synergy. We therefore sought to understand why so many companies have failed in their efforts to gain synergies, and to search out what guidance is available. This book captures what we have learnt from the management literature. It is the book we would have liked to have read at the start of our research. We have also produced a guide for practitioners. 'Synergy: Why links between business units often fail and how to make them work', (Andrew Campbell & Michael Goold, Capstone 1998) gives practical guidance that we believe helps managers make better decisions.

The first challenge is understanding the concept itself. Just what can companies gain from creating horizontal relationships across different businesses? Part I focuses on this question, with the readings exploring both the meaning of synergy for multibusiness companies and some of the evidence on synergy effects. At this general and somewhat abstract level, the potential benefits of synergy are truly impressive and help to explain why the concept has been so robust. In theory, synergy permits companies to make more of their resources and skills, opening up seemingly countless opportunities. If skills developed in one area can be applied in new areas, then a company has the attractive option of entering new businesses – where it can acquire new skills as well, thus enabling it to expand into still other areas. Synergy means that a company can continually enlarge its scope if it has the creativity and determination to recognize the opportunities available. As profitable growth has always been a major objective of corporate management, it is no wonder that synergy is beguiling.

It is not, of course, as easy as it looks and we do not think that the authors we have included in Part I mislead managers on this score. They take pains to point out that it is easy to misidentify potential interrelationships across different businesses, and they provide examples of just how some companies have got it wrong. The consequences of misguided efforts to gain synergies can be catastrophic. Getting it wrong does not just mean that 2 + 2 fails to equal 5. It can mean that 2 + 2 equals less than 4: that the corporate portfolio is worth less than the sum of its parts. This sobering reality is emphasized in both the theoretical and empirical approaches to synergy that are included in Part I.

One of the reasons synergy proves elusive, in our view, is that managers fail to identify correctly the potential benefits. Benefits are too often defined in general and abstract terms, causing managers to seek benefits that either do not exist, or that they cannot capture. A key challenge for managers is to identify the specific opportunities available in their company. This can be a demanding task since it requires analysis at a sufficient level of detail to be meaningful in a particular situation. Consultants and academics have developed a number of frameworks which provide managers with specific guidance in this difficult area, and this work is the focus of Part II. The frameworks we have included cover different situations: identifying opportunities in existing portfolios of businesses, in acquisitions, and in multinationals. The common theme of the authors in Part II is that the analysis of opportunities has to be detailed, and that it must take into account not just the potential benefit but also the costs. The authors define stringent criteria for assessing synergy opportunities: such opportunities must confer significant competitive advantage, they must add value to either the unit or to the corporation as a whole, and the cost must not outweigh the potential benefits. This means that managers have to be highly selective in deciding which opportunities to pursue. Although these frameworks focus mainly on identifying common activities, they can also help managers identify critical skills common to several businesses, and the article by Andrew Campbell in Part III includes a framework for identifying such core skills.

The next step is to make it happen, and this is the focus of Part III. We found a puzzling discrepancy in the management literature on the issue of implementation. On the one hand, the tools and frameworks available encourage managers to identify specific opportunities. On the other hand, much of the advice on implementation focuses on gaining synergies in general. The authors of two of the selections in this part – Rosabeth Moss Kanter and Christopher Bartlett of Harvard, and Sumantra Ghoshal of INSEAD – argue that organizations successful at promoting synergies have similar characteristics and the challenge for managers is to create these kinds of organizations. For many corporations this means overcoming formidable barriers, and developing new management processes and even cultures that support many different kinds of interrelationships across all the units of a company.

While much of the work on implementing synergy strategies focuses on ways to encourage the sharing of skills or know-how within an organization, managers confront similar issues when they seek to gain benefits through alliances or joint ventures. Often, joint venture partners have different strategic expectations or 'do business' in different ways. It can be frustrating to work with a partner whose decision-making processes or leadership style vary from your own, whether or not that partner is another business within your corporation or an external supplier or even competitor. The reading by Joseph Badaracco on alliances examines how managers have to seek a fine balance between sharing critical knowledge and capabilities with a partner and protecting their own firm's strategic interests and position. Badaracco describes some of the changes in organizational culture and values which are necessary to benefit fully from alliance strategies.

Creating new organizational cultures is a long-term endeavour and such advice may not be very relevant to managers grappling with specific synergy issues in their organizations. Our own research findings, which we have included in Part III in the article by Andrew Campbell, suggest that the issue managers often confront is not how to gain synergies in general, but how to gain a specific benefit. Sometimes the benefit is so substantial and the barriers so considerable that fundamental organizational change is the only option. Frequently, though, substantial benefits can be gained within the existing organizational constraints and Campbell suggests a framework to help managers understand the variety of approaches available to them without radical organizational change.

Part IV, 'Synergy in practice', further explores the issue of implementation, a critical issue because the failure of synergy strategies is often attributed to managerial and organizational deficiencies. Much of the current management literature focuses on the potential of synergy. Managers are encouraged to recognize all the opportunities available and to create the management processes and organizational culture required to achieve benefits from interrelationships across business units. Michael Porter, for example, argues that, 'Successful international competitors in the future will be those who can seek out competitive advantages from global configuration/co-ordination anywhere in the value chain, and overcome the organizational barriers to exploiting them.'[17] In Porter's view, a new kind of organization – the 'horizontal organization' – has to evolve if companies are to reap advantages from interrelationships. Such an organizational form has the structures, systems and practices required to support complex linkages across business units.[18] Similarly, Christopher Bartlett and Sumantra Ghoshal, in their study of multinationals, conclude that many companies recognize the many available opportunities, but need to create the capabilities to exploit them:

The disappointments and failures some of those companies have encountered in their international operations were not due primarily to inappropriate strategic analysis, but to organizational deficiencies. Throughout our five-year study, we were continually impressed by the fact that most managers of worldwide companies recognized what they had to do to enhance their global competitiveness. The challenge was how to develop the organizational capacity to do it.[19]

The solution they advocate is the development of 'transnational' organizations which are capable of capturing the manifold opportunities available to globally spread companies. The transnational is an integrated network, where components, products, resources, people and information flow freely between the interdependent units. This type of organization is capable of exploiting all the strategic opportunities available. The transnational is able to realize scale economies through global scale operations, like global corporations; the transnational can diffuse knowledge and skills throughout its world-wide operations, like the international company; the transnational is responsive to national differences, like the multinational.

Horizontal or transnational organizations, though, are only theoretical possibilities – such organizations do not yet exist. What we do know is that many organizations find it difficult, or even impossible, to overcome organizational barriers. The readings in Part IV, therefore, focus on the experiences of particular companies in pursuing synergy benefits. These in-depth studies give us insights not only into the reasons why managers find synergy a compelling concept and how they go about identifying opportunities, but also into what does and does not work.

In the case literature we mostly found examples of companies that failed to gain advantages from interrelationships, even though some of them used a variety of mechanisms to encourage co-ordination and co-operation among business units. Robert Grant's study of diversification in the financial services industry in Part IV examines why this is so. His article focuses on a group of companies – including Sears, American Express and Citicorp – that tried to implement strategies based on a broad concept of synergy. These companies diversified outside their core business to provide customers with a range of financial services. Potentially, there were many synergy opportunities from cross-selling products, using common sales forces and exploiting common technology. Most of these benefits, though, proved impossible to capture. Culture clashes between commercial and investment bankers, and between insurance sales people and stockbrokers, as well as a host of other difficulties, resulted in disappointing performance and negative net benefits from diversification. Grant argues that the strategies of the companies he studied were based more on vision and ambition than on careful analysis of what the benefits actually were and how they could be achieved.

While we have found little evidence to support the theory that companies are capable of organizational transformation on a grand scale, there are examples of companies gaining benefits from interrelationships when their efforts are closely targeted. The other readings in Part IV focus on the detailed and even painstaking efforts of managers to gain benefits from specific opportunities. Varun Bery and Thomas A. Bowers describe the rebuilding of an alliance between an American firm and its Japanese partner. The authors show how the two firms overcame initial failures in co-operation by re-examining the strategic reasons for the alliance and reaching a general agreement on common objectives. Once this was accomplished, a working team could then focus on practical steps to achieve these goals, and determine the contributions of each firm. The authors observe that the two companies did not attempt to define every eventuality or even aim for a legal contract in the initial stages of the process. Rather, managers were given time to try different approaches and to revise their initial plans. While restructuring this alliance took time, the efforts paid off in a more focused alliance with specific competitive objectives which both companies supported.

The message that synergy benefits result from clear objectives and targeted efforts is also supported by Phillippe Haspeslagh and David Jemison in their work on acquisitions in Part IV. These authors examine how ICI integrated the smaller entrepreneurial businesses of Beatrice Chemicals into their much larger organization. This was a gradual process, requiring ICI to take a hands-off approach for a year after the acquisition, and then to move slowly in integrating the Beatrice businesses into ICI's existing businesses. The authors argue that this incremental approach allowed Beatrice managers time to adjust to the changes and to discover how they could contribute to ICI. While ICI had a clear idea of what it wanted to accomplish with the acquisition, it recognized that moving too quickly could undermine the benefits it sought from the Beatrice companies.

The final reading in Part IV is by Therese Flaherty of Harvard. She examines co-ordinating projects in companies with international manufacturing facilities. Many of the projects were relatively modest, undertaken by local managers because they were 'doable' and the benefits readily identified in terms of improved performance. In several cases the initial projects led on to more complex ones, as managers gained experience in working with other units and confidence in the benefits available from sharing skills and know-how. Flaherty argues in favour of this 'bottom-up' approach, pointing out that local managers have the most detailed understanding of their own operations, and can therefore best judge what types of sharing will work in their units.

The evidence available on how companies achieve benefits from inter-relationships suggests that success depends on detailed analysis of the opportunities and a carefully targeted, incremental approach to implementation. Synergy is a broad concept, encompassing many kinds of potential benefits, but in practice managers need to define the specific opportunities available within their own organizations.

REFERENCES

1 Quelch, J. and Hoff, E. J., 'Customizing Global Marketing', *Harvard Business Review*, May-June 1986, pp. 59–68.
2 *Financial Times*, 26 February 1990.
3 Porter, M. E., *Competitive Advantage*, Free Press, New York, 1985, pp. 318–19.
4 Kanter, R. Moss, *When Giants Learn to Dance*, Simon & Schuster, London, 1989, p. 100.
5 Barney, J. B., 'Firm Resources and Sustained Competitive Advantage', *Journal of Management*, vol. 17, no.1, 1991; Peteraf, M. A., 'The Cornerstones of Competitive Advantage: A Resource Based View', *Strategic Management Journal*, 1993 (14), pp. 179–91.
6 Prahalad, C. K. and Hamel, G., 'The Core Competence of the Corporation', *Harvard Business Review*, May-June 1990, pp. 79–91.
7 We have discussed the work on core competences in detail in *Core Competency-Based Strategy*, Andrew Campbell and Kathleen Sommers Luchs, International Thomson Business Press, London, 1997.
8 Rumelt, R. P., *Strategy, Structure, and Economic Performance*, Harvard Business School Press, Boston, 1974.
9 Rumelt, R. P., 'Diversification Strategy and Profitability', *Strategic Management Journal*, vol. 3, 1982, pp. 359–69.
10 Bettis, R. A., 'Performance Differences in Related and Unrelated Diversified Firms', *Strategic Management Journal*, vol. 2, 1981, pp. 379–93; Christensen, K. H. and Montgomery, C. A., 'Corporate Economic Performance: Diversification Strategy Versus Market Structure', *Strategic Management Journal*, vol. 2, 1981, pp. 327–3; Johnson, G. and Thomas, H., 'The Industry Context of Strategy, Structure and Performance: The UK Brewing Industry', *Strategic Management Journal*, vol. 8, 1987, pp. 343–61.
11 Seth, A., 'Value Creation in Acquisitions: A Re-examination of Performance Issues', *Strategic Management Journal*, vol. 11, 1990, pp. 99–115.
12 Goold, M., Campbell, A. and Alexander, M., *Corporate-Level Strategy*, John Wiley & Sons, Inc., New York, 1994.
13 Fortier, C., Cook, D. Smith, Khodjamirian, A. and de la Torre, J., 'BOK Finishes', in Davidson, W. H. and de la Torre, J., *Managing the Global Corporation: Case Studies in Strategy and Management*, McGraw-Hill inc., New York, 1989.
14 Bartlett, C. A. and Yoshino, M. Y., 'Corning Glass Works International', (A-D), Harvard Business School Case Studies, 1981.
15 Porter, M. E., 'From Competitive Advantage to Corporate Strategy', *Harvard Business Review*, 65 (3), 1987, pp. 43–59.

16 Sirower, M. L., *The Synergy Trap*, The Free Press, New York, 1997.
17 Porter, M. E., 'Competition in Global Industries: A Conceptual Framework', in Porter, M. E., ed., *Competition in Global Industries*, Harvard Business School Press, Boston, 1986, p. 56.
18 Porter, M. E., *Competitive Advantage*, Free Press, New York, 1985, Chapter 11.
19 Bartlett, C. A. and Ghoshal, S., *Managing Across Borders; The Transnational Solution*, Harvard Business School Press, Boston, 1989, p. 4.

Part I

What is synergy?

Chapter 1

Introduction to synergy

The first reading in Part I, by H. Igor Ansoff, is one of the earliest attempts to address the issue of synergy. Since the 1950s, Ansoff has been a consultant and professor in both Europe and America. He has written numerous articles and books over this period, focusing on strategic planning and strategic management. 'Synergies and capabilities' is drawn from *Corporate Strategy*, first published in 1965. The framework presented in this book is logical and analytical, and although Ansoff has written widely on the subject of corporate strategy in the last 25 years his concept of synergy is largely unchanged even in his recently revised and enlarged book, *Corporate Strategy*.[1]

The 1960s was a time when many corporations were rapidly becoming larger and more diversified, and Ansoff's purpose was to help managers make better decisions on questions of growth and diversification. Should a business enter new product-markets? What new areas provide the best opportunities for a particular business? Ansoff's model of strategy aims to help managers answer these questions. He identifies four components of strategy: product-market scope; growth vector; competitive advantage; synergy.

Any, or all, of these components could provide coherence to the firm and guidance to its managers in their decisions on the firm's future. The product-market scope defines the industries in which a firm competes; the growth vector indicates the direction of a firm's growth according to what combination of new products and markets it selects; and competitive advantage identifies the kind of opportunity the firm seeks, such as a dominant position in an emerging industry, or one where the cost of entry is so high that there are only a few competitors. Synergy, the last component, defines how a company is going to succeed in new ventures, by identifying the match between its capabilities and the opportunities available. Some firms, such as conglomerates, may have no synergy component to their strategy, and other firms may decide to forgo some joint effects if achieving them would require restructuring of the firm or refocusing management efforts. Synergy, therefore, is one of the possible key components of corporate level strategy.

Ansoff establishes the economic basis of synergy – how it can be possible for different businesses to add up to more than the sum of their parts. The synergy equation is based in part on the economic benefits gained through economies of scale. For example, it may be possible to lower costs across two businesses by increasing the capacity utilization of plant, using a common sales force, or combining purchasing volumes. Synergy, however, also encompasses more abstract benefits, which Ansoff terms 'managerial synergy'. Managers might be able to apply the experience and knowledge they have in one business to a new area. If this results in better guidance and better decisions for the new business, then synergy results. Just the opposite occurs if managers enter unfamiliar businesses they do not understand, or if they try to apply inappropriate solutions. The result is likely to be poor guidance for the business, and this means that synergy effects will be negative.

Therefore, Ansoff argues, managers must understand both the upside potential and downside risks of entering new areas. The procedure suggested by Ansoff is first to identify potential synergies across businesses in different industries, and then to compare these to a company's capabilities profile. The first stage reveals potential joint effects in areas such as general management, manufacturing, or sales across different businesses. At this point, however, these broad possibilities are only theoretical. The potential for a particular company to achieve these synergies depends on its own capabilities in each area, and so managers also have to analyse their company's particular strengths and weaknesses. The capabilities profile of a company identifies the resources and skills it possesses in each functional area. Companies have the best chance of achieving synergies if they are able to capitalize on their strengths, and so Ansoff's framework helps managers identify the capabilities they might be able to exploit in new areas.

Ansoff's explanation of synergy emphasizes its economic basis, the potential for tangible as well as intangible benefits and its close relationship to the firm's capabilities. Other authors have a similar understanding of synergy. The second piece in this section, though, provides a more restrictive definition of synergy, separating Ansoff's concept of synergy into a 'complement effect' and a 'synergy effect'. The Japanese strategist Hiroyuki Itami is the author of 'Invisible assets', a chapter taken from his book *Mobilizing Invisible Assets*. Itami, a professor at Hitotsubashi University, originally published his book for Japanese managers in 1980. Thomas Roehl of the University of Washington translated Itami's work and helped prepare it for an English speaking audience, and Itami acknowledges him as his collaborator in the English edition, published in 1987.

In his book Itami argues that a firm's strategy should seek fit in five areas: three external areas – customers, competition, and technology; and two internal areas – resources and organization. Itami discusses each of these areas in turn, raising the issue of synergy in each area. The aim of the strategist is to make best use of all the firm's resources and create adequate resources, and Itami views synergy as a process of making better use of resources. He defines two types of resource: physical assets, such as manufacturing facilities, and invisible assets. An invisible asset is an intangible resource; it may be a brand name, customer knowledge, expertise in a technology, a strong corporate culture that inspires employee commitment. Itami argues that such invisible assets are a company's best long-term source of competitive advantage because they are unique to the firm. They cannot be purchased, they can be put to multiple uses across the firm, and they can be combined or used in new ways that enable a firm to grow.

A company must strive to get the most out of all its resources. One means of doing this is to improve capacity utilization of the physical resources, as when a firm adds a second product to utilize more efficiently its manufacturing facilities, or enters a new market because its production capacity outstrips demand in its current markets. The firm saves costs, or improves sales, by getting more out of its physical assets and this Itami terms the 'complement effect'. Although worthwhile, the complement effect seldom provides lasting advantage to a firm because it is easily duplicated by competitors. They, too, can produce additional products in their factories to achieve cost savings. Itami concludes that the complement effect is not the true source of synergy.

It is when a firm exploits its unique resources – its invisible assets – that it achieves the 'synergy effect'. A firm that uses an established brand name to launch a new product successfully gains synergy, because it is using an invisible asset to create something new. Synergy, according to Itami, is a 'free ride' because the invisible assets developed in one part of the company can be used elsewhere at the same time, without being depleted. Many companies, he argues, overlook their invisible assets and thus forfeit their opportunities to gain synergy benefits. At the same time, companies also have to exercise some caution, since it is easy to assume that any joint use generates synergy benefits, but this is not the case. A firm known for its superior products may be able to capitalize on its image and enter the mass market with a lower cost product, but it may also damage its reputation in doing so. Furthermore, Itami observes that because the payoff from synergy is potentially high, there is a temptation for managers to overestimate the benefits and to justify unprofitable products because of potential synergies.

In narrowing the definition of synergy to the use of invisible assets, Itami deliberately departs from the Ansoff view which includes benefits gained from economies of scale (the 'complement effect') as well as the sharing of intangible assets such as expertise or image across a portfolio. Itami admits that complement effects and synergy effects often occur together. His purpose in distinguishing between them is to encourage managers to consider more explicitly the synergy potential of assets such as technological expertise or reputation. This approach, he argues, is justified because a firm's invisible assets provide the foundation for its growth and prosperity.

Itami's approach to strategy and synergy is theoretically similar to the resource-based view of the firm.[2] Proponents of this view, which has become increasingly influential, argue that instead of seeing firms as discrete businesses, we should regard them as bundles of tangible and intangible assets, or resources. J. B. Barney categorizes a firm's resources as physical capital, human capital and organizational capital.[3] These categories encompass a company's skills and capabilities, its organizational routines and values as well as its physical assets such as plant, machinery or land. Whilst every firm has many resources, the critical ones are those which can be exploited for competitive advantage. Competitively valuable resources cannot be imitated by competitors, they have no readily available substitutes, and they have significant value in the market-place. A patent, a superior retail location, or a unique expertise in a particular technology are examples of resources that may be exploited for competitive advantage. The work of the resource-based theorists, like that of Itami, puts as much emphasis on the internal sources of competitive advantage as on external factors such as market position or industry attractiveness. In this view, synergy results when valuable internal resources are exploited in different end products, or businesses.

The concept of synergy, in both its broader and narrower definitions, has had a powerful impact on management thinking. In a review of the vast literature on diversification, Friedrich Trautwein, a professor at the University of Bochum in Germany, found that managers almost always explain mergers in terms of the synergies available, and most of the advice in the management literature rests on the assumption that mergers are justified only if they can capture synergy. At the same time, Trautwein found little empirical evidence that mergers actually do result in synergies.[4] Other researchers and practitioners have also written sceptically about synergy effects, including Harold Geneen, the founder of ITT, whose recent book on management is entitled *The Synergy Myth*.[5]

The fact that many synergy efforts fail is well recognized, but this has not caused supporters to reject the concept itself. Igor Ansoff, in a later book, reflected on the gap between theory and reality:

In the early days of the synergy concept, some observers of mergers and acquisitions claimed that synergy was not a useful concept, because potential synergies, diagnosed during merger investigations, failed to materialize after the merger. But experience showed that the difficulty lay not in the synergy concept, but in the failure by the corporate management to pay sufficient attention and exercise sufficient authority to make sure that the potential synergies were realised by SBU managers, whose natural inclination is to 'row their own boat' and avoid dependence on other parts of the firm.[6]

Other management authorities, such as Michael Porter, agree that synergy is a sound concept. Thus, Porter writes, 'The failure of synergy stemmed from the inability of companies to understand and implement it, not because of some basic flaw in the concept.'[7]

It is not just blind faith that leads management authorities to reaffirm the concept of synergy – there is some evidence that synergy works. For example, Gary Hamel of London Business School and C. K. Prahalad of INSEAD have written admiringly of Japanese corporations which are able to build and exploit core competences, especially technological expertise, across their businesses, and they urge western companies to emulate their successful Japanese competitors.[8] NEC has been frequently cited in the literature for the advantages it gains from synergy. Its strategy is based on the link between computers and communication and its businesses have many interrelationships in technologies, channels, production and procurement.[9] Banc One's detailed reporting system, which ranks its affiliates' performance on a number of measures, has encouraged the spread of best practice within the organization. Unilever's human resource system allows its managers to gain experience in its different businesses and also facilitates the spread of product knowledge and know-how across the company.[10] These companies do gain benefits from interrelationships across their businesses, indicating that synergy is not necessarily a chimera.

Broad statistical studies examining synergy effects are another source of evidence about the existence of synergy, but many studies have proven ambiguous or inconclusive. Richard Rumelt compared the performance of a large sample of companies, finding that related diversifiers outperformed conglomerates, but later studies suggested that performance differences he found were largely caused by industry effects rather than the type of diversification. One problem with large-scale statistical studies is that they can only test if, overall, a group of related diversifiers outperforms a group of unrelated diversifiers. This is a blunt way to test for synergy effects. Within a group of 'related diversifiers', some companies may be gaining synergy benefits, but others may not. These differences would not show up in the overall performance of the category. Furthermore, this methodology often has not distinguished between the sharing of strategically important resources, and the sharing of resources which have little or no strategic significance.[11]

One way to overcome this problem is to look for synergy effects at the level of the SBU, and the third reading included here explores a methodology for doing this. 'Integrating strategies for clusters of businesses' is by Robert Buzzell, of Harvard Business School, and Bradley Gale. Both authors have long been associated with PIMS, the acronym for Profit Impact of Marketing Strategies. The PIMS database includes information on market conditions, competitive position, and operating and financial performance for thousands of business units. Researchers have used the database to investigate a wide range of marketing and strategic issues over the last 20 years, and Buzzell and Gale report the major findings in their book *The PIMS Principles*. The selection included here is largely based on the research of John Wells, who used the PIMS database to investigate synergy effects for his 1984 Harvard doctoral dissertation 'In Search of Synergy'.

Insights into the benefits of synergy are gained by comparing the actual performance of a corporate portfolio with the expected profitability of the businesses if they were stand-alone entities. The expected profitability of a business is derived from the data on the thousands of businesses in the PIMS database. Wells and other researchers have used various approaches to examine the impact of shared activities, shared skills and knowledge, and shared image, discovering that synergy effects depend in part on what is being shared. For example, there are significant economies of scale available if the costs of R&D can be spread across a group of businesses, but such savings will only impact overall profitability if R&D is, in fact, a significant cost to the businesses. The sharing of unimportant activities yields little advantage. To explore the effect of relatedness in a portfolio where businesses could share similar skills and knowledge, Wells identified portfolios where the businesses had similar characteristics, such as marketing- or technology-intensive businesses, and compared their performance with that of unrelated clusters of businesses. Businesses that were related in terms of their capital intensity, technology, marketing intensity, or industry concentration did outperform unrelated clusters, but portfolios with businesses in high-growth markets and those with a strong emphasis on new products performed worse than unrelated clusters.

In investigating the results of shared image, Wells used quality as a measure. He found that portfolios with a high-quality image had higher profitability than predicted for stand-alone businesses, suggesting that some businesses do gain bottom-line advantages from sharing a positive image. In contrast, portfolios with a poor quality image performed worse than expected – in other words, the portfolio performance was worse than the sum of its parts. According to these authors, the lesson for managers is that synergy or sharing effects can be negative as well as positive, a possibility also raised in the work of Igor Ansoff and Hiroyuki Itami.

The fact that synergy can be negative as well as positive means that seeking synergies is like crossing a minefield – there is a way across, but the failure rate is high. Professors Ansoff and Itami give reasons why managers should consider taking this risk. How to traverse this minefield is the subject of later chapters.

REFERENCES

1 Ansoff, H. I., *Corporate Strategy*, revised edition, Penguin Books, 1987.
2 For a discussion of the resource-based view of the firm see Peteraf, M. A., 'The Cornerstones of Competitive Advantage: A Resource Based View', *Strategic Management Journal*, 1993 (14) pp. 179–91.
3 Barney, J. B., 'Firm Resources and Sustained Competitive Advantage', *Journal of Management*, vol. 17, no. 1, 1991, pp. 99–120.
4 Trautwein, F., 'Merger Motives and Merger Prescriptions', *Strategic Management Journal*, vol. 11, 1990, pp. 283–95.
5 Geneen, H., *The Synergy Myth*, St. Martins Press, 1997; see also Sirower, M., *The Synergy Trap*, Free Press, New York, 1997.
6 Ansoff, I. H., *Implanting Strategic Management*, Prentice Hall International, 1984, p. 81.
7 Porter, M. E., *Competitive Advantage*, Free Press, New York, 1985, p. 318.
8 Prahalad, C. K. and Hamel, G., 'The Core Competence of the Corporation', *Harvard Business Review*, May-June 1990, pp. 79–91.
9 Bartlett, C. A. and Ghoshal, S., 'Managing Across Borders: New Organizational Responses', *Sloan Management Review*, Fall 1987, pp. 45–53; Porter, M. E., *Competitive Advantage*, Free Press, New York, 1985.
10 Goold, M., Campbell A. and Alexander, M., *Corporate-Level Strategy*, Chapter 7 'Linkage Influence', John Wiley & Sons, Inc., New York, 1994.
11 For a discussion of this issue, see Markides, C. C. and Williamson, P. J., 'Related Diversification, Core Competences and Corporate Performance', *Strategic Management Journal*, vol. 15, pp. 149–65, 1994.

Chapter 2

Synergy and capabilities

H. Igor Ansoff

'Speak English!' said the Eaglet. 'I don't know the meaning of half those long words, and what's more, I don't believe you do either!'

Lewis Carroll

THE PROBLEM

In this chapter we begin to explore *synergy*, which is one of the major components of the firm's product-market strategy. It is concerned with the desired characteristics of fit between the firm and its new product-market entries. In business literature it is frequently described as the '2 + 2 = 5' effect, to denote the fact that the firm seeks a product-market posture with a combined performance that is greater than the sum of its parts.

In item three on the list of requirements presented in Chapter 2 [of Ansoff: *Corporate Strategy*] for a strategic decision method, we described synergy as a measure of joint effects. It will be recalled that this requirement arises from practical rather than theoretical needs. If it were practically possible in each instant to compute the *marginal* cash flows into and out of the firm for each new project, the requirement would not exist, since this aspect of project evaluation would be adequately covered by capital investment theory. Nor would it exist if it were possible to compute quickly and efficiently the new flows for the entire firm each time a new project came along.[1]

As a substitute for these infeasible approaches, we shall derive a method for qualitative estimation of joint effects. In the process it will be shown that measurement of synergy is similar in many ways to what is frequently called 'evaluation of strengths and weaknesses'. In synergy, joint effects are measured between two product-markets; in strength and weakness evaluation, the firm's competences are rated relative to some desired performance level. The former contributes to the decision to make a new entry; the latter, to the decision to exploit certain strengths or to remedy certain deficiencies within the firm. Thus the difference is largely one of viewpoint.

With this in mind we shall develop an estimation technique which is applicable for both purposes. This will be accomplished by means of *capability* profiles. At the end of the chapter we shall have a multipurpose technique which can be used to

1 evaluate any internal strengths and weaknesses within the firm;
2 derive synergy characteristics which the firm can use in its search for opportunities;
3 measure the synergy potential between the firm and a possible acquisition.

CONCEPT OF SYNERGY

Use of simple mathematical symbols is helpful for a quick summary of the meaning of synergy. Each product-market makes a contribution to the overall profitability of the firm. Each product brings in annual sales of S dollars. Operating costs of O dollars are incurred for labour, materials, overhead, administration and depreciation. To develop the product, to provide facilities and equipment, and to set up a distribution network, an investment of I dollars must be made in product development, tooling, buildings, machinery, inventories, etc.

The annual rate of return, ROI, on product $P1$ can be written in the form

$$\text{ROI} = \frac{S_1 - O_1}{I_1}$$

Expressed in words, the formula states that the return on investment from a product can be obtained by dividing the difference between operating revenues and costs during a period by the average investment which is needed to support the product. A similar expression can be written for all products in the product line: $P_1, P_2, \ldots, P_n$.

If all the products are unrelated in any way, the total sales of the firm will be

$$S_T = S_1 + S_2 + \ldots + S_n$$

And similarly for operating costs and investment

$$O_T = O_1 + \ldots + O_n$$
$$I_T = I_1 + I_2 + \ldots + I_n$$

The return on the investment for the firm as a whole will be

$$(\text{ROI})_T = \frac{S_T - O_T}{I_T}$$

This condition obtains whenever the revenues, the operating costs, and the investments are unrelated. Therefore, their totals can be obtained through simple additions. In practice this is very nearly true in an investment firm which holds unrelated securities, or in a holding company in which there is no interaction among the operating units. A picture of the total profitability is obtained through a simple consolidation of the individual statements.

In a majority of firms, advantages of scale exist under which a large firm with the same total sales as a number of small firms can operate at a cost which is lower than the sum of the operating costs for the separate enterprises. The investment in a large firm can be similarly lower than a simple sum of the respective investments. Using symbols, this is equivalent to saying that for

$$S_s = S_T$$

we have

$$O_s \leqslant O_T$$
$$I_s \leqslant I_T$$

where subscript s denotes the respective quantities for an integrated firm and subscript T, the sum for independent enterprises.[2] As a result, the potential return on investment for an integrated firm is higher than the composite return which would be obtained if the same dollar volumes for its respective products were produced by a number of independent firms

$$(ROI)_s > (ROI)_T$$

A similar argument can, of course, be made by keeping the total investment fixed. In this case

$$S_s \geqslant S_T$$
$$O_s \leqslant O_T$$
$$I_s = I_T$$

For a given level of investment, a firm with a complete product line can usually realize the advantages of higher total revenues and/or lower operating costs than competing independent firms.

The consequences of this joint effect are clearly very far-reaching. A firm which takes care to select its products and markets so as to optimize the effect has great flexibility in choosing its competitive stance. It can gain a larger share of the market by lowering prices, it can choose to make a larger investment in research and development than its competitors, or it can maximize its ROI and attract growth capital to the firm. All this can be done while remaining fully competitive with firms whose product-markets are not as carefully chosen.

TYPES OF SYNERGY

This effect, which can produce a combined return on the firm's resources greater than the sum of its parts, is frequently referred to as '2 + 2 = 5'. We shall call this effect *synergy*.[3] One way to classify the several types of synergy is in terms of the components of the ROI formula:

1 *Sales synergy.* This can occur when products use common distribution channels, common sales administration, or common warehousing. Opportunity for tie-in sales offered by a complete line of related products increases the productivity of the sales force. Common advertising, sales promotion, past reputation can all have multiple returns for the same dollar spent.

2 *Operating synergy.* This is the result of higher utilization of facilities and personnel, spreading of overhead, advantages of common learning curves, and large-lot purchasing.

3 *Investment synergy.* This can result from joint use of plant, common raw materials inventories, transfer of research and development from one product to another, common tooling, common machinery.

4 *Management synergy.* Although not immediately apparent from the formula, this type is an important contributor to the total effect. As will be shown below, management in different types of industry faces different strategic, organizational, and operating problems. If upon entering a new industry management finds the new problems to be similar to the ones it has encountered in the past, it is in a position to provide forceful and effective guidance to the newly acquired venture. Since competent top-level management is a scarce commodity, very positive enhancement of performance can result in the combined enterprise. Thus synergy will be strong.

If, on the other hand, the problems in the acquired area are new and unfamiliar, not only will positive synergy be low, but there is a distinct danger of a negative effect of top-management decisions. For example, management of a firm in the defence industry would be at an actual disadvantage if it attempts, without prior experience, to assume responsibility for pricing and advertising decisions in a highly competitive consumer area, such as the cigarette or the automobile industry.

This example points to the fact that management synergy, as well as the other types, can be negative as well as positive. An attempt at joint use of a facility which is not suited for manufacturing of a new product (e.g. use of aircraft factories for consumer aluminium products) or of an organization which is not set up to perform a new function (e.g. use of a consumer sales organization to sell to industrial customers) can result in total profitability which is *lower* than the combined profitability of two independent operations.

Table 2.1 demonstrates the possibility of negative synergy through a comparison of competences in the principal functional areas found in typical firms in different industry groups. For purposes of comparison we are assuming that a firm in one of the groups shown in the first column diversifies into an industry group shown in the first line.

It is seen that the best transfer of functional competence will occur in general management, where many practices and skills in accounting, finance, industrial relations, and public relations are common among industries. However, even here the differences in the competitive environment and in basic resource allocation problems have led us to give unequal ratings to different pairs of industrial areas. In manufacturing and marketing where organizational forms, cost controls and individual skills become more specialized, greater differences in synergy appear among the groups. The differences become so great between space defence and consumer groups as to create potentially negative synergy.

It should be noted that this table describes potential (rather than actual) synergy. Whether the indicated joint effects will, in fact, materialize depends on the manner in which the new acquisition is integrated into the parent organization. (This problem of management control will be discussed in Chapter 8 [of Ansoff: *Corporate Strategy*]).

Table 2.1 Functional synergy between industry groups

Diversifying industry	Functional capability	New Industry		
		Defence-space	Producers	Consumers
Defense-space	GM	High	High	Moderate
	R&D	High	Moderate	Low
	Mfg.	High	Low	Negative
	Mkt.	High	Low	Negative
Producers	GM	High	High	Moderate
	R&D	Moderate	High	Low
	Mfg.	Low	High	Low
	Mkt.	Low	High	Low
Consumers	GM	Moderate	Moderate	High
	R&D	Low	Low	High
	Mfg.	Negative	Low	High
	Mkt.	Negative	Low	High

Legend
  GM – general management
  R&D – research and development
  Mfg. – manufacturing
  Mkt. – marketing
Source: H. I. Ansoff and J. F. Weston, 'Merger Objectives and Organization Structure', *Review of Economics and Business*, August 1963, pp. 49–58.

START-UP SYNERGY AND OPERATING SYNERGY

As discussed above, the synergistic effect can be measured in either of two ways: by estimating the cost economics to the firm from a joint operation for a given level or revenue, or by estimating the increase in net revenue for a given level of investment. In this section we shall take the first approach and discuss the nature of synergy through analysis of cost economies and dis-economies.

Acquisition of a new product-market area goes through two successive phases: start-up and operating. In addition to identifiable physical costs, such as the costs of facilities and inventories, the costs associated with start-up include the highly intangible costs of learning a new kind of business: setting up a new organization, establishing new rules and procedures, hiring new skills and competences, paying for mistakes in developing organizational relationships and for early bad decisions made in an unfamiliar business environment, and costs of gaining customer acceptance. Although these are one-time costs, most of them are not capitalized, but charged to operating expense during the start-up period. They are difficult to pinpoint, since many of them are not identified (no firm is likely to have a special account labelled 'management blunders made in start-up'), but are evident only indirectly through substandard operating efficiencies.[4] During the period in which they are incurred they put the firm at a disadvantage with respect to the established competitors in the field, since the latter no longer incur any of these costs.

Whether the firm will, in fact, have to incur these start-up costs depends on how well its skills and resources are matched to the requirements of the new product-market area. If the required new capabilities are very different from those of the firm, then, as discussed earlier, cost dis-economies may result in any of the major functional areas. Thus start-up in new business can have potentially negative as well as positive synergy; a firm with positive synergy will have a competitive advantage over a firm which lacks it.

In addition to the direct and hidden dollar costs, start-up in a new product-market often carries a penalty for time delay. A firm which has the requisite skills and resources, such as suitable production facilities or the appropriate distribution channels for a new market, can quickly transfer them to new activities and thus get a head start on firms which have to build from scratch. The timing advantage in synergy becomes particularly desirable when the new entry is in a dynamic fast-growth stage. Rapid response will have less significance if the firm is considering an entry into a latent demand market (such as RCA's early entry into colour television), or if the new market is stable and slow growing (which would be the case if, for some strange reason, a new firm sought an entry into the textile industry).

Thus, during the start-up phase, synergy can occur in two forms: in the form of dollar savings to the firm thanks to the existence of competences appropriate to the new line of business, and in the form of time savings in becoming fully competitive.

The second category of costs incurred in a new entry is the costs of a going concern: the operating costs and the investment required to support the operation. Here two basic effects operate to produce synergy. One is the advantage of scale – many operations will produce at a lower unit cost when the total volume is increased. For example, purchasing in large quantities offers the advantage of discounts; production in large quantities makes possible more efficient methods and procedures and hence lower direct costs. Many other well-known examples can be given.

A more subtle effect in synergy is a distribution of the burden of overhead expenses over a number of products. This arises from the fact that most overhead functions require a certain minimum level of effort for a wide range of business volume. If volume can be added through a type of diversification which makes use of the existing overhead services, economies will be effected in both the new and the old business. For example, a sales management and administration function must be staffed regardless of whether the firm has one product or a full line; the same research must be conducted regardless of whether it supports one or many products (so long as the products are all based on the same technology).

If top-management talent in a firm is not fully utilized in running the present business, and if its training and experience are relevant, it can provide the most critical ingredient to the new operation. Unfortunately, this potentially strongest component of synergy is also the most difficult to measure. Many diversification histories can be cited in which an erroneous estimate was made, either through failure to realize that top management was already fully committed and that new responsibilities resulted in a thin spread of talent or through failure to realize that new business called for different types of talent and experience and that synergy, in fact, did not exist.

In general, synergy effects during start-up will go hand in hand with operating synergy. For example, a firm with a fully developed position in an area of consumer merchandising, say, in clothing, would have a strong bid for an entry into the toy industry, where similar merchandising experience and talent are required. However, the new entry would require setting up and operating different sales organizations, different manufacturing facilities, different purchases, and different product development. Thus while start-up synergy will be strong in the advantages of timing and basic business know-how, operating synergy will be limited to sales administration and to general management. On the other hand, a firm in women's clothing which adds a line of swimming apparel would have both strong start-up and operating synergy.

SYMMETRY AND JOINT EFFECTS

For convenience the preceding discussion has been presented from the viewpoint of the advantages which the diversifying firm can offer to a new product-market entry. It should be made clear that the effects of synergy are symmetric. While the diversifying firm offers benefits to the new product line, it may receive substantial benefits in return. For example, while the parent may strengthen the new subsidiary's research capability, the latter may offer new marketing outlets for the parent's products.

Further, while the viewpoint of cost and investment economics used above is convenient, it fails to account for a full range of potential synergistic benefits. Rather than permit lower cost in support of previous sales volumes, synergy is most frequently sought as a quick way to accelerate growth without additional major investments. This may come from the mutual contributions of *existing* skills and capacities which otherwise might take a long time to acquire and for which start-up premiums might have to be paid.

A less frequent, but much sought after, effect occurs when by combining resources the joint firm gains access to product-markets to which neither could previously gain access without a major investment. Thus the merger of the Remington Rand Company, an office machine company, with Sperry, an electronics concern, provided a foundation for the electronic computer entry by Sperry-Rand. The merger of Puget Sound Bridge and Dry-dock, a shipbuilding company, into Lockheed, which is highly sophisticated in many fields of technology, provided a basis for the former's efforts to get into the atomic submarine business.

A FRAMEWORK FOR EVALUATION OF SYNERGY

In principle, all synergistic effects can be mapped on one of three variables: increased volume of dollar revenue to the firm from sales, decreased operating costs and decreased investment requirements. All three are viewed in the perspective of time; therefore, a fourth synergistic effect is acceleration of the respective changes in the three variables. If this mapping could be carried out in practice, the total effect of synergy could be reflected in the return on investment formula (or some other cash-flow scheme).

In practice, the mapping is frequently not possible, particularly when strategic moves contemplate product-markets in which the firm has little previous experience. Under such conditions, although the primary variables affecting synergy can be identified, as we have done before, it is not possible to quantify and combine their effects.[5]

As was discussed in Chapter 2 [of Ansoff: *Coroporate Strategy*], this problem is not unique to measurement of synergy. It occurs in many other parts of the strategic decision process. Our general approach to it in this book is to construct a separate measurement of each important effect and, in a later chapter, to construct a method for applying these measures jointly to overall evaluation of a project.

A framework for assessing synergy is shown in Table 2.2, which in effect summarizes the developments of this chapter. Synergy effects are first grouped by the primary functional areas of the firm: general management, research and development, marketing, and operations (which includes manufacturing, purchasing, inventory control, distribution, and warehousing). Some firms may prefer a finer breakdown of categories. For example, firms which deal heavily in money, securities, and financing will benefit by separating finance from general management. Within each functional area three possible symmetric effects are considered:

1 The contribution which the new product-market entry can make to the firm. (This is a very important effect when the entry is sought through an acquisition of a firm which is comparable in size to the parent. The effect may be negligible when the acquisition is small or the entry is through internal product development.)
2 The contribution from the parent to the entry.
3 Further product-market moves which the two will be able to undertake as a result of the consolidation.[6]

The columns in the table list the variables to be considered in connection with each of the categories. The headings of the columns list the various ways in which synergistic effects may manifest themselves and are self-explanatory in the light of the preceding discussion. It will be noted that a column labelled 'investment' is provided under both start-up and operating synergy. The intent is that a firm will use the former to assess one-time learning costs which do not result in tangible physical facilities, such as marketing start-up costs. The investment entries under operations reflect economics of acquisition of tangible physical assets.

The entries in Table 2.2 should be measurements of the strength of a particular effect. Wherever possible, they should be assigned a numerical value, such as 'reduction of 40,000 square feet in plant requirements' or '20 per cent increase of sales on same investment base'. Failing this, the entries will be relative qualitative ratings. A column is provided for the overall synergy rating, most likely a qualitative one, for each functional area. These in turn can be combined into one overall rating for the prospective entry. Before discussing these entries we need to consider a

Table 2.2 Measurement of synergy of a new product-market entry

		Start-up economies			Operating economies		Expansion of present sales	New product and market areas	Overall synergy
	Effects due to pooling of competences								
Functional area	Symmetry effects	Investment	Operating	Timing	Investment	Operating			
General management and finance	Contribution to parent								
	Contribution to new entry								
	Joint opportunities								
Research and development	Contribution to parent								
	Contribution to new entry								
	Joint opportunities								
	Contribution to parent								
Marketing	Contribution to new entry								
	Joint opportunities								
	Contribution to parent								
Operations	Contribution to new entry								
	Joint opportunities								

problem very similar to estimation of synergy, which is frequently called estimation of the firm's strengths and weaknesses.

STRENGTHS AND WEAKNESSES

Management literature dealing with problems of product-market change suggests that one of the early steps following the formulation of objectives should be an analysis of 'strengths and weaknesses' or, as more appropriately described by Staudt, 'an audit of the tangible and intangible resources for diversification'.[7]

The audit has two purposes. First, it can identify deficiencies in the firm's present skills and resources which can be corrected *short* of diversification. Second, it can identify strengths from which the firm can lead in pursuing diversification and/or deficiencies which it may wish to correct through diversification.

The strengths from which the firm wishes to lead are readily identified from the preceding discussion as the *synergy* component of the firm's strategy. By searching out opportunities which match its strengths, the firm can optimize the synergistic effects. Thus the problem of strengths and weaknesses and the problem of synergy are seen to be related.

It is also apparent that the estimates made in both problems are relative. In the first part of the audit the firm's deficiencies are compared with those of its successful competitors. In the second part the strengths can only be identified relative to the industries into which the firm seeks to diversify. Thus, for example, a superior competence in design of lightweight strength but expensive structures which is a 'strength' in the aircraft-missile industry, is a weakness when applied to design of industrial machinery (as was shown by the venture of Bell Aircraft into industrial wheelbarrows).

In order to accommodate synergy and strengths and weaknesses within the same analytic framework, we shall use the method of profile comparison. As the first step we shall develop the framework for a *capability profile* which rates a particular pattern of skills and facilities relative to some reference level. We do this by first constructing a grid which matches functional areas in the firm against its skills and competences, and then by providing a checklist for entries into the grid.

Grid of competences

The framework we seek must possess two key features. To be widely applicable, it must be constructed in terms of competence areas which are common to most industries; to be applicable to a single firm, these areas must list specific skills and resources which differentiate between success and failure in different types of business. In other words, we are seeking a common framework with differentiated contents within it. Since a fully integrated manufacturing firm has the most comprehensive framework of capabilities, we shall use it as a point of reference. Frameworks for analysis of firms in trade, finance, and services can be obtained through simplification of the general model.

The individual skills and resources can be organized along the same major functional areas as in the preceding table:

1 *Research and development* is defined to encompass the entire process of creating a marketable product. Included are pure and applied research, construction of breadboards and prototypes, industrial design and preparation of manufacturing drawings. Also included is development of manufacturing processes and techniques. Market research is included in so far as it is concerned with determining the price-performance characteristics of the product and the size and structure of the market.
2 *Operations* is concerned with procurement of raw materials, scheduling and controlling production, tooling, manufacturing engineering, quality control, inventory, and manufacturing the product.
3 *Marketing* is taken as a broad activity concerned with creating product acceptance, advertising, sales promotion, selling, distributing the product (including transportation and warehousing), contract administration, sales analysis and, very importantly, servicing the product.
4 *General management and finance* is taken to include three areas of activity:
   a Determining the overall pattern of relationships between the firm and its environment. This includes determination of strategy and the total resource allocation, acquisition of new product-market positions for the firm, obtaining necessary financing, and maintaining public relations.
   b Providing integrated decision making, guidance, and control to the functional areas – particularly in areas of pricing, inventory levels, production levels, capital expenditures, and individual functional goals.
   c Providing various staff services to the functional areas, such as accounting, industrial relations, personnel training, and performing functions which are most efficiently carried out at centralized levels, such as purchasing.

Within each of these functional areas we recognize four categories of skills and resources:

1 *Facilities and equipment.*
2 *Personnel skills.*
3 *Organizational capabilities* – this includes specialized organizational

units, such as mass production or large systems management, established standards, policies and procedures for performance of specialized functions.
4 *Management capabilities* – this is described by the types of decisions and actions for which the management is specially qualified by virtue of training, experience and present responsibilities. For example, an ability to live with cyclical demand conditions, such as those encountered in the machine tool industry or the textile industry, is a management skill acquired with experience; another is knowledge and understanding of doing complex prime contractor work for the government.

Contents of the grid

The dual classification presented above offers a refined grid for assessing a firm's competences. We must next concern ourselves with the contents. The purpose is to develop a master list of entries which will contain the different kinds of capabilities encountered in American industry. In view of the great variety of competitive structures such a list cannot be made exhaustive. The purpose is, rather, to provide a master checklist which can be refined by each firm. The following discussion is organized around typical characteristics of three principal industrial groups in the United States economy: producers of durables and non-durables, consumers of durables and non-durables, and products and systems for military combat and for space missions. Each appears to have a different 'success function' – a different combination of capabilities required of successful competitors.

A major difficulty in determining the success function of consumer products is that customer acceptance is seldom based on measurable performance characteristics of the product. More frequently it is determined by a complex of factors (the interaction of which is imperfectly understood): apparent performance advantage conveyed to the customer through advertising and sales promotion, price advantage, ready availability of product, fashion, social pressure, artificial obsolescence of preceding products. Since customer acceptance is relatively insensitive to actual performance characteristics, and since quality differences among brands tend to be small, capabilities which are of greatest importance in consumer business lie in the area of merchandising skills – in advertising, product styling, promotion, distribution, and selling. Since demand is sensitive to price, cost-conscious engineering design philosophy is also an important factor.

In industrial products the interaction tends to be somewhat less complex. The critical factor in product acceptance is its economic justification: demonstrable ability of the product to make money for the buyer (in the form of savings or increased income). Price differential is important, but is related to quality. It is not uncommon in industry to pay a high price for a proven and reliable product. Of great importance is a demonstrated ability of the product to perform reliably. Among key competitive skills in industry are knowledge of customer's economic justification levels and an ability to design to them, ability to translate new technology into reliable products, special process and manufacturing competences, patent protection, sensitivity to customer needs and requirements, and an ability to provide quick and efficient product service.

End products sold to military and space missions succeed primarily if their performance capabilities are in excess of anything which had been previously available. In addition, they must be virtually failure-free during intermittent periods of all-out performance under extreme environmental conditions. A major competitive skills is an ability to apply the most advanced state of the art to products and systems. Organizational competence to manage development and manufacturing of technologically advanced, highly complex systems is another central skill. A very substantial share of military and space business differs from the industrial in that the customer usually buys a design (and a very preliminary one at that) instead of an existing product. This puts emphasis on a very special kind of marketing competence required in the US Department of Defence (DOD) and National Aeronautics and Space Administration (NASA) business. Technical quality of the design, past performance on similar contracts, technical and scientific reputation, and geopolitical advantages enjoyed by the firm all play an important role in marketing. The salesman is frequently a middleman between engineering and the customer, rather than an active merchandiser.

While these three groups exhibit important differences, their boundaries are not sharply drawn and there are many overlaps. Many industrial products (components, for example) have competitive characteristics closely resembling those in the consumer business. The DOD and NASA customers buy vast quantities of industrial-type material. The large and growing non-military government market (Federal, state, municipal) has features in common with both military and industrial markets.

In filling out the grid, it is therefore desirable to forgo reference to the respective groups and instead to compile a checklist of characteristics of the facilities, skills, organization, and management which may be encountered. The result of such an approach is shown in Table 2.3. An effort was made to make this list comprehensive enough to enable each firm to find items which describe the pattern of its major competences. It is to be expected, however, that many firms will identify additional entries which apply to their particular cases.

As an example, if the checklist is used by an American firm in road-building machinery the following distinctive entries may be singled out.

Table 2.3 Checklist for competitive and competence profiles

	Facilities and equipment	Personnel skills	Organizational capabilities	Management capabilities
General management & finance	Data processing equipment	Depth of general management Finance Industrial Relations Legal Personnel recruitment and training Accounting Planning	Multi-divisional structure Consumer financing Industrial financing Planning and control Automated business data processing	Investment management Centralized control Large systems management Decentralized control R&D intensive business Capital-equipment intensive business Merchandising intensive business Cyclical business Many customers Few customers
Research and development	Special lab equipment General lab equipment Test facilities	Areas of specialization Advanced research Applied research Product design: industrial consumer military specifications Systems design Industrial design: consumer industrial	Systems development Product development industrial consumer process Military specifications compliance	Utilization of advanced state of the art Application of current state of the art Cost-performance optimization

	Facilities and equipment	Personnel skills	Organizational capabilities	Management capabilities
Operations	General machine shop Precision machinery Process equipment Automated production Large high-bay facilities Controlled environment	Mass production Tool making Assembly Precision machinery Close tolerance work Process operation Product planning	Continuous flow process Batch process Job shop Large complex product assembly Subsystems integration Complex product control Quality control Purchasing	Operation under cyclic demand Military specifications quality Tight cost control Tight scheduling
Marketing	Warehousing Retail outlets Sales offices Service offices Transportation equipment	Door-to-door selling Retail selling Wholesale selling Direct industry selling Department of Defense selling Cross-industry selling Applications engineering Advertising Sales promotion Servicing Contract administration Sales analysis	Direct sales Distributor chain Retail chain Consumer service organization Industrial service organization Department of Defense product support Inventory distribution and control	Industrial marketing Consumer merchandising Department of Defense marketing State and municipality marketing

In the *facilities and equipment* column: high-bay assembly plant, medium-precision large general-purpose machine tools, up-to-date materials test laboratory, large heavy-duty test truck for completed machines, nation-wide direct sales and service offices. Under *personnel skills*: engineering skills in design and manufacture of rugged, medium-tolerance, large machinery, requiring marginal maintenance. *Organizational skills*: job shop for handling large medium-tolerance assembly, strong sales, and field service. *Management skills*: knowledge of dealing with Federal government, states, and municipalities, experience in running a cyclical business subject to the variations of capital goods cycle and vagaries of Federal and state budgets.

COMPETENCE AND COMPETITIVE PROFILES

The example describes a part of what we shall call the firm's *competence profile*. It is a list of the major skills and competences in the firm (identified with the aid of Table 2.3) rated with respect to other firms which have the same capabilities. Although most firms would prefer to make the comparison with their own competitors, it is desirable to rate the respective capabilities also with respect to other industries in which they exist. Thus the high-bay large product assembly facilities in the example above would also be found in firms which build railway equipment rolling stock and in materials-handling firms. In assigning the relative ratings some firms may prefer to use a simple two-valued strength or weakness classification. Others would rank the capabilities as outstanding, average, or weak; still others may construct bar-chart profiles.[8]

The competence profile is the basic reference profile for the firm. It is relatively permanent and will need updating only when major changes occur in the capabilities. The competence profile is a strength and weakness profile only relative to specific areas of competences and skills. It does not necessarily denote strengths and weaknesses with respect to a particular product-market position, since different industries require different balances of capabilities. The major use of the competence profile is in assessment of this balance in four different parts of the strategic problem.

1 *Internal appraisal.* As will be discussed in detail in Chapter 8 [of Ansoff: *Corporate Strategy*], one of the early stages in strategy formulation is to assess the firm's capability to meet the objectives without a change in strategy. For this purpose a *competitive profile* is conducted which presents the capability pattern of the most successful competitors in the industry.[9] The competence and the competitive profiles are now superimposed to determine the areas in which the firm is either

outstanding or deficient. *These are the strengths and weaknesses relative to the present product-market posture.*

2 *External appraisal.* In a later step in strategy formulation, a broad field of outside industries is surveyed to determine attractive areas for the firm. A part of the evaluation will measure the growth and profitability characteristics of the various industries; another part measures the synergy potential between the firm and each new industry, since synergy determines the firm's ability to make a successful and profitable entry. This requires a competitive profile for each industry, describing the pattern of skills required for success. Such profiles can be constructed through a combined use of general industry data and competence profiles of the most successful firms in the industry. Superposition of our firm's competence profile with the respective competitive profiles measures the 'fit' with each new industry and hence the chances of a successful entry.

3 *Synergy component of strategy.* In Chapter 9 [of Ansoff: *Corporate Strategy*] product-market strategy of the firm will be determined through several key components, each of which have specific rules for search and for evaluation of opportunities. Synergy is one of these components. To derive it, a procedure like the above is used, but the competence profile is now compared with competitive profiles for a few selected industries. The major relative strengths and weaknesses of the firm are identified and specified as rules for search. The management has a choice of an *aggressive strategy,* in which the strengths are used as search criteria or a *defensive strategy,* in which the search is directed toward remedying the weaknesses, or both. The strategy will be chosen subject to availability of opportunities which can match the firm in areas of both strength and weakness.

4 *Evaluation of individual opportunities.* Once search has uncovered a promising acquisition or a new product, a final evaluation must be made. A part of this evaluation is a measurement of synergy as a contributing factor to potential joint profitability. This requires completion of Table 2.2 presented earlier in this chapter. Profiles of the firm and of the acquisition are constructed and superimposed. Then:

   a The resulting pattern is compared with the competitive profile of a successful competitor in the firm's own business developed in item 1 above to determine whether the pattern of reinforcements will make any significant contribution to the parent firm's competitive position. The results can be used to determine the entries in the line 'contribution to parent' in Table 5.2 (see Table 5.2 in *Corporate Strategy*).

   b The superimposed profiles are similarly compared with a profile of a successful firm in the new entry's industry, thus giving material for the line in the table labelled 'contribution to new entry'.

c Finally superimposed profiles are compared with typical profiles developed under item 2 in the list above to see whether the combination of the two firms' skills will provide an entry into an industry which neither could enter alone. This provides date for the line in Table 2.2 labelled 'joint opportunities'.

This procedure of using paired profiles to fill in Table 2.2 is laborious and should be used primarily at the 'short strokes' of an acquisition. For a preliminary analysis, profiles can usually be dispensed with and Table 2.2 filled in on a judgement basis.

REFERENCES

1 It would appear, at first glance, that this could be done by 'computerizing' the internal operations of the firm, i.e. by programming its planning process on a high-speed computer. While this step certainly provides for some of the synergistic interaction, it still falls short of the total requirement. To meet the complete requirement we shall require much better models of the firm than are currently available. In particular, models are needed which can measure the potential of the firm as a result of radical changes in its product-market posture.
2 The symbol $\leq$ means less than or equal to; the symbol $\geq$ means greater than or equal to.
3 Combined action or operation, as of muscles, nerves, etc. *Webster's New Collegiate Dictionary*, G. & C. Merrian Company, Springfield, Mass., 1961.
4 This is one major reason for the difficulty encountered in determining marginal cash flows for new product-market entries.
5 Part of the reason is the simple fact that models relating these variables quantitatively are largely unavailable.
6 Anderson, T. A., Ansoff, H. I., Norton, F. E. and Weston, J. F., 'Planning for Diversification through Merger', *California Management Review*, vol. 1, no. 4, Summer 1959, pp. 24–35.
7 Staudt, T. A., 'Program for Product Diversification', *Harvard Business Review*, vol. 32, no. 6, November–December 1954, pp. 121–31.
8 Similar types of profiles have been used by some firms in evaluation of research and development proposals.
9 If the firm is already diversified, several competitive profiles may be needed, one for each distinct product-market line.

Reproduced from Ansoff, Igor, 'Synergies and Capabilities Profile', first published in *Corporate Strategy*, 1965, reprinted in *New Corporate Strategy*, John Wiley, 1988 by permission of Igor Ansoff.

Chapter 3

Invisible assets

Hiroyuki Itami

Up to this point I have discussed the external factors (customers, competition, and technology) with which strategy must fit. In the next two chapters [in *Mobilizing Invisible Assets*] I present the internal factors – corporate resources and the organization – necessary for fit. This chapter will consider the issues underlying effective utilization and efficient accumulation of resources and strategies for achieving these goals. In each case I will discuss not only static, one-period resource fit but also ways to keep resource fit over time.

Why discuss internal factors, when it is obvious that a firm lives or dies on its ability to match effectively and continuously its external environment? The answer is that to match the external environment, a firm must have good internal fit. Strategy is the linchpin that connects the internal and external factors and finds the most desirable shape for these interrelationships. Strategy must look both outward to the environment and inward to the firm itself through resource fit and organizational fit.

To fit the environment effectively, a person must live within his physical and psychological limits. At a minimum, he must set his existing limits to a level appropriate for the environment. The city dweller who goes to live in the Arctic must be sure he is in good physical and mental condition; he must adapt to different eating habits and must toughen himself for the stress of long periods of darkness. The situation is similar for a firm trying to match its internal factors to the environment. The company's resource levels and organizational climate limit its adaptiveness, much as a person's physical and mental limits restrict his ability to fit the environment.

STRATEGY AND EXISTING RESOURCES

A firm's strategy is made up of the current and future elements in its product-market portfolio, its operations mission, and its corporate resource portfolio. Resource fit can be approached in two ways. One way is for the strategist to look for preferred relationships between resources and strategy. From this perspective there are three key questions: Does the firm have sufficient *resource backing* to carry out its strategy? Does the firm's current strategy *effectively utilize* its current resources? Is the firm *efficiently accumulating* resources for the future?

The other approach is to focus on relationships within the strategy elements, evaluating various mixes of these elements to find the mix that effectively uses and efficiently accumulates corporate resources. Some mixes will improve performance, and others will not. The appropriate mix of strategy elements produces what I call a *combinatorial benefit*. Figure 3.1 shows the relationships to be examined in this chapter.

Backing strategy with sufficient resources

Good strategy is often said to capitalize on a company's strengths and to conceal its weaknesses, which is certainly true. This statement becomes

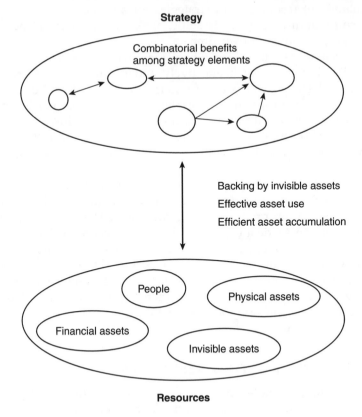

Figure 3.1 An overview of resource fit

more meaningful if one thinks about the relationships between current resources and strategy. Before a firm can decide how to accumulate and use its corporate resources, it must ascertain whether it has the resources to carry out a given strategy. Surprisingly, many companies undertake a strategy without realizing that they lack the necessary resources. During World War II the Japanese army at one time decided that it did not have to carry many supplies to carry out a campaign in Burma, since it would be capturing supplies as it went along. This strategy failed dismally, wasting thousands of lives.

There seem to be three reasons for firms choosing a strategy without having sufficient resources to carry it out: lack of careful analysis, difficulty in predicting future needs, and overestimation of current resources.

In the first case, those who designed the strategy may simply not have thought it through carefully. Strategy in this case becomes just a slogan. A more serious variation of this carelessness is shown when managers are unduly optimistic about the level of resources necessary to carry out the strategy.

A second blind spot is forecast error. If it is hard to project the required resources, mistakes may be made as the environment changes. Even a careful and conscientious manager may end up with insufficient backing for a strategy. Even if sufficient resources become available, they may not be accumulated in time to support the strategy. Forecasting is not easy. The strategist may be able to come close most of the time in deciding on the personnel, financial resources and production facilities necessary for a given strategy, but that may not be enough. Invisible assets are often the most important resource for a successful strategy and they are difficult to forecast. Such invisible assets as sensitivity to fashion may make or break a firm in the apparel industry; cosmetics success may be based on the ability to project a particular image. Each of these invisible assets has to be identified and its necessary level forecast. The greater the changes in the competitive environment, the more difficult this forecasting becomes.

An example will make the point. As the electronic calculator moved from the growth stage, in which it was a new and relatively expensive product, to the mature stage, in which it could be bought at the local drug store, companies were forced to develop various products from the basic one. The companies had to change to mass production, find ways to market the output, and develop production equipment that would handle a wide variety of products. Sharp and Casio were among the few firms that prepared the necessary resources to carry out their strategies.

Aida Engineering, a Japanese machinery company, illustrates how a company can define its product correctly and be prepared with the resources to meet key customer demands. Keinosuke Aida, the president of the firm, put it this way:

Our company started out making machines, but we never thought of machines as mere chunks of metal, but rather as a tool for firms to use for efficient production. We even chose as our name, Aida Engineering, a name that stressed the provision of the software necessary to make the chunks of metal work for our customers. That is where we make our profits. Engineering implies we have the tools for problem solving. Customers do not come to us for a new machine unless they are facing some type of problem that they cannot solve with their current equipment.

The firm might want to find ways to increase product quality or to do small lot production of a variety of products on an automated line. They know what they want their tools to do. We sell that performance through our lines of machinery.

(Industrial Bank of Japan, 1979).

Aida Engineering had to do more than build machinery well. It realized that its key corporate resource was its ability to build systems that matched customer desires. Aida built and maintained its competitive position by consulting with clients and solving their problems.

The third reason for firms failing to prepare sufficient resource backing is that they misread their level of resources, especially invisible assets. Even if the strategist correctly calculates the level of resources *necessary* for a strategy, it may fail if the present level of resources has been misjudged. It is not difficult to find examples. When a Japanese sewing machine company decided to add consumer electronics to the products it sold door-to-door, it miscalculated the resources available for selling two completely different lines of products. At first the salespeople put more effort into selling the new electronics product line, since that seemed easier to sell. Sales of sewing machines dropped. But the salespeople were not able to sell the electronic appliances well, since they had insufficient knowledge and were not able to provide adequate service after the sale. As a result, the company lost its top ranking in sales of sewing machines and failed in its diversification moves.

This mistake is often made by American firms trying to enter the Japanese market. They assume that their invisible assets of worldwide reputation and well-known technology will be sufficient to enter the market. Safeway's initial attempt to develop an American-style super-market in Tokyo without adjusting for higher land costs reflects their overestimation of the brand name's value. Procter & Gamble's initial attempt to sell detergent in Japan using exactly the same methods as in the United States also failed because they misread the competitive power of their internationally proven marketing assets.

Utilizing resources effectively

A strategist might think that the firm should pile up enough resources to be absolutely sure that the backing is sufficient. The cost of that kind of safety is too high, however. As the old Japanese proverb says, 'Too much is just like too little', because the firm cannot use those resources to gain some other strategic goal.

Even with sufficient backing for a strategy, some firms fail because they do not effectively use their resources to build successful strategies. A firm's resources are effectively utilized if none are idle, as long as the technology to apply them is available, and if the full potential of each resource is tapped. Every company must check for idle resources. If a plant is typically shut down during the winter, the company should consider developing a new product that would use the plant in that slack period. Not all idle resources are so easy to spot, however, and the firm has to pay special attention to identifying them. For example, a transport firm may not realize that its truck is running empty over some portions of the route. Once it spots this idle resource, it can look for new products to fill the empty slot.

Much harder than achieving full utilization, however, is taking full advantage of each resource. It is especially difficult to find the potential and choose strategies to take advantage of the most important set of resources, invisible assets. Managers often agonize over such questions. 'What's the technical potential of my firm?' 'How much can we push through our distribution channel without straining its capacity?' If a company misreads the potential of its current resources, a strategy designed to utilize that potential will have insufficient resource backing. The sewing machine company's attempt at diversification illustrates this point. By misjudging the potential of its distribution capability and by not adjusting to this problem, the strategy was doomed to failure.

Some firms solve these problems smoothly. Both Casio and Sharp correctly read the potential of their invisible assets in integrated circuit technology, which they had nurtured with electronic calculators and similar products. Using this technology, Sharp successfully developed electronic home appliances and office information systems and Casio developed digital watches and electronic musical instruments.

In the 1950s several Japanese textile trading companies (for example, C. Itoh, Marubeni) that had developed sophisticated international trading systems found that some of their international resources (market information, shipping capacity, overseas offices) could be more fully utilized. By having an office in the United States, they could gather market information and handle other products. They predicted that customers who were unfamiliar with most Japanese companies would know their names and might rely on them to help market other products. These companies developed a wider portfolio of products and in the process became general trading companies.

Accumulating resources efficiently

Effective utilization of invisible assets implies that the firm must work only with the resources it currently possesses. It is easy to get caught up in this and be trapped into wrongly assuming that resources cannot be changed. But resources *do* change, and strategy is often the source of that change. When firms use their resources effectively, they create new invisible assets. Resource fit thus requires more than effective utilization of existing resources; efficient accumulation of new resources is just as important. New resources must be accumulated at *low cost, quickly, and in a timely manner.* It may be idealistic to try to achieve all three conditions at once, but each contributes to the ideal of efficient resource accumulation.

A system that efficiently accumulates resources usually shows one of the following patterns: either new resources are created as a by-product of a one-period strategy or resources developed in one strategy element are consciously used for the next element.

When new resources are a strategy by-product, they can be accumulated at low cost. Examples were presented in Chapter 2 [of Itami: *Mobilizing Invisible Assets*] in the discussion of invisible asset accumulation. To use resources developed in carrying out one strategy in other strategic areas – the second pattern – the supply of resources and the demand for them within the firm must be effectively matched, both in magnitude and in timing. When the profits generated from mature products are used to develop new products, the resources of one area of the firm are the base for the firm's entry into new product lines.

Combinatorial benefits

When resources and strategy fit well together, there are combinatorial benefits in both resource utilization and asset accumulation. The right combination of product/market segments or elements of the firm's operations mission in a strategy produces various benefits relating to the firm's resources. If a firm can use a single resource (say a plant, or some technology or skill) in more than one product/market segment, there is a combinatorial benefit from the two segments. Resources developed for one product can often reduce the required accumulation of resources for another product, either at the same time or in the future. Similarly, a combinatorial benefit results when operations in one area develop resources that can be used in other areas of the firm.

When a firm sells several types of products, another kind of combinatorial benefit occurs. Consumer confidence in the firm and the appeal of the product line increase. Panasonic, with its full line of electronics products, relies on its well-recognized brand name to sell a greater variety of products than Sony, which has a narrower product line. Recognizing the importance of this kind of diversity, Sony has established a series of stores that sell foreign brand-name electrical products. This enables Sony to get more benefit from its market reputation, a key invisible asset. A department store that stocks a wide range of products or an electronics manufacturer that provides a full line of products is realizing this type of combinatorial benefit, building up the invisible asset of consumer confidence.

A firm can combine strategy elements in many different ways: in products, in markets, in elements in the operations mission, or in current and future strategies. Figure 3.2 illustrates these relationships.

A combination of several strategy elements at one time uses a firm's assets more effectively. A combination of strategies at two different times enables the firm to more efficiently accumulate invisible assets for the future. In other words, effective utilization of resources springs from static combinatorial benefits; efficient accumulation, from dynamic combinatorial benefits.

Efficient   accumulation   is   closely   connected   to   the   dynamic

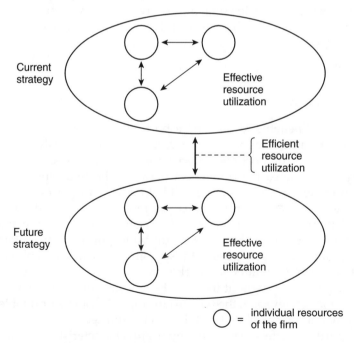

Figure 3.2 Combinatorial benefits and resource fit

combinatorial effect between current and future strategy for two reasons. First, it takes time to accumulate resources. If a current strategy leads to efficient accumulation, those resources have value only as the basis for later utilization. The Sony success (both in brand name and in technology) in transistor radios was the base for later success in television and other areas. Experience in selling textiles in developing countries gave Japanese trading companies knowledge about political and economic situations and the market information necessary for developing more complex deals such as industrial equipment contracts. Resource accumulation is inescapably tied to current and future strategy.

Current strategy has many spillover effects that affect future strategy as well. If current strategy generates cash flow or market information, for instance, these resources will affect the firm's future strategy. Braun, the German electronics firm, has had its own subsidiary to sell shavers in Japan since 1968. Hans Pauli, the president of the subsidiary, said about the benefits of the office for global strategy information:

Certainly we are also a listening post for a European organization about what is going on in Japan, because this is the market from which the competition is coming. Japan has five or six major electrical appliance manufacturers, all of them producing electric shavers. They are competing against each other very heavily and in the process competing against us, too. They are also looking more toward Europe and the United States, so developments here have a big impact on what is going to happen elsewhere.

(Murray, 1984)

PORTFOLIO EFFECTS

Combinatorial benefits result from a portfolio of strategy elements utilizing and accumulating resources effectively and efficiently. I will consider two types of portfolio effects: the complement effect and the synergy effect. Since the differences between the two types have not yet been made clear, an example will help. The manager of a ski resort hotel whose market is primarily skiers must be concerned about the seasonal nature of the business. Off season the facilities are idle. To deal with this problem the resort might build golf and tennis facilities to attract summer resort guests. By so doing it creates a combinatorial benefit between the winter ski market and the resort market, providing for stable profits throughout the year. Even if neither group by itself can generate enough revenue, the two groups together can be profitable. The firm's physical resource, its hotel, is effectively used.

This portfolio effect has two important characteristics. First, both markets use the same resource. Each market fills a void left by the other, putting excess resources to work. But there may be no further interaction between the two markets. In this sense they are complements. Improvement in one market will have no effect on the other market; if ski traffic increases, it will not affect summer resort occupancy.

But the combinatorial benefit of the two sets of hotel visitors may not be limited to the complement effect. If skiers find that the hotel is a good place to stay, some may return in the summer. And summer guests may decide to try the ski resort next winter. One market is able to ride free on the invisible asset (the hotel's reputation) developed by the other. Sales in one market (skiers) are no longer independent of those in the other (summer guests). The effect may be positive or negative, but it is very different from the complement effect discussed above. It is multiplicative rather than additive: this is synergy.

Previous studies have defined synergy as merely the whole portfolio effect, but I use the term in a narrower sense that is more in keeping with its original meaning. This requires the use of an additional term (complement effect), but the discussion in terms of these two types of portfolio effects enables us to dig more deeply into the portfolio effect. The synergy effect is one strategic level above the complement effect. With synergy something new is created, whose effects are more significant and wide-ranging than those of just full utilization. It obviously takes more than adding markets to achieve this result.

Compared to the complement effect, the synergy effect is difficult to achieve and the strategist must make a greater effort to capture these benefits. A careless company might never be aware that they exist. Yet the difference between two companies in resource fit may be in the ability of one to ferret out synergy effects.

Complement effect

The complement effect almost always focuses on full capacity utilization of some kind. Just as the ski resort becomes a summer hotel, some Japanese auto carriers are filled with logs for the return voyage to Japan from the west coast of the United States. A personal computer manufacturer gets full use from the cash flow generated by an established model when it uses those funds to develop the next generation of models. Of course a complement effect can work with several products; the objective is always to combine elements so that resources are fully used.

Unless a firm has more than one product or market, its resources may not be used to capacity, resulting in lower sales or profits. Permitting two unrelated strategy elements to coexist, usually through the utilization of the same physical or financial assets, is the essence of the complement effect.

The most easily observable and perhaps most widespread complement effect is the use of the same physical asset to serve more than one market. A single product market might not be sufficient because optimal resource capacity does not match the size of the market, or because resources are not used with equal intensity over time, or because the required resource capacity fluctuates.

In the first case there is a gap between the logically optimal size of the firm's resource commitment and the volume of the operation in a single market. For example, it may not be possible to build a plant with just the right capacity to manufacture a single product; the gap can be filled by adding a second product. A good example is General Motors' auto engine plants. If an automobile division cannot use all of their capacity, GM permits the engine plants to build engines for its other divisions. Falling sales of one product may provide an opportunity to use part of the plant to produce another product.

Another opportunity to produce a complement effect arises when facilities are not used with equal intensity over a cycle, daily or seasonal. We have seen that in the hotel case, but a restaurant that serves an after-theatre meal or a Sunday brunch is doing the same thing.

A third type of complement effect can be obtained when the level of physical resources necessary to operate in a given market fluctuates. A firm with several markets or products can be more confident that the total level of required resources will remain relatively stable. Each market has sales variability, but by operating in several the firm reduces the total variability. Again, the GM engine plant is a good example. GM is able to forecast its overall sales better than sales of individual models. Having the flexibility to occasionally supply Chevrolet engines to other divisions helps GM maintain full operation of its engine plants. To take another example, as the domestic economies of Japan and the United States experience more variation, more and more firms are trying to enter export markets. Any firm can find potential areas for complement effect benefits if it pays attention to the problem.

The three conditions described for the complement effect for physical assets also apply to financial resources, but with a significant difference: financial resources are both an input and an output; they are *generated by* and *utilized in* business activities. This special characteristic will require some adjustments in the analysis. The first condition, underutilization of the resource, here means that funds generated by one product or market cannot be effectively recycled in that area. This idle money has to be funnelled into other products or markets. Few companies are in that enviable position, but it is an important complement effect to keep in mind.

The second condition, inability to use a resource with the same intensity over a cycle, also applies to money, but the cycle is of longer duration because of the input/output nature of this resource. If the financial resources input in a product line do not match the cash flow generated, the potential exists for the second type of financial complement effect. A company that has a strong cash flow can use this resource to expand into new markets. The reverse situation can also exist. A computer leasing company frequently must search for short-term financing. One US firm bought an insurance company to have access to current funds.

The imbalance between inflow and outflow may be in short-term or long-term funds or it may be seasonal, but it may also be between products at different life cycle stages. During the product development period funds are poured into the product line. In the growth period, more money flows in as investment in production and product development increases. When the product reaches the mature stage, however, little investment is needed and money flows out. A firm that is conscious of this dynamic imbalance of cash inflow and outflow can design a multiproduct strategy to achieve a complement effect.

The third condition for complement effects, uncertainty about the future use of resources, also applies to the flow of financial resources. Thus firms choose to operate in several market segments to make balanced cash flows more likely. A firm that successfully deals with uncertainty in the use of its physical assets will create the potential for complement effects with its financial resources.

Synergy

The goal of synergy is to get a free ride. This happens when the resources accumulated in one part of the company are used simultaneously and at no additional expense by other parts. Ajinomoto, the Japanese condiments company, had developed a strong brand image and distribution network. It used those resources to sell other food products, such as salad oil, mayonnaise and bouillon cubes, and become a more diversified manufacturer. In addition, it used the amino acid technology developed for its condiments in a new pharmaceutical products division.

The potential for free rides is just as important in marketing as in production. Supermarkets advertise loss leaders to draw customers into stores, where they will also buy products with a higher mark-up. What they lose on these loss leaders is offset by the profits from the sales of other goods. Loss leaders and high mark-up goods have to be present together to create synergy.

Sometimes two areas work together to take advantage of each other's strengths. In the hotel example the two market areas, ski customers and resort customers, take a free ride on the invisible assets such as the hotel's reputation, but the result is more than the sum of the two markets when they are put together.

Most physical resources do not offer the potential for a free ride or simultaneous usage. When two distinct areas of a plant are used to produce two different products, no synergy is created. Financial resources cannot be used simultaneously in two segments either. If money is poured into development of one product, less is available for other products.

Invisible assets are different. Unlike physical and financial resources, an invisible asset like technology can be used in more than one area simultaneously without reducing its value in other areas. When the Ajinomoto amino acid technology is used in a pharmaceutical product, it can still be used to develop products in other areas. This is a true free-ride situation. Not only do invisible assets hold their value with simultaneous multiple use, in some cases their value is enhanced. The invisible asset of the ski lodge's reputation may increase in value as more customers take advantage of the facility and its summer reputation spreads. Synergy results when several areas are free to use the resources without taking anything away from other parts of the firm. The complement effect is created by utilizing visible assets; the synergy effect, by utilizing invisible assets.

The essence of invisible assets is information, and it is this characteristic, which is not shared by other resources, that makes a free ride possible. Only information-based assets can be used in multiple ways at the same time. Information has three characteristics that make synergy possible: it can be used simultaneously, it does not wear out from overuse and bits of it can be combined to yield even more information.

For example, if one of the firm's technical people knows a lot about a particular process, she can pass along that knowledge to colleagues in another department. She can still use it herself, and it is available for others within the firm to use. In fact, this technology may increase in value as people share the results of their research. One department may know of a development that will enable them to combine two pieces of information to create additional valuable technology. Eventually the value of the information to other areas may lessen as it is dispersed, but the value of the information itself will not decline.

Synergy from information-based assets often enables a company to create a competitive edge. This can happen as the firm operates in new products and markets or as it chooses new strategies in established markets. A company that can call on the synergy from invisible assets such as product name or distribution channel control will have a competitive edge over a company without such assets. Ajinomoto, with its invisible assets in condiments marketing and production, was able to enter the mayonnaise market successfully when other companies failed.

The synergy from invisible assets enables the firm to build a competitive position at lower cost. Of course good product design and careful implementation of strategy are important, but the basis of the success is synergy.

The complement effect also has potential for forging a competitive edge, but it is much more limited. Using an idle plant for a new product saves capital equipment costs and reduces the time needed to enter a new market, but these benefits stop when the new production line starts up and the plant is producing at full capacity. The limits on physical resources set the limits on the contribution of the complement effect. Financial resources are similarly limited. The benefits of a cash flow balance may be negated if competitors also have access to extra financial resources. This asset may not give the firm the competitive edge it is seeking.

With invisible assets, on the other hand, the competitive benefits from synergy can be both continuous and substantial. In Chapter 2 [of Itami: *Mobilizing Invisible Assets*], I stressed that invisible assets cannot be purchased but must be created within the firm over the long term. These assets give the firm a strong advantage over new competitors, who will need considerable time to create similar resources. With effective use of synergy, the strategist can make even better use of this competitive advantage. By taking a free ride on the synergy inherent in invisible assets, the firm can create very effective and long-lasting competitive weapons.

The potential for achieving resource fit is reduced substantially if synergy benefits are not considered. Thus, a strategist has to keep invisible assets constantly in mind by asking questions like the following. 'What kind of invisible assets does this product or market create?' 'Can the assets be used in other areas of the firm?' 'Am I making the best possible use of the invisible assets I have?' 'Is this strategy limited to be the complement effect benefits?' 'Am I falling into the trap of being satisfied with just the complement effect?'

A strategy based on synergy can fail for various reasons, including the following: overestimating the benefits of synergy, assuming that all joint uses generate synergy, and developing too many unprofitable 'synergy-creating' products. A company that overestimates the synergy benefits will find that the effect is much smaller than it anticipated, and the strategy may fail. Because it is difficult to estimate synergy benefits, it is best to be conservative in projections.

A second pitfall is to assume that any joint use of invisible assets will benefit the firm. The Nikon case shows the danger here. In marketing the Nikon EM, a less expensive, mass-produced camera, Nikon was able to take a free ride on its high-quality brand image, the Nikon mystique. But there was a risk that the Nikon EM might damage Nikon's reputation for superior quality. A firm must be aware of the potential for damaging its invisible asset base and try to anticipate any potential negative repercussions.

There is yet a third pitfall. A product may contribute to a firm's overall portfolio, even if it is not profitable. There may be a temptation to justify an unprofitable product by suggesting that it will enable other products to take a free ride. Any such suggestion should be examined carefully to ensure that it is justified.

Even though the payoff is higher for synergy, a strategist might argue that the return from complement effects is still important for competitive edge. After all, it is easier to keep track of physical assets than invisible assets. An idle plant is easily noticed; if money is available, people will want to make use of it. Taking advantage of the complement effect is certain to pay off. Unfortunately, this is one reason that the competitive benefits from the complement effect are not long-lasting: all the competitors are doing it. It pays to seek out synergy effects, for they will be longer-lasting and harder to duplicate.

In fact, a firm may not have to choose between complement and synergy effects because in many cases they can be pursued simultaneously. Potential complement and synergy benefits are often closely related, as the hotel example showed. Still, many companies satisfied with the complement effect tend to miss opportunities to take full advantage of the synergy potential within their firm. The cost of this oversight is high.

DYNAMIC RESOURCE FIT

Over time, a company's accumulation of resources changes, and as a result its strategy must change. A company must recognize the dynamic nature of both its environment and of its resources. Dynamic combinatorial benefits result from combining present and future strategies; the two must mesh well to achieve this effect. Effective strategy in the present builds invisible assets, and the expanded stock enables the firm to plan its future strategy, bridging the gap between present and future strategy. A current strategy has to create enough resources for future strategy to be carried out. And the future strategy must make effective use of the resources that have been amassed. With these two steps, a firm has the dynamic combinatorial effect, which is the basis of dynamic resource fit.

A static combinatorial effect comes from the combination of different strategy elements at the same time. The dynamic combinatorial benefit, in contrast, is based on the combination of two strategies at different points in time. This is a very different type of portfolio effect.

Current resource accumulation strategy has to satisfy both present and future strategic requirements. When a company chooses a strategy, it is in fact making certain changes in its invisible asset portfolio for the future. A company that decides to advance into a new operation and makes the appropriate investment in plant, equipment and research and development, with the necessary financing, has changed the set of resources available for use in the future. The future stock of resources is thus set by current policy.

Resources may also be accumulated as a by-product of current strategies in the product/market portfolio and the operations mission. In this way both financial resources and invisible assets are created without any direct effort by the firm. Matsushita's overseas strategy for batteries, discussed in Chapter 2 [of Itami: *Mobilizing Invisible Assets*], is an example of this route. The company created invisible assets in knowledge of the market, trained workers, and skills developed through producing and distributing simple batteries. These assets then became sources of dynamic synergy. Invisible assets and financial resources can be accumulated via both routes, but physical assets can be accumulated only through the first.

The future stock of resources is the variable that connects present and future strategies. Dynamic resource fit thus is, in essence, the creation of the most effective combinatorial benefit of these two strategies. The firm has to decide what current strategy is necessary to obtain this effect, and then how to frame its future strategy to capitalize on the effect. If the current and future strategies mesh well, they create either a dynamic complement effect or a dynamic synergy effect, or both. The effects are essentially the same as in the static case.

Dynamic complement effect

The two key points for realizing the dynamic complement effect from physical resources are using resources effectively over time and securing the appropriate level of resources for strategy at each point in time. The complement effect depends on current and future strategies sharing the same assets or on current resources being reused for future strategy goals. Reusable physical assets are strategically valuable, and a firm should try to accumulate such resources.

For example, if a firm must decide whether to build a specialized assembly line for some of its products, it could design the plant with the potential for changing over to production of another product. This may make it much less efficient, however. In that case it may be better to design the assembly line so that it can be easily scrapped when it becomes outmoded, and to create a corporate culture that accepts change when a scrapping decision has to be made.

The important point about dynamic resource fit is that resource inputs and outputs must match. Cash flow is one measure of that matching, since it compares the total financial resources for all operations (the money outputs) with the cash expenditures for reinvestment within the firm (the money as an input). If financial resources are to be balanced in a dynamic sense, the strategist must consider not just where the flow of resources will come from within established operations, but also what financial resources the firm's divisions will require. For example, if a firm undertakes several operations with potential growth simultaneously, the strategist must be aware that after two or three years each one will require more investment if growth is to continue. Present strategies must generate enough cash to support the expected growth later, or the strategist must be willing to accept outside financing.

The cash flow requirements of a given product or market segment vary according to the stage of the product's life cycle, the size and growth rate of the market, and the product's competitive edge. At any one time, a product may be either a net user or a net generator of cash flow.

At the early stages in its life cycle, the product is most likely to use cash flow. As the cycle progresses, it should generate cash flow. Without holding constant the other two factors, however, the exact pattern cannot be determined. A segment with a faster rate of growth will require a large investment over a short period, slowing the shift to cash flow generation. The third factor is competitive edge. Other things being equal, a firm with a strong competitive position can generate a given sales volume at lower cost because it has lower production costs, based on accumulated knowledge or large-scale facilities, or lower sales cost, based on an established brand image. To change that firm's position, a competitor would have to commit substantial resources.

To get the dynamic complement effects from cash flow, a firm must first choose products and markets with different cash flows. The next step is to preserve that complementary pattern over time. Conventional wisdom says that the ideal balance of product or market segments is struck when all cash-draining elements with no future are purged from the portfolio, except for a few unprofitable but promising new areas where the cash flow from current successes can be used. Since many of the currently unprofi-table but growing areas may have an uncertain future, some should be kept, just in case. This is the basic message of the now famous Product Portfolio Management (PPM) techniques. The purpose of this method is to create the dynamic complement effect of cash flow by systematically combining different products and selecting matching strategies.

Dynamic synergy

There is always the potential for dynamic combinatorial benefits from synergy, with future strategies getting a free ride on the invisible assets generated by current strategy. If the future strategy can start before the

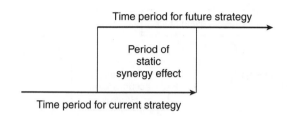

Figure 3.3 Dynamic synergy and static synergy

current strategy has exhausted all potential use of the invisible asset, so much the better. Where the periods of use overlap, contemporaneous use of the resources creates a static synergy effect, too. This use of invisible assets over time is illustrated in Figure 3.3.

The Casio example presented in Chapter 2 [of Itami: *Mobilizing Invisible Assets*] is a good illustration of this effect. The company was able to take advantage of the semiconductor chip technology accumulated in its electronic calculator business to advance into digital watches. At present Casio is also getting the benefit of the static synergy effect shown in Figure 3.3, since currently both calculators and watches are reaping benefits from this semiconducctor technology. Current strategy calls for using semiconductor chip technology to develop office automation equipment and electronic musical instruments.

As I emphasized in Chapter 2 [of Itami: *Mobilizing Invisible Assets*], invisible assets are accumulated through implementation of the firm's strategy in the operations route and through competitive pressures in the market. For example, Casio's semiconductor chip technology was a response to competition in electronic calculators. This produces the pattern shown in Figure 3.4.

Ricoh's decision to re-enter the camera market illustrates a strategy aimed at dynamic synergy. Ricoh was once a leading camera manufacturer in Japan; 65 per cent of its sales in 1955 were in camera equipment. After a long period in which the company focused on the copy machine market, their camera market share was down to 3 per cent in 1977. At that time Ricoh decided to re-emphasize cameras. Ricoh's president, Takeshi Ohue, said:

The camera is Ricoh's only consumer product. Consumer goods are better at building brand image than capital goods. If Ricoh is to achieve the goal of becoming a multinational company, we have to build up our own brand image, and the camera is a good way to do that.

(Michida, 1979)

Because Ricoh had not exported its copy machines under its own name (Savin bought them to sell under its own name in the United States), the

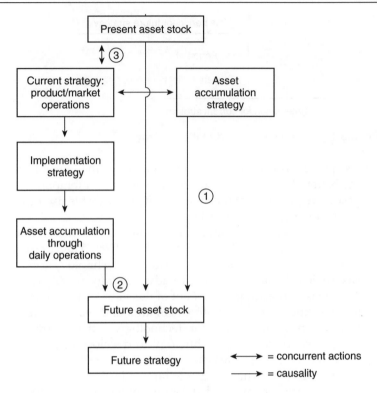

Figure 3.4 A basic framework for dynamic synergy

company's brand name was not established overseas. By building brand name recognition through camera sales, Ricoh has been able to take a free ride on that reputation for other products.

The key to corporate growth lies in generating this dynamic synergy. Whenever the strategies that have resulted in superior growth are analysed, one finds this basic principle at work. Dynamic synergy is essential for two reasons. First, invisible assets can be effectively accumulated and used over a long period only by taking advantage of dynamic synergy giving firms the resources to actively adapt to the ever-changing environment. Second, dynamic synergy between two product or market segments makes it easy to create a dynamic complement effect for financial resources at the same time. As Figure 3.3 shows, when the life cycles of two products overlap, it is often possible to match the cash flow inputs and outputs. By aiming at dynamic synergy, dynamic complement effects often emerge naturally.

To generate dynamic synergy, a firm should choose activities that create invisible assets, design strategy with dynamic synergy in mind, and go beyond its current abilities to develop these invisible assets.

The choice of product or market portfolio elements or operations mission can influence the future level of invisible assets. The flow of invisible assets does not come automatically. If a firm selects product or market portfolio elements only on the basis of cash flow or return on investment, without considering resource accumulation, it will never reap this synergy benefit. Careless application of product portfolio management will often lead to this result.

Kirin Beer chose to further develop its market for non-alcoholic drinks by accepting Coca Cola's offer of a bottling franchise when the American company entered the Japanese market after World War II. Coca Cola's world-wide strategy was to choose firms with bottling expertise and strong financial positions as franchise bottlers rather than owning the facilities itself. At that time Kirin Beer did not have much experience in nonalcoholic drinks, but through its Coca Cola franchise, Kirin developed a better knowledge of the market and the production process. These invisible assets eventually enabled Kirin to enter the soft drink market and eat into Coca Cola's market share by catching the switch in Japanese tastes to fruit and juice drinks earlier than its partner.

Operations mission decisions can sometimes have a greater effect on the accumulation of invisible assets than product or market decisions. If a firm puts too much emphasis on the latter, it may neglect operations-based avenues to resource accumulation, as happens when a firm bases its entire strategy on marketing considerations.

My second point is that the strategy for dynamic synergy requires designing the flow of events, setting out the dynamic changes step by step and determining the timing and order of those changes. The flow of strategy cannot be designed by considering only a single period. Product and operations mission decisions at any one time have to be seen in light of the overall flow of strategy. Each step must be designed with the overall flow in mind, achieving dynamic equilibrium as well as development within the design.

Casio's flow of strategy succeeded because the digital watch came after the electronic calculator; the reverse would not have worked. This is true also of the company's entry into the electronic musical instrument market. In Matsushita's foreign plants, battery production as an end in itself would not have had much meaning. As part of the company's strategic design, however, it was a very significant first step. A firm that develops a strategic design will find the hidden benefits of dynamic synergy within it. Then the door to the next market will be easier to unlock, as Casio found.

A company that does not design a strategy to generate a positive flow of resources can find itself in a vicious circle. If present strategies fail to generate the resources necessary for future strategies, the firm will be forced to eat into its resource base, reducing its options for future strategic moves. Chronically troubled companies are often trapped in this type of pattern.

The dynamic aspect of strategic design leads to my third point: the necessity for *imbalance* at times. Less than adequate backing for a strategy may not always be damaging and can be quite beneficial over the long haul, leading to the realization of the overall strategic design. I call this strategy *overextension*. In the cycle of dynamic synergy, a current lack of resources forces a firm to generate new invisible assets that will assure the success of future strategy. It would be ideal if these invisible assets could be created without overextension, but that is seldom possible in the reality of the business world. To achieve its strategic design, a firm may have to enter a new product area or operations mission activity before it is completely ready. Something I often hear in talking with successful strategists sums up this point well: *'Overextend yourself, but don't get reckless.'*

Dynamic imbalance

Sometimes strategy must take a calculated risk. In Figure 3.4, short-term resource matching requires that current resources be sufficient for the strategies chosen. Overextension requires that the firm consciously violate the principle of static resource fit. This is not as contradictory as it sounds. Of course, some resource backing (physical resources, short-term capital) is essential for a strategy to be operative. Invisible assets, however, are important for effective strategy implementation so in the short term a strategy can make do with a little less than the necessary level of invisible assets. The short-term strategy may not be a winning one, but it may be worthwhile. Competition will toughen and train the people in the firm, and quite possibly some invisible assets will be acquired along the way.

Casio's semiconductor chip strategy illustrates the overextension strategy. Faced with fierce competition in the electronic calculator market, Casio had to jump into integrated circuit design to survive, even though it did not have the best technology in that area. That technology was forged in the heat of competition, eventually leading to Casio's current position in the market. Casio began with less than adequate resource backing, less than fully balanced resources. This short-term imbalance led to the creation of a solid base for future strategy that enabled Casio to beat back the competition in this market. This I call *dynamic imbalance*.

I do not advocate static resource imbalance for its own sake. I believe, however, that imbalance is usually beneficial, especially for invisible assets and for companies that are growing rapidly. The short-term imbalance works as an impetus to achieve dynamic resource fit. If resources are *not* matched in a static sense at key times in the life of the firm, this imbalance can be the basis for corporate growth and strategy.

The Japanese auto industry is a good illustration of the potential payoff from dynamic imbalance. In the early 1950s some Japanese thought that the industry did not have the resources necessary to be competitive internationally. Bank of Japan Governor Ichimada argued that Japan would have to compete on too large a scale and over too wide a range of market segments. He argued that the industry lacked the skills for international competition. Japan could not produce high-quality sheet steel for automobiles and the domestic machine tool industry could not build the machines to grind the engine blocks. The Japanese automobile industry could not compete because it needed so many supporting industries, he thought. An imbalance existed between corporate resources, especially invisible assets, and the automobile production strategy. Proponents argued that the wide scope of supporting industries was an attraction. As the industry grew, they argued, the related industries would grow with it. These spillover effects could not be ignored. Producing cars would be the only way to eliminate the short-term imbalance gradually and the accumulated resources would enable the firms to be competitive.

The proponents won the debate, and the Japanese auto industry was protected from international competition long enough to develop the needed resources. Of course it could not produce internationally competitive cars right away. The first Japanese cars tested on American roads could not stand the sustained speeds and failed miserably. This sort of situation is now in the past for cars and many other Japanese products, but the lesson is worth remembering. In each of these industries an overextension strategy was crucial to accumulating sufficient resources to become competitive in world markets. By creating a static imbalance between resources and operations (route 3 in Figure 3.4), the flow of additional resources for use in future strategy (route 2) is increased. There is no assurance that successive short-term imbalances will lead to the desired long-term balance. Still, avoiding all short-term imbalances means giving up the potential for dynamic synergy.

If there is potential for long-term balance through short-term imbalance, a strategist should not be content as the benefits from previous imbalances work through the system and the system settles down. Such a situation should be seen as a signal for new overextension initiatives for an even higher level of long-term balance through imbalance. This logic says: *destroy balance*.

Chapter 4

Integrating strategies for clusters of businesses

Robert Buzzell and Bradley Gale

For individual business units, strategy involves creating a sustainable competitive advantage (better technology, superior perceived quality, larger market share, lower capital intensity) in the product/market segments that the business has chosen to serve. In Chapters 3–11 [of Buzzell: *The PIMS Principles: Linking Strategy to Performance*] we have shown how these and other strategic and market factors affect the performance of individual SBUs. In addition to formulating strategies at the business-unit level, a primary goal of corporate strategic management is to create sustainable competitive advantages by carefully building clusters of interrelated business units that reinforce each other. (We use the term 'cluster' to designate either an overall company portfolio or, in a larger corporation, a group or 'sector' of related SBUs.) The goal is not to invest in isolated projects that produce incremental benefits, but to develop well-positioned business clusters whose synergy creates advantages that beat the cost of capital and build lasting shareholder value. To achieve this goal, management must develop strategies for related business clusters, not just for one business at a time. Companies that have benefited from the powerful impact of synergies based on the interrelatedness of their businesses include General Electric, General Motors, Phillips, and RCA.[1]

Early portfolio matrix displays were designed to focus corporate management's attention on the need to invest in individual businesses whose competitive positions and strategies have a good chance of beating the cost of capital, rather than investing in individual projects based solely on financial analysis. These matrix approaches were useful for appraising questions of cash flow balance, but they didn't really deal with the issues of relatedness, sharing, synergy, and the need to integrate strategies for clusters of interdependent businesses. Whilst they bore the name portfolio matrices, they were really only systems for classifying individual business-unit data on such dimensions as market growth and relative market share.

Heightened global competition and merger, disposition and leveraged buyout activity in the 1980s all point to the need for focusing more attention on the broader portfolio issues of interrelatedness, sharing, synergy, and dedicated roles for specific businesses. What is synergy? How does synergy create value? How can the effects of synergy on performance be measured? How can a cluster of businesses be analysed systematically to uncover pervasive problems or opportunities? How can a cluster of businesses be assessed relative to competitors? What specialized roles should be assigned to specific units so as to strengthen the overall cluster effectively?

SYNERGY

What is synergy? We define synergy as the performance of a cluster relative to what its performance would be as the sum of its components. How would its effects show up in operating results? Ongoing synergistic benefits are those sources of value that allow the business units in a portfolio to achieve higher profitability levels than they would normally achieve as stand-alone operations. For instance, when business units share the costs of a particular activity, economies of scale will probably allow each to enjoy lower unit costs than if it had been operating independently. This reduced cost would be reflected in a higher level of profitability than indicated by the strategic position of each business unit.

There are four basic mechanisms through which ongoing synergies create value:

1 *Shared resources/activities.* Common activities (R&D/engineering, procurement, production/operations, pooled sales forces, marketing programmes, distribution channels) that are shared to achieve scale economies.
2 *Spill-over benefits of marketing and R&D.* Even when marketing and R&D activities aren't shared, businesses in a cluster often capture some of the indirect benefits of marketing and R&D expenditures that are made by sister businesses. For example, GE's research in turbine engines helped its aircraft engine business.
3 *'Similar' businesses.* Knowledge and skills (both technical and managerial) can be shared across businesses in similar domains of knowledge (high technology industries or situations where marketing skills are the key).
4 *Shared image.* Individual business units in a company gain in value by being strongly identified as members of the highly-regarded corporate whole.

The research insights summarized below are based on an analysis of a data base of sixty companies that have performed a PIMS portfolio analysis across all or most of their businesses.[2]

Shared activities and spill-overs

Shared functional costs represent a key type of potential synergy across units. How much synergy can be attained depends on the following:

- Which functional components of the value chain are most subject to scale economies across units. (A value chain is the collection of activities that a business performs to design, produce, market, deliver, and support its product-service offering.)
- How important each function is in the cost structure of the value chain.
- The degree to which functional costs can be shared across units.

Production and purchasing costs are variable in the sense that they are closely tied to a business's level of output. By contrast, R&D and marketing costs are relatively fixed and decline more rapidly on a per unit basis as a business's rate of output gets larger. This *a priori* knowledge of which costs are relatively fixed, and strong evidence from the SPI data base of portfolios of businesses, together indicate that R&D and marketing (advertising and sales) costs are more subject to scale economies across units; on the other hand, production and purchasing costs are usually more important components of the cost structure (Table 4.1). Portfolios whose value chain is relatively intensive in marketing and R&D achieve above-average synergy and therefore outperform the profitability they might achieve if they were stand-alone businesses. These results reflect not only the effects of economies in shared functional costs, but also the spill-over benefits that businesses in a cluster receive from the marketing and R&D expenditures of sister businesses. By contrast, portfolios whose value chain contains relatively little marketing and R&D activity realize below-average synergy.

Table 4.1 Assessing potential synergy across the value chains of related business

Cost Element	Activities included	Relative importance in cost structure	Opportunities	
			Scale economies	Sharing costs
R&D	Product and process development	Very low	High	High
Marketing	Advertising, promotion, sales	Medium	High	Medium
Production	Manufacturing distribution	High	Low	Low
Purchases	Purchased goods and services	High	Very low	High

Note: double line separates value-added costs from purchases.

Similar businesses: shared knowledge, skills

Some companies seem to develop a distinctive competence that enables their units to perform effectively in certain business contexts or knowledge domains. For example, a company might be particularly good at operating in high-technology industries (Hewlett-Packard), or in industries where marketing skills are key (Procter & Gamble), or in labour-intensive industries where people skills are especially important.

If a company consciously focuses on the business context that it has mastered, it should be able to outperform corporate portfolios that include several dissimilar kinds of businesses. Companies that stray outside their domain of knowledge usually have difficulty developing a recognized corporate competence or a 'culture' that accommodates all the businesses in their portfolio. As one might expect, they have trouble trying to run high-tech businesses in tandem with low-tech businesses, or labour-intensive businesses alongside capital-intensive businesses.

Research on related versus conglomerate diversification strategies has produced mixed results.[3] Rumelt found that firms that diversified horizontally into areas closely related to their core skills were more profitable than conglomerates or companies whose units were vertically related. But two groups of academics have disputed Rumelt's findings. One group took a subsample of Rumelt's data and corrected for market structure effects. Once these corrections had been made, they found no significant differences in performance. They found that companies following a closely-related diversification strategy happened to have strong positions in each of the markets in which they operated and it was this that explained why they performed so well. Another pair of academics found no statistically significant difference in profitability between related and unrelated companies once they had taken into account what they thought to be the undue influence of the pharmaceutical industry on their own results and Rumelt's.

Looking at the PIMS data base of start-up businesses, Ralph Biggadike found that financial and market-share performance depended on the type of relatedness between the venture unit and its parent.[4] He classified start-up businesses into three categories:

1 forward integration;
2 technology link;
3 marketing link.

Using the median performance of businesses in each category, Biggadike found that start-up businesses with marketing links to sister businesses outperformed, on all performance measures (cash flow, ROI, ROS, and relative market share), start-ups that had technology or upstream vertical links.

Table 4.2 Start-up success depends on type of relatedness between venture unit and parent

Performance measures (%)*	Type of relatedness		
	Forward integration (n = 31)	Technology (n = 28)	Marketing (n = 54)
Cash flow/investment	−83	−73	−69
Return on investment	−33	−47	−22
Return on sales	−38	−70	−16
Relative market share	7	3	14

*The results were achieved during the first two years of entry by start-up businesses.

Biggadike's findings were based on a sample of 29 of the 40 units in the PIMS start-up business data base in 1976. Using a sample of 113 of the more than 200 businesses in the 1986 start-up data base, we replicated Biggadike's research and found that this larger sample confirmed his original results (Table 4.2).

For several dimensions of portfolio relatedness, research on the PIMS portfolio data base indicates that clusters of businesses competing in similar environments outperform those clusters competing in dissimilar environments. Portfolios of businesses that have roughly comparable marketing intensity, or R&D spending levels, or capital intensity almost inevitably outperform portfolios that try to accommodate both high tech and low tech, or both marketing-intensive and non-marketing-intensive, or both capital-intensive and non-capital-intensive businesses. They generally do so by about three points of ROI (Table 4.3).

Table 4.3 Portfolio profitability and the degree of similarity among business units*

Characteristic	Measure	Profit performance of consistent versus dissimilar clusters of business units
Marketing intensity	Marketing/sales	+3.5
Technology	R&D/sales	+2.9
Capital intensity	Fixed capital/sales	+3.5
Industry concentration	Share of top 4 companies	+1.8
Innovation	% sales from new products	−2.4
Growth	Real market growth	−0.2

*The degree of similarity was captured by using the standard deviation of the measure in question within each portfolio. For each characteristic, the portfolios were divided into similar and dissimilar groups on the basis of the average degree of similarity for the 60 portfolios.
Source: John Wells, 'In Search of Synergy', doctoral thesis, Harvard Business School, 1984.

Innovation, however, is one key characteristic that thrives on dissimilarity. The evidence indicates that in introducing new products, portfolios in which each business introduces some new products earn lower returns than portfolios composed of a balance between businesses that actively introduce new products and those that do not (Table 4.3).

Shared image

A business unit's reputation for superior (or inferior) quality may spill over on to its sister businesses in the cluster. If a portfolio is made up of businesses that are consistently superior in quality relative to their competition, we would expect that portfolio to achieve performance levels that exceed par projections based on individual business-unit characteristics. Conversely, if relative quality is consistently inferior across a portfolio, the portfolio will tend to underperform the par of its individual units.

The SPI portfolio data base confirms these expectations (Figure 4.1). Portfolios with consistently superior quality outperform par by 2.5 points of ROI. Portfolios with consistently inferior quality underperform par by 2.9 points of ROI.

Notice what we have just observed. 'Synergy' can be negative as well

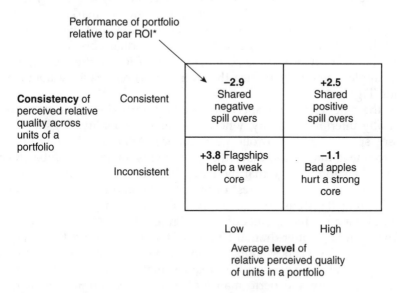

Figure 4.1 How the level and consistency of relative perceived quality affects portfolio performance
*Actual ROI earned minus Par ROI
Source: Wells, John, 'In Search of Synergy', doctoral thesis, Harvard Business School, 1984

as positive! Most executives (and researchers) focus on positive synergies – not negative synergies. When stand-alone businesses are clustered
together they hope for

1 economies of scale in shared activities;
2 spill-over benefits from marketing and R&D expenditures of sister
  businesses;
3 economies of shared knowledge and skills in running similar
  businesses.

Many people even define synergy as 2 + 2 = 5. But our definition of
synergy focuses on the performance of a cluster as such, relative to what
its expected performance would be as the sum of its components.
Clearly, a portfolio made up of businesses that were suffering from the
spill-over effects of their inferior quality reputations would be better off
broken up. This two-edged sword of shared-image synergy may be one
reason why researchers have not been very successful in finding significant performance differences between the related and conglomerate
categories of diversified companies.

The more intriguing effects of shared image are seen in portfolios that
contain a mix of inferior and superior quality businesses. There are two
very interesting manifestations.

At one end of the spectrum, we find portfolios where nearly all the
business units are superior in quality but a few are markedly inferior.
These 'bad apples' benefit from the excellent image of the core of the
portfolio and therefore outperform their individual pars. But they also
drag the performance of the core below par. The net effect is negative.
'Bad apples' generally reduce the overall portfolio ROI by about one
point (Figure 4.1).

At the other end of the spectrum, we find portfolios of business units
typically inferior in quality, whose few superior-quality, flagship businesses spark overall portfolio performance. Although the low quality
environment may undermine the profitability of the flagships themselves, the strong image that the latter SBUs project is sufficient to pull
up the performance of the rest of the portfolio and more than compensate. Strong flagships can generally pull up overall portfolio performance by almost four points of ROI (Figure 4.1).

These findings offer dramatic proof of the need to track the competitive positions of business units in a portfolio rather than just focusing on
their financial performance. Companies that don't track the relative
perceived quality and performance of their business units versus their
par ROI may allow 'bad apples' to make a deceptively good showing
and, what's worse, pull down the performance of the entire business
cluster. Alternatively, companies may under-reward the spark-plug performance of flagship units.

REFERENCES

1 Heaney, D. F., and Weiss, G., 'Integrating Strategies for Clusters of Businesses', *Journal of Business Strategy*, Summer 1983, pp. 3–11.
2 Wells, J. R., 'In Search of Synergy', Doctoral Thesis, Harvard Business School, 1984.
3 Rumelt, R. P., *Strategy, Structure and Economic Performance*, Boston: Division of Research, Graduate School of Business Administration, Harvard University. (For a summary of the follow-on research, see Wells, pp. 95–108).
4 Biggadike, F. R., *Corporate Diversification Entry Strategy and Performance*, Cambridge, MA: Harvard University Press 1976. (See Chapter 7, 'The Impact of Relatedness on Performance.')
5 Loomis, W., 'Strategic Planning In Uncertain Times', *Chief Executive*, Winter 1980/81.
6 Mitchell, R., 'Dow Chemical's Drive to Change Its Market – and Its Image', *Business Week*, June 9, 1986, pp. 92–6.

Part II

Identifying opportunities

Chapter 5

Introduction to identifying oppportunities

Synergy takes a prominent place in many companies' strategies. Daimler Benz, for example, explained its diversification into aerospace and electronics by pointing to the synergies it would gain by applying technologies from these new areas in its auto businesses.[1] Sony, Matsushita, and Toshiba took stakes in US entertainment companies because they anticipated synergies between their electronic hardware and the software of films and music.[2] Philips gave Product Divisions precedence over its country managers to facilitate the exchange of expertise and technology across the company.[3] Synergy efforts, though, often prove disappointing, either because the benefits do not really exist, or because the costs of the linkage prove to be higher than the benefit gained. Recognizing broad synergy opportunities takes a company only so far; it also has to scrutinize these opportunities in detail.

Consultants and academics have developed a number of frameworks to identify synergy opportunities. In field research at Ashridge Strategic Management Centre, however, we discovered that few companies undertake formal analyses of synergy opportunities across their businesses. One reason is that many managers are unaware of the frameworks that are available. The purpose of the chapters in this part is to make the analytic tools described in the management literature more accessible and better known to practising managers.

The first chapter, 'Interrelationships among business units', is by Michael Porter of Harvard Business School. Porter's contributions to the subject of strategy are widely recognized, and he is a pre-eminent authority in the field. In the selection included here, Porter presents a framework for analysing interrelationships based on sharing activities or skills across different businesses. This reading is taken from *Competitive Advantage*, in which Porter explores how a company creates and sustains a profitable position in an industry or across several industries. Porter identifies two generic strategies for competitive advantage in an industry: cost leadership and differentiation. A third generic strategy, focus, is based on either cost leadership or differentiation in a particular segment of an industry. It is the firm's activities that are the source of competitive advantage, and Porter explores how each activity affects the firm's overall strategy, using value chain analysis. Porter defines value chain activities as primary activities (inbound logistics, operations, outbound logistics, marketing and sales, service) and as support activities (firm infrastructure, human resource management, technology development, procurement). He argues that the value chain provides a more precise understanding of a firm's activities, and its sources of competitive advantage, than do broad functional areas such as R&D, manufacturing, marketing.[4]

This is the approach used to analyse interrelationships across businesses. Porter first explains how tangible interrelationships, or shared activities, can lead to competitive advantage, and the costs associated with such sharing. He then explores the many different activities that can be shared across businesses. Potentially, businesses can share any activity in the value chain, from component manufacturing to a sales-force. Porter examines each activity in detail, providing comprehensive lists of the important types of shared activities in each part of the value chain, the competitive advantage gained, and compromises that can be necessary to make the sharing occur.

When it comes to intangible interrelationships, or shared skills, Porter takes a cautious approach. While he acknowledges that there are examples of significant skills and know-how transfers across businesses, he claims that this is an area where many companies have gone wrong. One problem is that it is difficult to be precise about know-how or skills that are generic across businesses and Porter does not therefore attempt to identify the important kinds of intangible interrelationships in detail. Another problem is that it is harder to analyse just what advantage will be gained by sharing skills, and Porter suggests that there are actually few such interrelationships that are truly important to competitive advantage.

Porter's contribution is to demonstrate how synergy opportunities can be identified precisely enough for managers to judge better just what benefits are possible. By examining each activity in the value chain in detail, managers can specify how linkages result in cost savings or improved differentiation. What is surprising is Porter's chariness towards the sharing of skills and know-how, since this detailed approach can be equally insightful in identifying these kinds of opportunities. Companies such as Xerox, for example, use benchmarking to identify critical activities in areas such as logistics, customer service, or warehousing, and then examine the practices of sister businesses, competitors, and non-competitors who have superior performance in these activities to learn how to improve their own operations, and to set new performance targets for critical activities.[5] These transfers of know-how are not vague, ill-defined attempts to share a generic skill, but highly targeted efforts that can lead to higher performance in key activities. In Part III, Andrew Campbell's paper 'Building Core Skills' shows how companies can analyse the sub-components of skills to identify those that are critical to competitive advantage across different businesses.

Chapter 7, 'Evaluating interdependencies across businesses', provides a framework for managers to consider the organizational costs of potential linkages as well as their benefits. Written by C. K. Prahalad of the University of Michigan and Yves L. Doz of INSEAD, it is taken from their book *The Multinational Mission*. In their book, Prahalad and Doz use an 'integration-responsiveness grid' to help managers understand the balance of forces pushing for world-wide co-ordination on the one hand and local responsiveness on the other.[6] A company with businesses in an industry where the forces for global co-ordination are high will need strong interrelationships among its businesses. This framework can also be used to identify the requirements for co-ordination or differentiation of functions and tasks across different businesses. A group of businesses within a multinational may demand a high level of global integration in research and development, but their marketing functions may have to be more differentiated across countries.

In the reading included here, Prahalad and Doz discuss the many different kinds of interdependencies among the businesses of a multi-national company. Businesses may share common technologies, they may gain scale advantages through global manufacturing or co-ordinated distribution and marketing. The key issue for managers is to decide which of these linkages are critical, and the authors see this as a task that goes beyond value chain analysis. Even when interrelationships do provide quantifiable economic benefits, these have to be set against less easily quantifiable organizational and managerial costs. For example, in one multinational Prahalad and Doz discovered that managers spent 50 to 70 per cent of their time meeting and negotiating with managers of other businesses to co-ordinate activities and decisions, a heavy commitment of managerial time and attention. The costs of interdependencies identified by the authors include loss of top management focus, reduced innovation, loss of flexibility, and loss of visibility of business performance.

Prahalad and Doz agree with Michael Porter that many companies do have significant opportunities for interrelationships across their businesses. They argue, however, that the detailed analysis of economic benefits should not lead managers to overlook organizational costs. While these costs are harder to quantify, they can substantially affect the net benefit gained from an interrelationship. They suggest that a balance sheet approach to weighing costs and benefits can help managers sort out these complex issues.

Chapter 8, 'Four portfolios analysis', is by two strategy consultants, Christopher J. Clarke and Kieron Brennan. The authors argue that many diversification efforts of the 1970s and early 1980s failed not because managers misidentified synergies, or had too optimistic a view of the potential benefits, but rather because they neglected synergy opportunities altogether. Instead, encouraged by many different consultancies, corporate managers adopted portfolio planning, using growth-share matrices such as the one developed by Boston Consulting Group. In doing so, they focused too exclusively on SBU performance, acquiring businesses that were attractive as stand-alone entities but that often did not fit well with other businesses in the overall corporate portfolio.

Clarke and Brennan therefore encourage managers to move away from an SBU focus, and to take a broader perspective. Their methodology divides the corporation into four portfolios: products, resources, customers and technologies. Each portfolio is analysed on a matrix according to specific criteria; customers, for example, are assessed according to how fast their own businesses are growing and their relative market share, while the analysis of technologies takes into account the future importance of a specific technology and the firm's own competence relative to its competitors. These portfolio analyses are then compared with each other to identify the potential synergies between resources, products, customers, and technologies. For example, if a particular customer group is identified as becoming more important, the corporation will want to ensure that business strategies are co-ordinated so that they have adequate resources and appropriate technologies to serve those customers. In evaluating acquisitions, the authors suggest that there should be potential synergies across three of the four broad areas, providing opportunities for the corporation to exploit its existing strengths and also to develop new ones.

Corporate managers, according to Clarke and Brennan, must take a proactive role in identifying synergies, and their analytic framework provides a means of doing so. Their argument that companies should move away from an SBU focus supports the views of Gary Hamel and C. K. Prahalad.[7] The reasoning is that an SBU focus encourages individuality and parochialism and prevents managers from releasing the synergy benefits that exist. But there are opposing points of view. In Part I the chapter by Robert Buzzell and Bradley Gale provided evidence that some companies with an SBU focus do achieve synergy effects. Moreover, the value chain approach advocated by Porter suggests that a clear SBU definition is central to having a clear concept of synergy. In *Managing Across Borders*,[8] Christopher Bartlett and Sumantra Ghoshal also appear to come down in favour of SBUs. The authors support

Porter's analysis that clearly defined units can aid the sharing and linkage process. Perhaps the real challenge is integrating SBU concept with the synergy concept and this work has not been fully completed.

Identifying synergy opportunities is a complex and challenging undertaking. Managers need a wealth of data and a firm understanding of their businesses and their organization. The authors of this chapter argue that managers need to invest this effort if they are to avoid costly mistakes.

REFERENCES

1 *Financial Times*, 11 April 1991, p. 35.
2 *Financial Times*, 8 October 1991, p. 23.
3 Gerrit, J., 'Global Strategies of Philips', *European Management Journal*, vol. 7, no. 1, 1989, pp. 84–91.
4 Porter, M. E., *Competitive Advantage*, Free Press, New York, 1985, pp. 36.
5 Tucker, F., Sivan, S. and Camp, R., 'How to Measure Yourself Against the Best', *Harvard Business Review*, January–February 1987, pp. 8–10: Hayes, R. H., Wheelwright, S. C., Clark, K. B., *Dynamic Manufacturing: Creating the Learning Organization*, The Free Press, New York, 1988, p. 156.
6 Similar frameworks are used by other authorities on multinationals. See Bartlett, C. A. and Ghoshal, S., *Managing across Borders: The Transnational Solution*, Harvard Business School Press, 1989; Porter, Michael E., ed., *Competition in Global Industries*, Harvard Business School Press, 1986.
7 Prahalad, C. K. and Hamel, G., 'The Core Competence of the Corporation', *Harvard Business Review*, May–June, 1990, pp. 79–91.
8 Bartlett, C. A. and Ghoshal, S., *Managing Across Borders: The Transnational Solution*, Harvard Business School Press, Boston, 1989.

Chapter 6

Interrelationships among business units

Michael Porter

INTERRELATIONSHIPS AMONG BUSINESS UNITS

There are three broad types of possible interrelationships among business units: tangible interrelationships, intangible interrelationships, and competitor interrelationships. All three types can have important, but different, impacts on competitive advantage and are not mutually exclusive.

1 *Tangible interrelationships*. Tangible interrelationships arise from opportunities to share activities in the value chain among related business units, due to the presence of common buyers, channels, technologies, and other factors. Tangible interrelationships lead to competitive advantage if sharing lowers cost or enhances differentiation enough to exceed the costs of sharing. Business units that can share a sales force, for example, may be able to lower selling cost or provide the salesperson with a unique package to offer the buyer. Achieving tangible interrelationships often involves jointly performing one value activity while in other cases it involves multiple activities. When sister business units cross-sell each other's product, for example, they are sharing both of their sales forces.

2 *Intangible interrelationships*. Intangible interrelationships involve the transference of management know-how among separate value chains. Businesses that cannot share activities may nevertheless be similar in generic terms, such as in the *type* of buyer, *type* of purchase by the buyer, *type* of manufacturing process employed and *type* of relationship with government. For example, beer and cigarettes are both frequently purchased recreational products sold on the basis of image as well as taste, while trucking and waste treatment both involve the management of multiple sites.

Intangible interrelationships lead to competitive advantage through transference of *generic skills* or know-how about how to manage a particular type of activity or make it more unique and outweigh any cost of transferring the know-how. For example, Philip Morris applied product management, brand positioning, and advertising concepts learned in cigarettes to the beer business, substantially changing the nature of competition and dramatically enhancing the competitive position of the Miller brand. It performed marketing activities for cigarettes and beer separately, but used expertise gained in managing activities in one industry to manage them more effectively in another.

Often intangible interrelationships are manifested in a firm's use of the same generic strategy in a number of business units, reflecting management's skills in executing a particular strategy. For example, Emerson Electric and H. J. Heinz compete by using cost leadership strategies in many of their business units. Emerson and Heinz have learned how to manage many activities to achieve low cost, and transfer this know-how to similar but separate value activities in many business units.

3 *Competitor interrelationships.* The third form of interrelationship, competitor interrelationships, stems from the existence of rivals that actually or potentially compete with a firm in more than one country. These *multipoint competitors* necessarily link industries together because actions towards them in one industry may have implications in another. Whilst competitor interrelationships occur without tangible or intangible interrelationships being present and vice versa, the two often coexist because tangible and intangible interrelationships can provide the basis for diversification. Competitors in one industry, therefore, often expand in the same direction.

Competitor interrelationships make tangible and intangible interrelationships all the more important to recognize and exploit. A multipoint competitor may compel a firm to match an interrelationship or face a competitive disadvantage. Multipoint competitors can also have an overlapping but different set of business units linked by *different* interrelationships than the firm's, making the matching of such interrelationships difficult.

The three types of interrelationships can occur together, as has already been suggested. Tangible interrelationships involving some value activities can be supplemented by intangible interrelationships in others. Activities shared between two business units can be improved by know-how gained from similar activities in other business units. Both tangible and intangible interrelationships are often present when multipoint competitors are present. Each type of interrelationship, however, leads to competitive advantage in a different way.

Synergy is not one idea, then, but three fundamentally different ideas. Thus it is no surprise that what is meant by synergy has been vague. Synergy has most often been described in terms that suggest that what was meant was intangible interrelationships – transference of skills or expertise in management from one business unit to another. This form of interrelationship is perhaps the most ephemeral, however, and its role in creating competitive advantage often is uncertain though potentially significant. Hence it is not surprising that many firms have had great difficulty realizing the fruits of synergy in practice.

I will discuss all three forms of interrelationships in this chapter. Tangible and competitive interrelationships have the most compelling link to competitive advantage, and are easier to implement. Intangible interrelationships are fraught with pitfalls and are often difficult to implement, but can still be a powerful source of competitive advantage in some industries.

TANGIBLE INTERRELATIONSHIPS

The value chain provides the starting point for the analysis of tangible interrelationships. A business unit can potentially share any value activity with another business unit in the firm, including both primary and supporting activities. For example, Procter & Gamble enjoys interrelationships between its disposable diaper and paper towel businesses. Certain raw materials can be procured and handled jointly, the development of technology on products and processes is shared, a joint sales force sells both products to supermarket buyers, and both products are shipped to buyers via the same physical distribution system. The interrelationships are shown schematically in Figure 6.1. As this example illustrates, tangible interrelationships between two business units can involve one or many value activities. If most value activities are shared between two business units, however, they are not strategically distinct business units but in fact one business unit.

Sharing an activity can lead to a sustainable competitive advantage if the advantage of sharing outweighs the cost, provided the sharing is difficult for competitors to match. Sharing leads to a competitive advantage if it reduces cost or enhances differentiation. Sharing always involves some cost, however, that ranges from the cost of co-ordinating among the business units involved to the need to modify business unit strategies to facilitate sharing.

Sharing and competitive advantage

Sharing a value activity will lead to a significant cost advantage if it involves an activity that represents a significant fraction of operating costs or assets (I term this a *large* value activity), and sharing lowers the cost of performing the activity. Sharing will significantly enhance differentiation if it involves an activity important to differentiation in which sharing either increases the uniqueness of the activity or reduces the cost

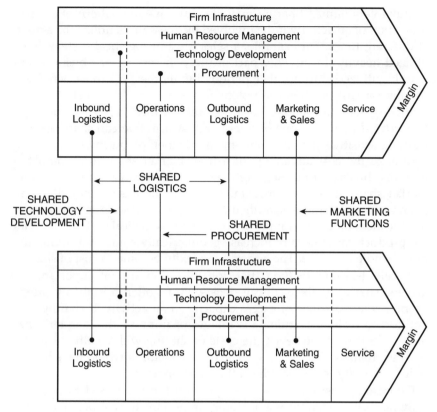

Figure 6.1 Illustrative interrelationships between value chains in paper products

of being unique. Thus sharing leads to a competitive advantage if it affects the drivers of cost position or differentiation described in Chapters 3 and 4 [in Porter: *Competitive Advantage*].

Sharing and cost

Sharing will have a material impact on overall cost position only if the value activities involved are a significant proportion of operating costs or assets, or will be in the future. In the Procter & Gamble example, the shared value activities add up to more than 50 per cent of revenues. Sharing does not necessarily lower cost, however, unless it favourably affects the other cost drivers of an activity. Sharing has the potential to reduce cost if *the cost of a value activity is driven by economies of scale, learning, or the pattern of capacity utilization.*[1] Sharing increases the scale of an activity and increases the rate of learning if learning is a function of cumulative volume.[2] Sharing may also improve the pattern of capacity utilization of an activity if the involved business units utilize the activity at different times. For example, a sales force or logistical system that is utilized heavily during only part of the year serving one business unit may be utilized during other periods by another. All three benefits of sharing for cost position can potentially occur simultaneously.[3]

Sharing activities among business units is, then, a *potential substitute for market share* in any one business unit. A firm that can share scale- or learning-sensitive activities among a number of business units may neutralize the cost advantage of a high market share firm competing with one business unit. Sharing is not exactly equivalent to increasing market share in one business unit, however, because a shared activity often involves greater *complexity* than an equivalent scale activity serving one business unit. The complexity of a shared logistical system involving ten product varieties may increase geometrically compared to one that must handle only five. The added complexity becomes a cost of sharing.

If scale, learning, or the pattern of utilization are not important cost drivers, sharing is likely to raise costs. Firms often mistakenly pursue sharing solely because of excess capacity in an activity. If sharing does not lead to scale or learning advantages or improve the long-term pattern of utilization, however, the costs of sharing will usually mean that sharing creates a disadvantage. The correct solution would have been to reduce capacity in the activity rather than share it.

Figure 6.2 illustrates how these principles can be used to highlight activities where sharing is potentially important to cost position. Interrelationships involving value activities in the upper right-hand quadrant of the diagram are of potentially greatest significance, due to their large costs and sensitivity to scale, learning, or utilization. Interrelationships involving value activities in the upper left-hand quadrant are not currently important because sharing will not reduce cost, though the value activities represent a large fraction of costs or assets. However, changes in the technology for performing such activities can quickly make interrelationships crucial if their cost becomes more sensitive to scale, learning, or utilization. The change in order processing technology from manual systems to on-line computers in many distribution industries, for example, has begun to create important advantages for sharing order processing across related product lines. Interrelationships involving value activities in the lower right-hand quadrant can become important for cost position if changes in the cost structure raise the percentage of operating costs or assets they represent. The increasing capital cost of a plant and supporting infrastructure, for example, will raise the potential advantage of sharing facilities.

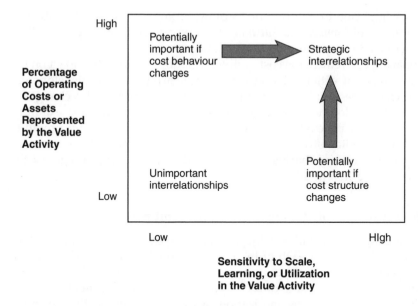

Figure 6.2 Shared value activities and cost position

Sharing and differentiation

Sharing affects differentiation in two ways. It can enhance differentiation by increasing the uniqueness of an activity, or it can lower the cost of differentiation. Chapter 4 [in Porter: *Competitive Advantage*] described how many activities can affect buyer value and, thus, differentiation. Sharing will be most important to differentiation if it affects value activities that are important to actual value or to signalling value. In consumer electronics, for example, sharing product development is important to differentiation because differentiation is heavily affected by product design. Sharing will also be important to differentiation where it reduces the cost of expensive forms of differentiation, such as an extensive sales and service network (e.g. IBM in office products).

Sharing can make an activity more unique both directly and through its impact on other drivers of uniqueness. Sharing enhances uniqueness directly if the shared activity is more valuable to buyers because it involves more than one business unit. Selling several products through the same sales force may increase convenience for the buyer, for example, or allow for the differentiation advantages of bundling (see Chapter 12 in *Competitive Advantage*). In telecommunications, for example, buyers want system solutions and one-vendor accountability. Similarly, joint product development may lead to greater compatibility among related products. Sharing may also increase uniqueness indirectly, through increasing scale or the rate of learning in an activity. As described in Chapter 4 [of *Competitive Advantage*], both scale and learning may allow an activity to be performed in a unique way.

Sharing can reduce the cost of differentiation through its impact on the cost drivers of differentiating activities. Sharing product development among business units can reduce the cost of rapid model changes if product development is subject to economies of scale, for example, whilst shared procurement can lower the cost of purchasing premium quality ingredients or components. The added complexity of a shared activity is a cost of sharing, however, that must be weighed against the benefits to differentiation.

The advantages of sharing and business unit position

Sharing an activity will usually not lead to an equal improvement in cost or differentiation for each of the business units involved. Differences in the scales of the business units are one important reason. A business unit that uses a large volume of a component may not gain much of a cost advantage from sharing fabrication of the component with a business unit that uses a small volume of it. However, the unit that is the smaller user may enjoy a tremendous improvement in cost position through gaining the benefits of the larger unit's scale. The advantages to the unit that is the smaller user may allow it to substantially improve its market position. Given such asymmetries, it should come as no surprise that larger business units are rarely enthusiastic about interrelationships with smaller units.[4]

Differences in the structure of the industries in which business units compete may also lead to differential benefits from sharing. A small improvement in cost position may be very important in a commodity industry, for example, but less significant in an industry where product differentiation is high and firms compete on quality and service. The significance of an interrelationship also depends on the strategies of the business units involved. An interrelationship may lead to uniqueness that is valuable for one business unit but much less valuable to another. It is rare, then, that all the business units involved in an interrelationship will perceive it as equally advantageous. This point has important implications for horizontal strategy and for the ability of senior managers to persuade business units to pursue interrelationships.

The costs of sharing

Interrelationships always involve a cost, because they require business units to modify their behaviour in some way. The costs of sharing a value activity can be divided into three types:

- cost of co-ordination;
- cost of compromise;
- cost of inflexibility.

The cost of co-ordination is relatively easy to understand. Business units must co-ordinate in such areas as scheduling, setting priorities, and resolving problems in order to share an activity. Co-ordination involves costs in terms of time, personnel, and perhaps money. The cost of co-ordination will differ widely for different types of sharing. A shared sales force requires continual co-ordination, for example, while joint procurement may require nothing more than periodic communication to determine the quantity of a purchased input required per period by each business unit. Different business units may also see the cost of co-ordination differently. The costs of co-ordination are often viewed as higher by smaller business units, who see a continual battle over priorities and the risk of being dictated to by larger units. Business units that do not manage a shared activity or are located at a distance from it also tend to fear that their best interests will not be protected.[5]

The cost of co-ordination will be influenced by the potentially greater complexity of a shared activity noted earlier. The added complexity involved in sharing will vary, depending on the specific activity. Sharing a computerized order entry system among business units will usually add little complexity, for example, in contrast to sharing a logistical system between two business units with large product lines. The added complexity of a shared activity can sometimes offset economies of scale or reduce the rate of learning compared to an activity serving one business unit. Thus sharing can both increase scale and/or learning at the same time as it alters the relationship between scale or learning and cost. This is important because changing the scale- or learning-sensitivity of an activity may benefit or hurt the firm's cost position depending on its circumstances. Computerization generally has reduced the cost of handling the complexity of sharing. That is one of the reasons why interrelationships are getting more important.

A second, often more important, cost of sharing is the *cost of compromise*. Sharing an activity requires that an activity be performed in a consistent way that may not be optimal for either of the business units involved. Sharing a sales force, for example, may mean that the sales person gives less attention to both business units' product and is less knowledgeable about either product than a dedicated sales force would be. Similarly, sharing component fabrication may mean that the component's design cannot exactly match one business unit's needs because it must also meet another's. The cost of compromise may include costs not only in the shared value activity but also in other linked value activities. Sharing a sales force, for example, may reduce the availability of salespeople to perform minor service functions, thereby increasing the number of service technicians required. Policy choices required to facilitate sharing, then, can adversely affect the cost or differentiation of one or more of the business units involved.

That business units must in some way compromise their needs to share an activity is almost a given. The cost of compromise may be minor, or may be great enough to nullify the value of sharing. For example, attempting to share a logistical system among business units producing products of widely differing sizes, weights, delivery frequencies, and sensitivities to delivery time may well lead to a logistical system that is so inappropriate to any of the business unit's needs that the cost savings of sharing are overwhelmed. However, sharing a brand name or sharing procurement of commodities may involve little or no compromise.

The cost of compromise to share an activity will often differ for each of the affected business units. A business unit with a product that is difficult to sell may have to compromise the most in employing a shared sales force, for example. The cost of compromise may also differ because the particular value activity plays a differing role in one business unit compared to another because of its strategy. The compromise involved in joint procurement of a common grade of milk or butter may be more serious for a business unit of a food manufacturer pursuing a premium quality strategy than it is for one attempting to be the low-cost producer if the common grade is not top quality.

The cost of compromise required to achieve an interrelationship is much less if the strategies of the business units involved are consistent with respect to the role of the shared value activity. Achieving such consistency often involves little or no sacrifice to the affected business units *if their strategic directions are co-ordinated over time*. A particular component can be highly effective in the products of two business units if both design their products with the component in mind, for example. If the design groups of the two business units are allowed to proceed independently, however, the chances are high that the common component will not meet either business unit's needs. Consistency among business units' strategies that facilitates sharing will rarely happen naturally. An example of both the opportunities to shape the cost of compromise and the indirect costs of compromise that must be weighed comes from General Foods' successful new Pudding Pops. Pudding Pops were designed to melt at a higher temperature than ice cream so that distribution then could be shared with General Foods' Birds Eye frozen vegetables. Whilst frozen foods are transported at zero degrees Fahrenheit, ice cream must be transported at 20 degrees below zero or it will build up ice crystals. While benefits in shared logistics were clear, however, sharing had some unforeseen consequences elsewhere in the value chain. Because Pudding Pops had to be ordered by supermarket frozen food managers along with vegetables, instead of with other free-zer case novelty items, Pudding Pops were often forgotten. As this example illustrates, the benefits and costs of an interrelationship must be examined *throughout the value chain* and not just in the activity shared.

The cost of compromise is frequently reduced if an activity is *designed for sharing* rather than if previously separate activities are simply combined or if an activity designed to serve one business unit simply takes on another with no change in procedures or technology. Recent events in financial services have highlighted this point. Merging computer systems initially designed for separate financial products has proven difficult, though a system designed to process many products would be effective. Similarly, attempting to sell insurance and other financial products through a distribution system designed for selling stocks and bonds has not served any of the products very well and has created organizational problems. However, a new conception of a brokerage office is emerging that combines brokers, customer service personnel to handle simple problems and screen clients, and specialists to sell other financial products together with a new shared information system. The cost of compromise in sharing distribution is likely to be much less as a result.

The third cost of sharing is the *cost of inflexibility*. Inflexibility takes two forms: (1) potential difficulty in responding to competitive moves, and (2) exit barriers. Sharing can make it more difficult to respond quickly to competitors because attempting to counter a threat in one business unit may undermine or reduce the value of the interrelationship for sister business units. Sharing also can raise exit barriers. Exiting from a business unit with no competitive advantage may harm other business units sharing an activity with it.[6] Unlike other costs of sharing, the cost of inflexibility is not an ongoing cost but a potential cost should the need for flexibility arise. The cost of inflexibility will depend on the likelihood of the need to respond or exit.

Some costs of co-ordination, compromise, or inflexibility are involved in achieving any interrelationship. These costs, particularly any required compromise to achieve an interrelationship, will be very real concerns raised by business units when sharing is discussed. They may appear far more obvious than the advantages of the interrelationship, which may appear theoretical and speculative. Business units will also tend to view a potential interrelationship in the light of their existing strategy, rather than weigh its cost if the strategies are modified to minimize the costs of sharing. Finally, the value of interrelationships is often clouded by organizational issues involved in sharing, including those of turf and autonomy which are addressed in Chapter 11 [of *Competitive Advantage*]. Thus business units can sometimes oppose interrelationships that may result in a clear competitive advantage to them.

The advantages of sharing an activity must be weighed against the costs of co-ordination, compromise and inflexibility to determine the net competitive advantage of sharing. The assessment of the competitive advantage from an interrelationship must be performed separately for each of the involved business units, and the value of an interrelationship to the firm as a whole is the sum of the net advantages to the involved business units. The net competitive advantage from sharing an activity will almost inevitably vary for each business unit involved. In some cases, the net value of an interrelationship may even be *negative* from the viewpoint of one business unit because of the required compromise, but will be more than offset by a positive net value for other affected business units. For this reason and because of the natural biases in approaching interrelationships noted above, then, business units will often not readily agree on pursuing interrelationships that will benefit a firm as a whole. Interrelationships will *only* happen under such circumstances if there is an explicit horizontal strategy.

While there are always costs of sharing, forces are at work to reduce them in many industries. The new technologies described earlier in this chapter are having the effect of reducing the cost of co-ordination, compromise and, to a lesser extent, the cost of inflexibility. Easier communication and better information systems make co-ordination easier. Low-cost computers and information systems also introduce flexibility into value activities, or the technical capability to minimize the cost of compromise. Programmable machines and robots can adapt to the different needs of business units sharing them. Many firms are only beginning to perceive these possibilities for lowering the cost of sharing, but continue to base their assessment of interrelationships on outdated methods.

Difficulty of matching

The sustainability of the net competitive advantage of an interrelationship will depend on the difficulty competitors have in matching it. Competitors have two basic options in matching the competitive advantage of an interrelationship: (1) duplicating the interrelationship, or (2) offsetting it through other means such as gaining share in the affected business unit or exploiting a different interrelationship. The ease of duplicating an interrelationship will vary depending on whether competitors are in the same group of related industries involved. The most valuable interrelationships from a strategic point of view are those involving industries that competitors are not in and that have high barriers to entry. For example, Procter & Gamble's advantage from the interrelationships between its disposable diaper and paper towel business units is quite sustainable because its paper towel competitors are blocked from entering the diaper business by enormous entry barriers. A competitor may also face higher or lower costs of co-ordination and compromise than the firm in achieving an interrelationship depending on the strategies and circumstances of its business units. Other things being equal, then, a firm should pursue most aggressively those interrelationships that its competitors will find the most difficult to match because of the costs of co-ordination or compromise.

The ability of competitors to offset an interrelationship is a function of whether they can find some other way of improving position in the affected business unit through changes in the strategy or by pursuit of *different* interrelationships.[7] Since nearly any value activity can potentially be shared, a competitor may be able to forge an interrelationship among a different group of business units or share different value activities among the same group of businesses. If a firm, through pursuing an interrelationship, causes a competitor to respond by pursuing different interrelationships, it faces the danger that the ultimate outcome will be an erosion in its relative position.

A final consideration in assessing the difficulty of matching an interrelationship is whether the same benefits can be achieved by a competitor through a coalition or long-term contract. Sometimes a firm can gain the benefits of sharing through a joint venture or other form of coalition with another firm, without actually entering another industry. While such coalitions may be difficult to forge, they should always be considered in assessing the value of an interrelationship and how to achieve it.

Identifying tangible interrelationships

To aid in identifying tangible interrelationships present in a firm, a useful starting point is to catalogue all the forms of sharing that occur in practice as well as the alternative ways they can create competitive advantage. Figure 6.3 divides forms of sharing into five categories: production, market, procurement, technology, and infrastructure. I have included shared human resource management as part of shared infrastructure. It is useful to separate these categories of interrelationships because they raise different issues in sharing. Interrelationships ultimately stem from *commonalities* of various types among industries, such as common buyers, channels, or production processes. These commonalities define potential interrelationships; whether the interrelationships lead to a competitive advantage is a function of the benefits and costs described earlier. The sources of each category of interrelationship and the possible forms of sharing to capture it are shown in Table 6.1.

Table 6.1 Possible sources of interrelationships

Procurement interrelationships		Technological interrelationships		Infrastructure interrelationships	
Source of interrelationship	Possible forms of sharing	Source of interrelationship	Possible forms of sharing	Source of interrelationship	Possible forms of sharing
Common purchased inputs	Joint procedure	Common product technology	Joint technology development	Common firm infrastructure needs	Shared raising of capital (financing)
		Common process technology	Joint interface design	Common capital	Shared cash utilization
		Common technology in other value activities			Shared accounting
					Shared legal department
		One product incorporated into another			Shared government relations
		Interface among products			Shared hiring and training
					Other shared infrastructure activities

Production interrelationships		Market interrelationships	
Source of interrelationship	Possible forms of sharing	Source of interrelationship	Possible forms of sharing
Common location of raw materials	Shared inbound logistics	Common buyer	Shared brand name
Identical or similar fabrication process	Shared component fabrication	Common channel	Cross selling of products
Identical or similar assembly process	Shared assembly facilities	Common geographic market	Bundled or packaged selling
Identical or similar testing/quality control procedures	Shared testing/quality control facilities		Cross subsidization of complementary products
Common factory support needs	Shared factory indirect activities		Shared marketing department
	Shared site infrastructure		Shared sales forces
			Shared service/repair network
			Shared order processing system
			Shared physical distribution system
			Shared buyer or distributor financing organization

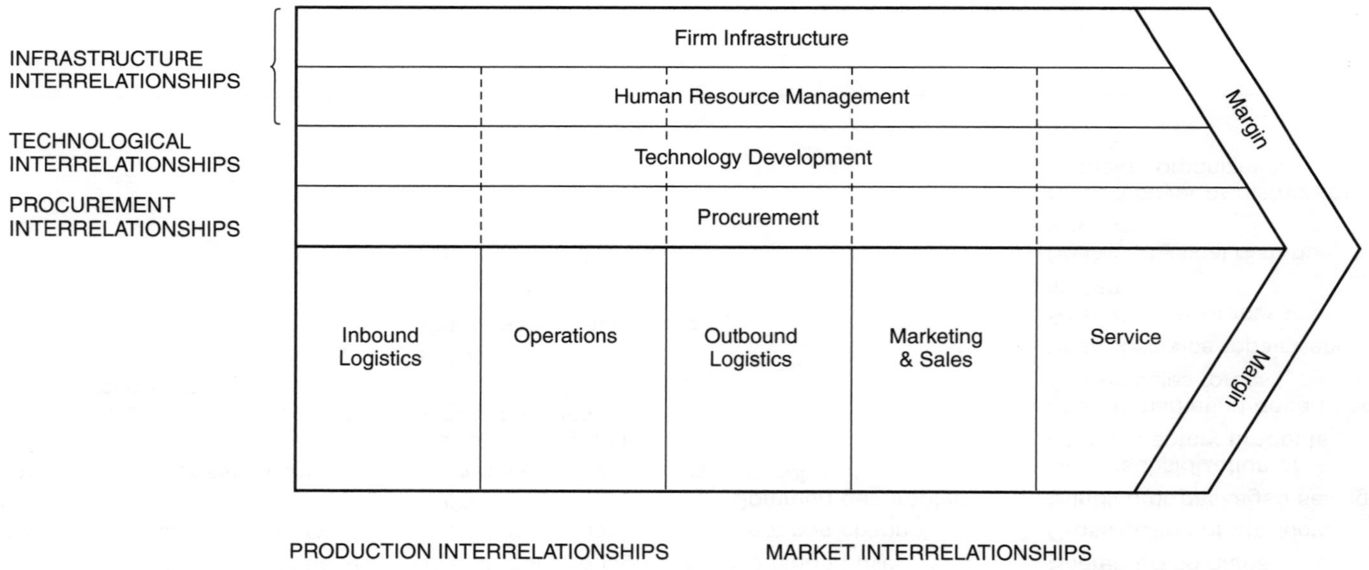

Figure 6.3 Categories of tangible interrelationships

Market interrelationships

Market interrelationships involve the sharing of primary value activities involved in reaching and interacting with the buyer, from outbound logistics to service. When business units have only the geographic location of their buyers in common, sharing is usually restricted to physical distribution systems, order processing, and to servicing and sales if the products have similar sales and servicing needs. Richer opportunities for sharing are present when business units also have common buyers, common channels, or both. If buyers or channels are the same, sharing of physical distribution or order processing systems among business units usually involves less complexity and lower costs of sharing. In addition, common buyers or channels open up a wide variety of other possible forms of sharing shown in Table 6.1.

The subtleties of identifying potential market interrelationships stem from the tendency to view the buyer or channel too broadly. A wide variety of products and services are sold to oil companies, for example, including drilling equipment, refinery equipment, and transportation equipment such as oil tankers and tanker trucks. Thus oil companies might be identified as a common buyer by business units in many industries. The various products are sold to different parts of the oil company, however, which often have little contact with each other. Even within a product category such as drilling equipment, equipment used in exploration is frequently sold to a different organizational unit than production equipment. Even in instances when the same unit of the oil company makes the purchase, the particular individuals making the purchase decision or influencing the decision maker will often differ for different pieces of equipment. Engineers may be responsible for choosing some high-technology equipment such as blowout preventers, for example, while purchasing agents often choose more standard items such as pipe.

Another example of viewing the buyer too broadly is becoming apparent from recent experience in financial services. The traditional buyer of stocks and bonds is a different individual than the average life insurance buyer. Both are different individuals than the typical buyer of futures. These differences are nullifying simplistic efforts to achieve market interrelationships in financial services. Meaningful opportunities for exploring market interrelationships among business units are usually present only where the decision makers for the products are the same or have some contact with each other.

The same issues arise in identifying common channels. Though two products might both be sold through department stores, few actual channel interrelationships are likely to be present if one is sold through discount department stores and the other through exclusive department stores such as Lord & Taylor and Neiman-Marcus. There are also often different buying executives responsible for different classes of products in the same channel. In most supermarket chains, for example, frozen foods are typically bought by a different buyer than meats, even though some frozen foods are meat products. Even if the decision makers are different, however, opportunities for sharing logistical and order processing systems may exist with both common buyers and common channels.

Whether products sold to a common buyer are substitutes or complements can also affect the advantage of sharing market-related activities. Shared marketing can yield less of a cost advantage when products are substitutes because the buyer will purchase either one product or the other but not both. However, offering substitute products to buyers can reduce the risk of substitution because losses in one product can be compensated in the other (see Chapter 8 [of Porter: *Competitive Advantage*]). Joint marketing of substitutes can also enhance a firm's differentiation.

When business units sell complementary products to common buyers, the advantage of sharing is often greater than if the products are unrelated or substitutes. Complementary products usually have correlated demand that facilitates the efficient utilization of shared value activities, and other practices such as common branding, joint advertising and bundling. The strategic issues raised by complementary products, a subset of market interrelationships, are treated separately in Chapter 12 [of *Competitive Advantage*].

The potential competitive advantages of the important forms of market interrelationships and the most likely sources of compromise cost are shown in Table 6.2. Indirect activities such as market research, sales force administration and advertising production (e.g. artwork, layout) can often be shared more easily than direct activities because they require lower compromise costs.[8] The benefits of market interrelationships can often be enhanced by changes in the strategies of the involved business units that reduce the cost of compromise. Standardizing sales force practices, repositioning brands to make their images more compatible, or standardizing delivery standards or payment terms may make sharing easier, for example.

Production interrelationships

Interrelationships in production involve the sharing of upstream value activities such as inbound logistics, component fabrication, assembly, testing, and indirect functions such as maintenance and site infrastructure. All these forms of sharing require that activities be located together. Doing so can lead to a compromise cost if the suppliers or buyers of the business units sharing the activities have greatly different geographic locations since inbound or outbound freight costs may be increased.

Table 6.2 Determinants of net competitive advantage from market
interrelationships

Form of sharing	Potential competitive advantages	Most likely sources of compromise cost
Shared brand name	Lower advertising costs	Product images are inconsistent or conflicting
	Reinforcing product images/reputations	Buyer is reluctant to puchase too much from one firm
		Diluted reputation if one product is inferior
Shared advertising	Lower advertising costs	Appropriate media or messages are different
	Greater leverage in purchasing advertising space	Advertising effectiveness reduced by multiple products
Shared promotion	Lower promotion costs through shared couponing and cross couponing	Appropriate forms and timing of promotion differ
Cross selling of products to each others' buyers	Lower cost of finding new buyers	Product images are inconsistent or conflicting
	Lower cost of selling	Buyer is reluctant to purchase too much from one firm
Interrelated pricing of complementary products	See Chapter 12*	See Chapter 12*
Bundled selling	See Chapter 12*	See Chapter 12*
Shared marketing department	Lower cost of market research	Product positionings are different or inconsistent
	Lower marketing overhead	Buyer's purchasing behaviour is not the same
Shared channels	Enhanced bargaining power with the channels leading to improvements of service, shelf positioning, maintenance/repair/ support, or channel margins	Channel gains too much bargaining power vis-à-vis the firm Channel unwilling to allow a single firm to account for a major portion of its sales
	One-stop shopping for the buyer improves differentation	Use of shared channel will erode support from other channels
	Lower cost of channel support infrastructure	

* See Chapter 12 of
  Porter: Competitive
  Advantage

Table 6.2 (continued)

Form of sharing	Potential competitive advantages	Most likely sources of compromise cost
Shared sales force or sales offices	Lower selling costs or sales force infrastructure costs	Different buyer purchasing behaviour
	Better quality salespersons	Buyer reluctance to purchase large amounts from a single salesperson
	More products to sell improves access to the buyer or enhances buyer convenience	Salesperson is not allowed adequate time with the buyer to present a number of products effectively
	Better sales force utilization if the pattern of utilization is not the same	Different type of salesperson is most effective. Certain products get more attention than others
Shared service network	Lower servicing costs	Differences in equipment or knowledge necessary to make typical repairs
	More sophisticated or responsive servicing, due to improved technology or denser service locations	Differences in the need for timeliness in service calls
	Better capacity utilization if demand for service is inversely correlated	Differing degrees to which the buyer performs service-in-house
Shared order processing	Lower order processing costs	Differences in the form and composition of typical orders
	Lower cost of employing improved technology that improves responsiveness or billing information	Differences in ordering cycles that led to inconsistent order processing needs
	Better capacity utilization if order flows are inversely correlated	
	One-stop shopping for the buyer improves differentiation	

Shared procurement is different from production interrelationships because merging facilities is not implied. Purchased inputs can be procured centrally but shipped from suppliers to dispersed facilities.

Production interrelationships can be illusory when apparently similar value activities are examined closely. For example, though the machines themselves are generically the same, a job-shop manufacturing process for one product may involve different machine tolerances than another, or lot sizes or run lengths can be quite different. As with market interrelationships, indirect value activities offer particularly attractive opportunities for sharing because the compromise costs are often low. For example, such activities as building operations, maintenance, site infrastructure, and testing laboratories can be shared despite the fact that the actual manufacturing processes are different.

Table 6.3 shows the potential competitive advantages of important forms of production interrelationships, and the likely sources of compromise cost. The balance will depend on the strategies of the involved business units. For example, two business units with differentiation strategies are more likely to have similar needs in terms of component specifications, manufacturing tolerances, and testing standards than if one business unit pursues cost leadership while another offers a premium product.

Procurement interrelationships

Procurement interrelationships involve the shared procurement of common purchased inputs. Common inputs are frequently present in diversified firms, particularly if one looks beyond major raw materials and pieces of capital equipment. Suppliers are increasingly willing to make deals based on supplying the needs of plants located around the world, and negotiate prices reflecting total corporate needs. Some firms go overboard in shared procurements, however, because they fail to recognize the potential costs of compromise or they establish a rigid procurement process that does not allow for opportunism in negotiating attractive opportunities.

The potential competitive advantage of shared procurement and the likely sources of compromise cost are shown in Table 6.4.

Technological interrelationships

Technological interrelationships involve the sharing of technology development activities throughout the value chain. They are distinguished from production interrelationships because their impact is on the cost or uniqueness of technology development, while production

98 Identifying opportunities

Table 6.3 Determinants of net competitive advantage from production interrelationships

Form of sharing	Potential competitive advantages	Most likely sources of compromise cost
Shared inbound logistical system	Lower freight and material handling costs	Input sources are located in different geographic areas
	Better technology enhances delivery reliability, reduces damage, etc.	Plants are located in differing geographic areas
	Sharing allows more frequent, smaller deliveries that reduce inventory or improve plant productivity	Varying physical characteristics of inputs imply that a logistical system which can handle them all is suboptimal
		Needs for frequency and reliability of inbound delivery differ among business units
Shared components (idenitical components used in different end products)	Lower cost of component fabrication	Needs for component design and quality differ among business units
	Better technology for component manufacturing improves quality	
Shared component fabrication facilities (similar or related components are produced using the *same* equipment and facilities)	Lower component costs	High setup costs for different component varieties
	Better fabrication technology improves quality	Needs for component quality or tolerances differ among business units
	Capacity utilization is improved because demand for similar components is not perfectly correlated	Flexible manufacturing equipment has higher cost than specialized equipment
		Larger workforce in one location leads to potential hiring, unionization or productivity problems
Shared assembly facilities (similar or related end products are assembled using the same equipment/ lines)	Lower assembly costs	High setup costs for different products
	Better assembly technology improves quality	Needs for quality or tolerances differ

Table 6.3 (continued)

Form of sharing	Potential competitive advantages	Most likely sources of compromise cost
Shared assembly facilities	Utilization is improved because demand is not perfectly correlated	Flexible assembly equipment is higher cost
	A shared materials handling system can feed different assembly lines	Larger workforce in one location leads to potential hiring, unionization or productivity problems
Shared testing/quality control	Lower testing cost	Testing procedures and quality standards differ
	Better technology increases the extensiveness of testing and improves quality control	Flexible testing facilities and equipment are higher cost
Shared indirect activities (including maintenance, plant overhead, personnel department, cafeteria, etc.)	Lower indirect activity costs	Differing needs for indirect activities among business units
	Improved quality of indirect activities	Larger workforce in one location leads to potential hiring, unionization, or productivity problems

Table 6.4 Determinants of net competitive advantage from procurement interrelationships

Form of sharing	Potential competitive advantage	Most likely sources of compromise cost
Joint procurement of common inputs	Lower costs of inputs	Input needs are different in terms of quality or specifications, leading to higher costs than necessary in business units requiring less quality
	Improved input quality	Technical assistance and delivery needs from suppliers vary among business units
	Improved service from vendors in terms of responsiveness, holding of inventory, etc.	Centralization can reduce the information flow from factory to purchasing, and make purchasing less responsive

interrelationships involve sharing activities involved in the actual production of the product on an ongoing basis.

It is important to recognize, however, that interrelationships in process development often occur together with production or market interrelationships. Interrelationships in process technology typically grow out of interrelationships in the primary activities.

As with other forms of interrelationships, apparently promising technological interrelationships can be illusory. Scientific disciplines that overlap for two business units may be of minor importance to success compared to scientific disciplines that do not overlap. Harris Corporation, for example, thought it could reduce the development expense involved in entering word processing through adapting software from its text editing system sold to newspapers. Harris discovered that the text editing system had so many features that were specific to the needs of newspapers that development of a word processing system had to start from scratch.

Truly significant technological interrelationships are ones involving technologies important to the cost or differentiation of the products or processes involved, as microelectronics technology is to both telecommunications and data processing. Many products have superficial technological similarities, making the identification of true technological interrelationships difficult. As with other types of interrelationships, the net competitive advantage of a technological interrelationship will differ depending on the industry and strategies of the business units involved. For example, the benefits of sharing microelectronics technology will tend to be greater for two consumer products business units than for a defence business unit and a consumer business unit. Rockwell International learned this lesson when it put a team of engineers from its defence business into its Admiral TV set division. The sensitivity to cost was so much greater in TV sets than in defence equipment that sharing did not succeed. The same thing occurred in business aircraft, where a design developed originally for military use (the Sabreliner) proved too expensive for the commercial market.

Table 6.5 shows the potential competitive advantages that can stem from sharing technology development as well as the most likely sources of compromise costs.

Infrastructure interrelationships

The final category of interrelationships involve firm infrastructure, including such activities as financing, legal, accounting, and human resource management. Some infrastructure activities are almost always shared in diversified firms, as described in Chapter 2 [of Porter: *Competitive Advantage*]. In most cases, the effect of sharing on competitive

Table 6.5 Determinants of net competitive advantage from technological interrelationships

Form of sharing	Potential competitive advantages	Most likely sources of compromise cost
Shared technology development (for separate products or where one product is incorporated into another)	Lower product or process design costs (including design time)	Technologies are the same, but the tradeoffs in applying the technology are different among business units
	Larger critical mass in R&D, or the ability to attract better people improves the innovativeness of product or process designs	
	Transference of developments among product areas enhances differentiation or allows early entry into new technologies	
Shared interface design for products with a technological interface	Lower interface design costs	A nonstandard interface reduces the available market
	Differentiation through superior and proprietary interface performance	Risks of bundling (Chapter 12*)
	Bundling opportunities created through a non-standard interface (see Chapter 12*)	
* See Chapter 12 of Porter: *Competitive Advantage*		

advantage is not great because infrastructure is not a large proportion of cost and sharing has little impact on differentiation. It is ironic, therefore, that the vast majority of literature on sharing has been on sharing infrastructure – principally finance and the utilization of capital. Interrelationships in finance, particularly, have been seen as a significant benefit the diversified firm contributes to its business units.

There are two basic sources of financial interrelationships: joint raising of capital and shared utilization of capital (primarily working capital). Economies of scale in raising capital may indeed exist, especially up to a certain quantity of capital needed. Efficient utilization of working capital is made possible by countercyclical or counterseasonal needs for funds among business units, which allows cash freed up by one business unit to be deployed in another. Financial interrelationships typically involve relatively few compromise costs that must be offset against any savings. Moreover, financial interrelationships are among the easiest to achieve if they are present, perhaps a reason why they are so frequently discussed.

The major limitation to the competitive advantage of shared financing is the *efficiency of capital markets*. Scale economies in financing appear to be moderate for most firms and lead to a relatively small difference in financing costs. Firms can also borrow to cover short-term cash needs and lend excess cash in the highly efficient markets for commercial paper and other instruments, mitigating the value of sharing working capital. Hence financial interrelationships are rarely the basis for creating a significant competitive advantage, unless the size and credit rating of competitors differ greatly. Other forms of infrastructure interrelationships can be important in particular industries. Shared infrastructure for hiring and training is important in some service industries, while shared government relations can be significant in natural resource firms.

INTANGIBLE INTERRELATIONSHIPS

Intangible interrelationships lead to competitive advantage through the transfer of skills among separate value chains. Through operating one business unit, a firm gains know-how that allows it to improve the way another generically similar business unit competes. The transference of skills can go in either direction, e.g. from existing business units to a new business unit or from a new business unit back to existing business units. The transference of generic know-how can occur anywhere in the value chain. Philip Morris transferred generic know-how in the marketing of consumer packaged goods from its cigarette business to Miller Beer, while Emerson Electric transferred plant design and cost reduction skills when it acquired the chain saw firm Beaird-Poulan. In both cases, the transference of skills *changed* the way that the receiving business unit competed and enhanced its competitive advantage.

Intangible interrelationships lead to a competitive advantage if the improvement in cost or differentiation in the business unit receiving the know-how exceeds the costs of transferring it. Know-how residing in one business unit has already been paid for, and hence transferring it may involve little cost compared to its cost of development. The actual transference of know-how always involves some cost, however, whether it be the cost of time of skilled personnel or perhaps the greater risk that proprietary information will leak out. Using the know-how that is transferred will also typically involve some cost in adapting it to the circumstances of the receiving business unit. These costs of transferring know-how must be weighed against the potential benefits to determine whether an intangible interrelationship will create competitive advantage.

Intangible interrelationships are important to competitive advantage when the transference of know-how or skills allows the receiving business unit to lower costs or enhance differentiation. This occurs if the transference of skills leads to policy changes that lower cost or enhance differentiation, or because the transference of skills gives the receiving business unit better insight into its other drivers of cost or uniqueness. The transference of skills from Philip Morris to Miller Beer, for example, resulted in policy changes in the way beer was positioned and marketed, as well as an escalation of advertising spending that increased scale economies in the industry and worked to the advantage of large brands like Miller.

Identifying intangible interrelationships

Intangible interrelationships arise from a variety of generic similarities among business units:[9]

- same generic strategy;
- same type of buyer (though not the same buyer);
- similar configuration of the value chain (e.g. many dispersed sites of mineral extraction and processing);
- similar important value activities (e.g. relations with government).

Although value activities cannot be shared, these similarities among business units mean that know-how gained in one business unit is valuable and transferable to another.[10]

Because of the myriad possible generic similarities among business units, it is not possible to be as complete in identifying the important types as it was with tangible interrelationships. However, the value chain provides a systematic way of searching for intangible interrelationships. A firm can examine the major value activities in its business units to unearth similarities in activities or the way the chain is configured that might provide the basis for transference of know-how or highlight generic skills that might be applied to new industries.

Intangible interrelationships and competitive advantage

Intangible interrelationships of one type or another are very widespread. It is always possible to point to some generic similarity in some value activity between almost any two business units. An airline is widely dispersed, has multiple sites and relies heavily on scheduling, characteristics shared by trucking companies, international trading companies and industrial gas producers. Widespread similarities of some kind make the analysis of intangible interrelationships quite subtle.

The key tests in identifying intangible interrelationships that are important to competitive advantage are the following:

- *How similar* are the value activities in the business units?
- *How important* are the value activities involved to competition?
- *How significant* is the know-how that would be transferred to competitive advantage in the relevant activities?

These questions must be answered together. The similarity of two business units is a function of how much know-how can be usefully transferred. The importance of the transferred know-how is a function of its contribution to improving competitive advantage in the receiving business unit. Transference of just one insight can sometimes make an enormous difference to competitive advantage, so even business units that are not very similar can have important intangible interrelationships. However, truly important intangible interrelationships are much less common than an initial search for them might imply. It is frequently difficult, moreover, to predict whether the transference of know-how will prove to be valuable.

The most common pitfall in assessing intangible interrelationships is to identify generic similarities among business units that are not important to competition. Either the know-how that can be transferred does not affect value activities that are important to cost or differentiation in the receiving business unit, or it does not provide insights that competitors do not already have. Philip Morris's acquisition of the Seven Up soft drink company provides a possible example of the latter. While the beer industry had historically been populated by family firms with little marketing flair, the soft drink industry has long been characterized by sophisticated marketing by the likes of Coke, Pepsi, and Dr Pepper. Philip Morris's marketing expertise appears to have offered much less of an advantage for Seven Up than it did for Miller.

Many firms have fallen into the trap of identifying intangible interrelationships that are illusory or do not matter for competitive advantage. Often, it seems, intangible interrelationships are forced, and represent more of an ex poste rationalization of diversification moves undertaken for other reasons. Intangible interrelationships were prominent in discussions of synergy. The difficulty of finding and implementing significant intangible interrelationships is one of the reasons synergy proved such a disappointment to many firms.

The effective exploitation of intangible interrelationships thus requires an acute understanding of the business units involved as well as the industries they compete in. The importance of an intangible interrelationship for competition can only be truly understood by identifying specific ways in which know-how can be transferred so as to make a difference. The mere hope that one business unit might learn something useful from another is frequently a hope not realized.

Even intangible interrelationships where the benefits of transferring know-how far exceed the cost of transferring it do not lead to competitive advantage unless the transference of know-how actually takes place. Know-how is transferred through interchange between managers or other personnel in the affected business units. This process does not occur without active efforts on the part of senior management. Personnel in the receiving business unit may be wary or unsure of the value of know-how from a 'different' industry. They may even openly resist it. Business units with know-how may be hesitant to commit the time of important personnel and may view the know-how as highly proprietary. Finally, transference of know-how is subjective and the benefits of doing so often are hard for managers to understand when compared to tangible interrelationships. All these factors imply that even important intangible interrelationships can be very difficult to achieve. Doing so requires a sustained commitment and the existence of formal mechanisms through which the required transference of skills will take place. A conducive organizational setting can greatly reduce the cost of transferring know-how.

NOTES

1 Economists have begun to use the term 'economies of scope' to refer to economies available to multiproduct firms (see Baumol, Panzar and Willing, 1982). The sources of economies of scope have not been operationalized, nor have the conditions that nullify them.
2 Sharing can increase the rate of learning in an activity by increasing its throughput. Intangible interrelationships are also a form of learning, but one in which knowledge gained in one business unit is tranferred to another though each business unit has separate activities.
3 Terms such as shared experience or shared resources are sometimes used to reflect the possibility that activities can be shared. Such terms are not well defined, however, nor do they grow out of a framework that specifies the potential competitive advantages of sharing and its costs.
4 The important scale differences among business units are those in the value activity being shared, which is not necessarily the same as the overall scale of the business unit. A small business unit may utilize logistics very intensively, for example.
5 The cost of co-ordination is clearly dependent on a firm's organizational practices. See Chapter 11.
6 See *Competitive Strategy*, Chapter 1 for a discussion of exit barriers.
7 For a summary discussion of the ways of gaining competitive position in an industry see Chapter 15.
8 See Wells (1984). [Wells, John R., 'In Search of Synergy', PhD dissertation, Harvard Graduate School of Business Administration, 1984.]
9 John R. Well's (1984) study contains important work on intangible interrela-

tionships that provides further insight into when and how they arise. [Wells, John, R., 'In Search of Synergy', PhD dissertation, Harvard Graduate School of Business Administration. 1984.]

10 There may be a fine line in some cases between transferring know-how and sharing technology development. The basis for separating tangible and intangible interrelationships is whether an activity is shared in some way on an ongoing basis, or whether know-how is transferred between essentially separate activities.

Chapter 7

Evaluating interdependencies across businesses

C. K. Prahalad and Yves L. Doz

In our discussion, so far, of top management's task in a DMNC (diversified multinational company) we have assumed that the basic unit for analysis and management is a discrete, stand-alone business. That is a valid assumption only if the various businesses in the DMNC's portfolio are not interdependent or if we can ignore, for purposes of strategic management, the interdependencies among them. In this chapter we shall identify the *source* of interdependencies among businesses in a DMNC and examine ways to determine *the criticality* of various interdependencies.[1]

SOURCES OF INTERDEPENDENCIES

The various sources of interdependencies in the portfolio of a DMNC can be illustrated by examining the high-fidelity audio business at Philips.[2]

Vertical integration and technology

Product and component flows across businesses (vertical integration) as well as technology linkages, such as sharing a common core technology across several businesses, can create interdependencies.

Let us take the hi-fi business as an example. Figure 7.1 illustrates the nature of component and technology linkages in the hi-fi business. Hi-fi, as a worldwide business, was part of the Audio Group, which included phonograph, radio, and tape businesses. Hi-fi products were created partly by various combinations of subassemblies from the phonograph, radio, and tape businesses. Further, the hi-fi business within Philips depended on the Components Group (Elcoma) for components. Elcoma also sold those components to third parties as a discrete business in its own right. Hi-fi was also dependent on another division, called ELA, which developed and manufactured specialized audio components. The simplified chart of product and technology flows among the various groups illustrates the nature of linkages. The managers of hi-fi could

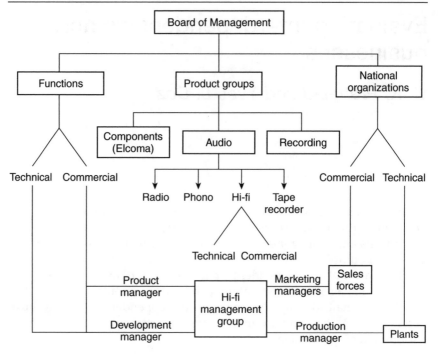

Figure 7.1 A schematic of linkages: hi-fi business

not start their day with the simplifying assumption that they were managing a discrete, stand-alone business.

Logistics

The logistics imposed by the product development and manufacturing system can create a series of interdependencies.

The market for hi-fi was world-wide. The manufacturing system supporting the hi-fi business was spread over several international production centres (IPCs) in France, Holland, Belgium, and Singapore. Those plants produced, in addition to the components needed for the hi-fi business, components and subassemblies for other businesses. That manufacturing configuration resulted as much from the firm's history of incremental commitments to the plant as the business expanded as from careful analysis of the total development and manufacturing costs associated with the system. As most manufacturing plants associated with the hi-fi business served other businesses as well, hi-fi management could not request drastic changes (either increases or decreases) in output from any location. In a sense, the manufacturing plants were selling capacity, and the hi-fi business group had to negotiate the capacity that would be assigned to it. Any changes in the negotiated allocation of capacity was contingent on the demands imposed by the other businesses the plants served. The agility with which the hi-fi business could respond to market demands was restricted by the very nature of the underlying manufacturing and development system.

Host governments

Host government demands can impose interdependencies across businesses that would otherwise be discrete and stand-alone.

The host governments – France, Holland, Belgium, and Singapore – where the IPCs of the hi-fi business were located, were also hosts to a large number of other businesses of Philips. For example, Philips had a significant presence in the defence and telecommunications businesses in France. The French government was concerned about Philips's maintaining component manufacturing capability in France. Any move on the part of either hi-fi management or Elcoma (Philips's component business) to reduce supplies of components from France, it was felt, could negatively affect the ability of Philips to maintain its presence in the defence and telecommunications business. As a result, the choice of manufacturing location in the hi-fi business (a strategic choice given the pressures for cost reduction in that business) was constrained by its possible impact on unrelated businesses like defence and telecommunications. The linkage between the two sets of businesses – hi-fi and defence systems – was the result of managerial perceptions of the possible reactions of the French government. The impact of a reduction in component capacity in France, brought about by the need to be cost competitive in the hi-fi business, on the ability of Philips to continue to sell defence systems in France was not easy to determine. The linkage was nebulous and hard to define. It was, however, a real issue for managers.

Philips was the largest employer in Holland. Reducing capacity, or 'out-sourcing', by Philips had serious implications for Holland's employment situation. As a result, the Dutch government did not look kindly on attempts to out-source. Philips's top management had to be sensitive to the political implications of reducing capacity in Holland, and no business could make that choice unilaterally without considering the implications of such a move on Philips's total operations.

The Belgian government was equally concerned about employment sustained in that country by businesses like hi-fi. Its approach to protecting employment was to link the purchase of Philips computer equipment by the Belgian public sector with Philips's continued manufacturing presence.

Singapore's government was less concerned about employment per se. It was more concerned with becoming a centre for high-technology manufacturing, thereby upgrading the skill levels in the country. Singapore's concern translated into its demand for locating product development centres there. The development could relate to any business requiring high technology, not just hi-fi.

Distribution and marketing

Competitive advantages derived from distribution and marketing considerations, as well as the costs of marketing, might force interdependencies across businesses that might otherwise be discrete and stand-alone.

In the case of the hi-fi business at Philips, managers had to make choices regarding the marketing of hi-fi products in various country markets. In all the important markets of Philips, the national organizations had built up an impressive distribution and service organization around the audio-video products, as well as major and small domestic appliances. Hi-fi managers could use the existing marketing infrastructure, including channels, salesmen, and promotion provided by the video business or the appliance business, or could start a dedicated marketing infrastructure for hi-fi. In some countries hi-fi products were sold partly through specialized dealers – a further complication in the choice of a marketing approach. The cost of a dedicated infrastructure in various countries was prohibitive. On the other hand, it was extremely difficult to interest the video marketing group in providing support for the relatively small hi-fi business when its chief concern was to maintain market share in the video business. The appliance business had a reputation for standard products rather than for high technology, state-of-the-art products, an image that the hi-fi business group was trying to promote in the minds of the consumer. The need to leverage distribution investments indicated an alliance with the established video group. This would make hi-fi's marketing strategies dependent on the strategies of the video group, an interdependence, the merits of which were not obvious.

Corporate image

The need to maintain and leverage a corporate image can and often does impose interdependencies across businesses.

Philips was concerned about the image hi-fi would create and its impact on the other consumer businesses in its portfolio. The hi-fi business represented state-of-the-art technology and corporate management felt that the benefits of that image had to be exploited by other businesses as well. That meant hi-fi managers would have to work closely with other businesses and pursue opportunities for leveraging the Philips brand in a variety of consumer businesses, yet another source of interdependency.

WHICH INTERDEPENDENCIES ARE CRITICAL?

The example of the hi-fi business at Philips illustrates the multiple sources of interdependencies. Depending on which interdependency is seen as critical, the position of the hi-fi business in the IR grid would change, as illustrated in Figure 7.2. If the hi-fi group felt that leveraging technology and the benefits of an in-house supply of components was critical to hi-fi's business success then the interdependency between the component business (Elcoma) and the hi-fi business would be critical. That would force the hi-fi business to take on the characteristics of the component business in the IR framework. Dominant strategic concerns would relate to cost reduction, technology transfer, economies of scale, and standardization of products and product modules. On the other hand, if the central strategic concern is market development, and if sensitivity to differences in customer tastes and preferences is seen as

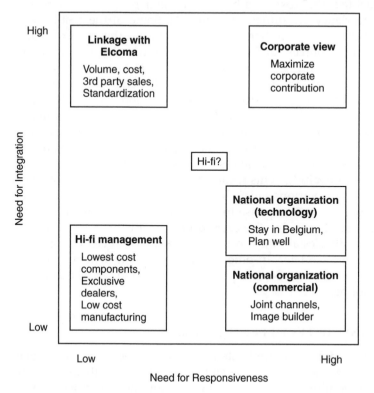

Figure 7.2 Multiple interdependencies: impact on hi-fi business

the critical element of success, then the hi-fi business would take on the characteristics of a nationally responsive business, as shown in Figure 7.2.

The desire of host governments to link 'unrelated' businesses together for public reasons, or the desire of corporate management to leverage a business along multiple dimensions (in the case of hi-fi along the technology dimension and the distribution dimension), can easily push the hi-fi business into a mode where the need for both global integration and local responsiveness are high at the same time. It is not uncommon in such circumstances for managers running the business to hope for an extreme stand-alone mode, where they are allowed to source components from anywhere, have a dedicated sales force, and primarily sell to OEM customers like Sears. The four possible configurations of the hi-fi business, depending on which is seen as the critical interdependency, as depicted in Figure 7.2, raise an important strategic question: how do we make a choice?

The difficulty in making explicit choices regarding the appropriate interdependency to leverage in a case like the hi-fi business arises from the fact that the 'costs and benefits' of managing or not managing an interdependency are difficult to estimate. Some of the cost-benefits are more readily identified than others. For example, the value of shared manufacturing resources can be computed by estimating the additional investment that would be required to get into that business as a stand-alone operation. On the other hand, the cost-benefits of a shared distribution and marketing infrastructure are much more difficult to assess. Some aspects of that choice, such as the additional salesmen required or the warehousing costs, lend themselves to analysis, but other aspects do not. Typically, judgments regarding the impact on distributors and the sales force of adding a new business to an existing line of businesses are difficult to quantify. Judgments regarding the possible reactions of a host government on the various salient businesses a DMNC may be involved in, in that country, as a response to its actions in a non-salient business are even harder to come by. The organizational costs of co-ordination of the interdependencies are the most difficult to assess, even though very real, as we shall see later. In other words, costs and benefits are both tangible and judgmental. Some aspects of the equation can be quantified, others cannot be.

EVALUATING INTERDEPENDENCIES

While it is very difficult to understand all the sources of interdependencies and identify the costs and benefits associated with them, strategic management requires that managers make some choices rather than try to manage all interdependencies as if all were crucial to success. While no one simple formula will provide the answer, we can identify a set of questions that can help in developing a comprehensive cost-benefit picture.

Costs associated with managing interdependencies

The costs associated with managing interdependencies tend to be primarily organizational and therefore difficult to quantify. Consequently, most firms ignore those costs. However, the costs are real. Some recurring symptoms of those costs follow.

Loss of top management focus on a business

The most basic cost associated with attempts to manage interdependencies is the loss of focus on the performance of a specific business. The quality of a discrete business – its investment requirement, quality of returns, growth potential, market share, product leadership, quality of management – can be measured. An interdependent set of businesses creates difficulties in measuring the quality of any one business. For example, the performance of a component business is likely to be influenced by the quality of other businesses. Investment requirements, for example, in the case of hi-fi business, may have to take into account the investment requirements of the component business as well. The minimum size required to be cost-efficient may be quite different in the component business as compared with the hi-fi businesses, in which case the firm may have to carry additional capacity in the component business or find suitable third party buyers.

A discrete business provides top management with the option of continued investment or divestment. It allows an opportunity to measure managerial performance, uncluttered by a maze of accounting complications caused by joint costs and transfer prices. The management group can identify its performance with the success of a discrete business much more easily than that of various interdependent organizational subunits.

Loss of flexibility

Increasingly, a large number of businesses require flexibility and quick response time to market needs. That is obvious not only in the consumer electronics industry, which is characterized by very short product life cycles, constant addition to and changes in features, and cost reduction, but also in such diverse industries as medical electronics, engineered materials, instrumentation, and information technology. Businesses that operate as discrete, stand-alone entities can respond quickly. If they are part of an interdependent set of businesses, then the response time to accommodate market needs – be it in product development or in increasing capacity – is constrained by the manager's ability in that business to convince others of both the need for and the urgency of the change. Strategic priorities of businesses that are part of the interdependent set may differ enough to make agreements on priorities difficult to negotiate.

Reduced innovation

Innovation and entrepreneurship tend to flourish when organizational arrangements allow for 'freedom to act'. In discrete, stand-alone businesses, where managers have control over most of the critical resources they need, such action is possible. DMNCs concerned with innovation, like Hewlett-Packard, 3M and Harris, have prided themselves on operating small, discrete businesses within the large umbrella of the corporation. Even IBM, whose mainline business was managed with probably one of the most interdependent management systems, created separate independent business units (IBUs) to provide the opportunity for new businesses, like the PC business, to emerge and grow. When innovative ideas have to be negotiated with several other businesses, and when resource commitments have to pass the test of several groups of managers not close to the market place addressed by the innovation, entrepreneurship is often the victim.

Loss of visibility of business performance

The performance of a stand-alone business is relatively easy to compute, as we can identify both the assets deployed in support of the business and the returns of that business. As a result, managerial motivation and performance evaluation are relatively easy. In an interdependent set of businesses, shared resources, joint costs, and transfer prices cause even the accounting for results to be 'muddy'. Further, as managers do not have the freedom to make business decisions like volume, location, levels of investment and prices pertinent to that business without concern for the impact on other interdependent parts, they cannot be held totally responsible for results. Both goal setting and performance measurement become confused. Confused perceptions of responsibility, based on responses of a set of managers, illustrated in Figure 7.3, result. It is obvious that no one feels particularly accountable for overall business performance results, like profitability or market share, even though they all feel responsible for selecting the scope of the business, like picking market niches in which to compete.

Key managerial tasks	National organization	Organizational units			Other product divisions
		Technical	Commercial	IPC	
Profit responsibility	X?		X?		
Market share	?	?	?	?	
P–M niche	X	X	X	X	X
Price	X	?	X		
Product specs		X		X	
New products		X	X		
Product line			X		
Market testing		?	?		
Volume	X				
Market/segment	X		X		
Distribution channels	X				
Sales force allocation	X		X		
Deliveries		X	X		
Advertising	?		X		
Emphasis on service			X	X	

Figure 7.3 A case study of managerial perceptions of responsibility

Costs of co-ordination

Co-ordination of interdependent businesses has other organizational costs. First, co-ordination means more management time, often more managerial layers, and more time spent in committee meetings. Often managerial attention is focused on 'oiling the wheels of the organization' rather than on competition. In one DMNC we studied, managers often spent 50 to 70 per cent of their time with managers from other businesses on which they were dependent. The process of negotiation on priorities, resource allocation, transfer prices and such issues consumes a significant amount of managerial attention and time. An internal focus is one of the costs of co-ordination.

Yet another cost of an interdependent system is the cost of carrying the inventory. The number and the complexity of interrelationships across businesses increases the difficulty of responding to changes in the market place. Changes in the demand for end products must be reflected in demand for subassemblies and components made in plants around the world. That results in a phenomenon best described as the 'internal business cycle'. Essentially, small shifts in the end product markets result in very large fluctuations in component demand as a result of a series of adjustments each stage makes to the forecast of the previous group as well as time lags in detecting the shifts in demand at various levels in the chain. The phenomenon, first described by Forrester during the early 1960s, is now well known.[3] A consequence of it is that inventories accumulate at different stages of the pipeline, even if only small shifts were required at the end product level. The inventory penalty can be considerable, often 25 to 50 per cent more for an interdependent system than for stand-alone businesses.

Benefits associated with managing interdependent businesses

One might get the impression that there are only costs associated with managing an interdependent system. There are also distinct benefits.

Cost reduction and control over value added

The most obvious benefit of managing interdependencies is that sharing resources reduces cost. The incremental investment required to enter a business may be considerably reduced by sharing the resource base.

A less obvious advantage is that a degree of vertical integration gives managers control over the value added chain. Such control can provide an opportunity for active price management. By capturing the margins that would normally accrue to middlemen or suppliers, the managers of an interdependent system can enlarge the margin they have at their disposal to fight competitive battles. We are assuming that the internal suppliers are as efficient as external suppliers, so that the margins are available to the firm for use in a competitive situation.

A degree of self-sufficiency also provides significant bargaining advantages with suppliers; it allows managers to understand the cost structures better and provides a creditable threat to suppliers.

Technological integrity

A technologically orientated DMNC is willing to pay the costs of co-ordination in return for the technological integrity that it can bring. For example, IBM managed its mainline businesses as one interdependent system, with all its attendant costs of corporate staff, because providing a compatible line of equipment was critical to IBM's strategy. IBM not only provided a whole line of equipment, it also ensured that the products were all compatible, which gave IBM customers a sense of security.

Technological integrity can also include the ability to keep critical know-how in-house. Often, proprietary know-how is contained in special purpose components. Further, keeping a critical mass of talent in related technical disciplines can lead to ease in product development.

Firms like AT&T, IBM, NEC and Philips have maintained core skills in-house for that purpose.

Sustaining a global infrastructure

As outlined in Chapter 3 [of Prahalad: *The Multi-national Mission*], global competition requires a strategic infrastructure – global brands, distribution coverage, manufacturing presence, sales and service support. Most often the costs of building and maintaining such an infrastructure are beyond the capabilities of a single business. DMNCs like Matsushita, Philips, Hitachi, and Sony have developed a family of products that can utilize the same strategic infrastructure effectively. On the other hand, RCA and General Electric do not have a global infrastructure in their appliance and consumer electronics businesses. At best they can boast of global sourcing. No single business unit, be it audio or video, in General Electric, for example, can support the massive investment required to build a global marketing network.

Nature of competition

Increasingly, the nature of global competitors is changing. In several businesses, such as consumer electronics, computers and telecommunications, medical electronics, machine tools and financial services, the largest competitors are broadening their product lines. A broad product line allows a competitor to cross-subsidize products and businesses, develop a bargaining advantage with distributors and dealers and pay for 'core technologies' common to several businesses. The costs of paying for 'core technologies', leveraging distribution advantages, and the opportunities for cross-subsidization are forcing firms wedded to the concept of decentralization, like 3M, Hewlett-Packard and Matsushita, to re-examine their ideology of decentralized management.

Bargaining leverage with host governments

DMNCs with a wide range of products, spanning a variety of levels of technology, can develop multiple bargaining theatres in their relationships with host governments. That essentially takes two forms. One, a DMNC could offer to manufacture a low- or medium-technology product in a developing country in exchange for getting privileged access to public sector markets and/or large contracts. A case in point would be the offer by Brown Boveri to manufacture small motors in developing countries as an inducement to obtain contracts for power systems and heavy equipment.

DMNCs can also use a broad product range as a bargaining tool with developed countries. For example, in return for guarantees to maintain a certain level of employment, a DMNC could get the government of France or Belgium to provide privileged access to public sector markets, balancing a high-cost production centre for radios with a respectable market share in computers or telecommunications equipment. That type of bargaining also takes on another form, known as 'offset agreements'. For example, General Electric, in return for an order estimated to be worth more than $1.2 billion for jet engines for the Canadian Air Force, agreed to an offset of more than £800 million dollars. The offset involved not only developing Canadian vendors for Canadian General Electric's requirement but also developing world product programmes for General Electric, from Canada. The world programmes involved such diverse businesses as electrical components, broadcast equipment and filaments.

In all three forms of negotiation, corporate managers tend to use a broad portfolio to create a bargaining advantage. In the process, they create a linkage between the strategies of otherwise unrelated, distinct businesses.

MANAGING INTERDEPENDENCIES: FINDING THE BALANCE

From the foregoing section it is obvious that evaluating the criticality of a set of interdependencies across businesses, like the hi-fi business at Philips, may not be a simple exercise in examining the value-added chain in tangible economic terms. That kind of analysis, derived from the analysis of vertical integration, is often suggested as the methodology appropriate to the analysis of interdependencies, a complex web of relationships, caused by a variety of considerations – competitive, organizational and political. We believe that assessing the value of a set of interdependencies deserves analysis of costs as well as not so easily quantifiable judgments. We suggest developing a balance sheet comprising the factors shown in Table 7.1.

Table 7.1 A balance sheet for evaluating interdependencies

Potential assets	Potential liabilities
Cost reduction and control over value added	Loss of top management focus on a business
Technological integrity	Loss of flexibility
Sustaining a global infrastructure	Loss of innovation
Matching key competitors and competition	Costs of co-ordination
Bargaining leverage with host governments	Loss of visibility to performance of a business

Table 7.1 illustrates the essential dilemma. The potential assets are primarily substantive items that are amenable to detailed economic analysis. Data can be gathered to justify a position on almost all the items listed on the assets side. In debates about how many interdependencies should one try to manage within a DMNC, the asset side of the balance sheet gets more attention. The potential liabilities tend to be primarily organizational, and the effects are hard to identify in the short run. It is also difficult to produce hard data to justify most elements other than the incremental inventory needs in an interdependent system over a stand-alone system. The liabilities, therefore, are more subject to a corporate ideology, such as decentralized operations, as in 3M, Hewlett-Packard, and Matsushita, or a totally integrated management, as in IBM.

The search for a balance

Increasingly, DMNCs are forsaking an 'either/or' position and recognizing that costs and benefits must be considered explicitly, even if not all aspects lend themselves to quantification. The tradeoff is between 'strategic advantages' and 'organizational costs'. This kind of soul-searching is leading to a series of significant reorganizations in a large number of firms.

- IBM has moved from a totally integrated DMNC, managing all interdependencies across its businesses (other than Federal Systems group), to one that manages most (not all) interdependencies across its mainline businesses; manages some as independent business units (IBUs) not subject to the same disciplines of staff review as the main line businesses; manages some as quasi-interdependent, which means only some aspects of the businesses are seen as linked; and engages in some joint ventures and collaboration agreements. The transformation of IBM over the last seven years is rendered schematically in Figure 7.4.[4]
- Hewlett-Packard, dedicated to decentralized management and individual entrepreneurship, has recently recognized the need to co-ordinate its efforts in its computer effort. Decentralization, as a philosophy, is giving way to centralization and co-ordination.[5] The transformation at Hewlett-Packard is shown schematically in Figure 7.5.

The implications of this search for balance – balance between the strategic advantages of co-ordinated effort and its organizational costs – are forcing large DMNCs to reconsider their approach to resource allocation. Instead of allocating resources to discrete businesses, DMNCs are examining ways in which the resource allocation process can be changed to consider those costs and benefits explicitly. In several

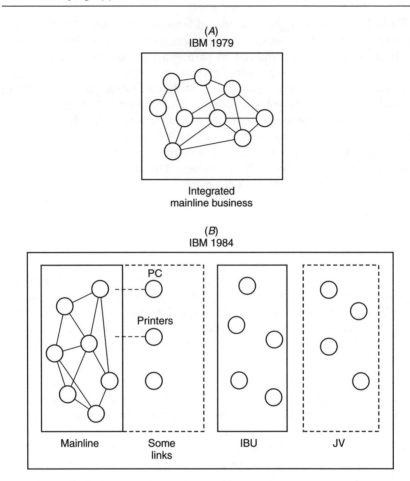

Figure 7.4 Transformation at IBM: a schematic

DMNCs it may be advantageous to move away from a 'discrete business' as the only unit of analysis for resource allocation decisions and examine the opportunities and costs from different perspectives. For example, core technologies that serve several businesses and distribution and brand investments that transcend any one business may be distinct units for resource allocation and corporate attention as well. Resources may be allocated to core technologies and distribution in addition to specific product-markets. For example, Philips may allocate resources to optical media (a core technology) as well as compact audio discs (a product-market using optical recording technology). Such an approach to resource allocation forces firms to deal explicitly with the costs and benefits of interdependencies.[6]

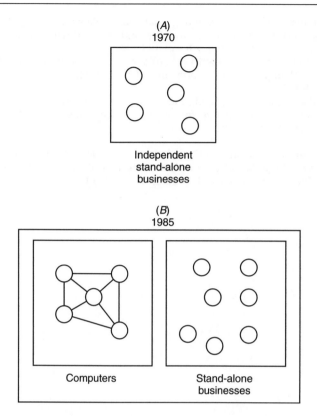

Figure 7.5 Transformation at Hewlett-Packard: a schematic

NOTES

1 Interdependencies have been discussed mostly as a sharing of costs between businesses based on common elements in their value chain; see Michael Porter, *Competitive Advantage*, New York: Free Press, 1984. While the economies and technological benefits of interdependencies are in principle relatively clear, their organizational costs are seldom fully appreciated. Among works that touch upon the organizational aspects are Porter, *Competitive Advantage*, chapter 11, and Bruce Kogut, 'Designing Global Strategies: Profiting From Operational Flexibility', *Sloan Management Review* 27, No. 1, Fall 1985, pp. 27–38.

2 This section draws on data published in Yves Doz, 'Background Note on Hi-Fi: Western European Markets and Industry' (revised by Kenneth Winslow), Harvard Business School, No. 4–337–193, 1977. See also Yves Doz, 'Philips M.I.G. Audio (A), (B) and (C)', Harvard Business School Cases Nos. 1–377–196 and 1–337–197, 1977.

3 Jay Forrester, *Industrial Dynamics*, Cambridge, Mass.: MIT Press, 1961.

4 The interpretation of IBM's evolution is based on 'IBM Corporation: Background Note', and 'IBM: The Bubble Memory Incident', Harvard Business School Cases Nos. 180–034 and 180–042; Abraham Katz, 'Planning in the IBM Corporation', 1983, 'Personal Computers: And the Winner is IBM', *Business*

Week, October 3, 1983; 'The Coming Shakeout in Personal Computers', *Business Week,* November 22, 1982, and the author's series of interviews with senior executives at IBM in 1979 and 1984–85.
5 The interpretation of Hewlett-Packard's evolution is based on 'Hewlett-Packard: Challenging the Entrepreneurial Culture', Harvard Business School Case No. 9–384–1983.
6 See Prahalad, C. K., Doz, Y. and Angelmar, R., 'Technological Innovation and Interdependence: A Challenge for the Large, Complex Firm', *Technology in Society* 7, Nos. 2–3 (1985) pp. 105–25.

Chapter 8

Four portfolios analysis

Christopher J. Clarke and Kieron Brennan

In the 1970s and early 1980s many multinational enterprises (MNEs) responded to the lack of growth in their core businesses by diversifying. Their response to the dead hand of corporate bureaucracy, which developed as an accompaniment to their size, was to set up separately directed strategic business units (SBUs). The intention was to focus performance measurement and management effort at the level of each separately defined business. These moves were encouraged by management consultancies, especially those using product/market portfolio approaches. For example, Bruce Henderson's famous product portfolio matrix is shown as Figure 8.1. The matrix has on its vertical axis the growth of a product market in the next planning period. On the horizontal axis is the market share of a firm in a defined product market divided into that of the largest competitor (relative market share). The circle sizes represent the revenue generated by each product for the firm. This matrix was often used to define strategic business units and then to encourage firms to move into new businesses (diversification). High growth sectors were often chosen, bearing no relationship to the capabilities of the existing business.

It has become increasingly clear that these diversification and portfolio strategies are failing in many companies. Peters and Waterman questioned them and suggested 'sticking to the knitting'.[1] Michael Porter and others have given evidence that diversification is unsuccessful.[2] Hamel and Prahalad criticized the SBU/portfolio approach for ignoring strategic intent and for being a snapshot of a moving target.[3] These last two laud the success of Japanese firms, giving examples of the many different ways they have overcome their Western counterparts. We agree with their argument, which demands an aggressive, dynamic and flexible corporate mission to overcome the competition.

More telling than academic argument has been the wave of breakup bids. KKR's recent acquisition of Nabisco Brands and Sir James Goldsmith's bid for BAT are typical examples. They are founded on the

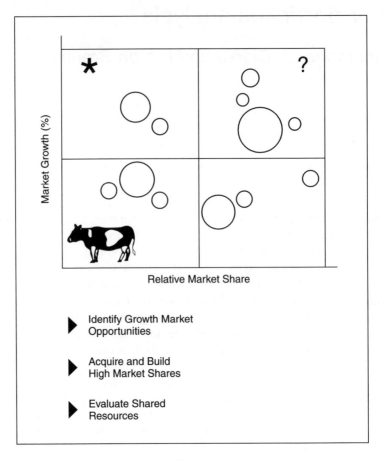

Figure 8.1 A product/market portfolio

concept that diversification often diminishes the value of the corporate whole and are intended to reverse the process.

Despite these criticisms of the popular approach to strategy, we are still meeting the CEOs who are about to embark on reorganization into SBUs or on major diversification programmes, because they believe there is no better strategy available. Only conglomerates such as Hanson Trust have consistently achieved success in diversification. One striking characteristic of Hanson and several similarly run companies is that they drive out synergies from between business units.

In this chapter we propose a practical framework which helps to improve their analysis and to implement an action programme capable of realizing their strategic intent. We first identify some of the problems associated with traditional portfolio approaches. Then we develop a methodology which takes account of their dangers to enable the organization to focus its efforts on achieving its intended goals. We argue that this can be achieved by 'Synergy Bonding'. By linking new products and business ventures using four portfolios, the synergies between businesses can be clearly identified and reinforced. Through such an analysis a firm's organizational structure, systems and culture can be redirected towards new goals which create 'synergy bonds'.

THE PRODUCT-MARKET PORTFOLIO

The underlying logic of the portfolio matrix in Figure 8.1 was based on the experience curve, Figure 8.2. In a wide number of industries, from limestone quarrying to electronics, it was observed that, over long periods of time, unit costs fell as cumulative volume increased. This occurred because:

- labour became more skilful (the learning effect);
- management identified superior production methods;
- simplified designs were developed;
- new production technologies were introduced, and production moved towards the optimal scale economies for the industry.

The link of the experience curve to the product portfolio matrix was that if an SBU's market share was greater than that of competitors it would have lower unit costs and would therefore generate more cash flow than

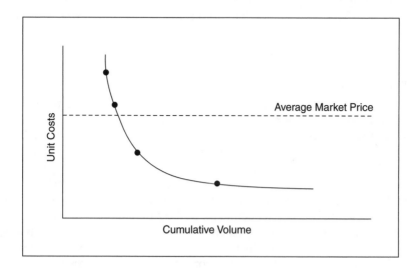

Figure 8.2 The experience curve for a German electronic product

they did. Equally, if it was in growth markets, cumulative volumes would increase more rapidly, reducing units costs even faster, to give the firm a competitive edge.

Early on, it was recognized that gaining market share did not necessarily improve profits, especially if achieved at the cost of lower prices, higher advertising spending or higher promotional costs. All of these approaches can be used pre-emptively to seize market share and drive down the experience curve, but the effectiveness of this depends on whether the share can be held in the long term.

The Henderson Portfolio[4] was used by his firm, Boston Consulting Group. Its use spread like wildfire. Like all simple prescriptive ideas, it was often used as a 'quick fix'. McKinsey and others introduced their own 'me too' portfolios, each claiming to overcome the shortcomings of the others. Their cumulative impact was to get multinationals into the mind set of separable SBUs and portfolio management.

LIMITATIONS TO THE PORTFOLIO APPROACH

In 1983 Wind and others described the results of running some standard data through four competing portfolio analyses.[5] The results were worrying. They offered completely conflicting strategies for the firms from which the data had been derived. The idea that a simple portfolio can be used to devise a company's strategy was clearly naive, though it spawned a host of highly profitable, specialist consulting firms.

The main shortcomings of the market grown/market share portfolio are worth examining. They give insights into what strategic tools are needed for MNEs to avoid the pitfalls in diversification and the SBU structure.

Using the experience curve

The first problem relates to the experience curve itself, the theoretical underpinning of the portfolio. As the curve falls steepest in its earliest stages, it is more relevant for high tech or short lifecycle products. Telling General Motors that it only needs to double its cumulative car volume to gain a 20 per cent unit cost reduction is not very helpful, as this is a very long-term task given the length of time GM has been in volume production. Equally, new market entrants can gain the cumulative experience of earlier entrants. This can be achieved by buying production technology, recruiting competitors' management or locating in an area where ready trained labour is available. In the UK credit card business, Barclaycard incurred the costs of pioneering the concept. The start up costs of second on the market, Access, and others were much lower. Retailers already understood the idea. Consumers had been made aware of the concept and computer systems had been developed.

Defining market share

A second problem is the definition of market share. Within which geographic and product definitions are we working? Wallace Smith's experience is that many firms have an inappropriate definition of their markets. A common fault is to persist in looking at a national market within a regionally or globally competitive industry. This is easily rectified by identifying the importance of cross border product flows and the international activities of competitors.

Synergy and shared resources

The biggest problem of the product portfolio strikes at the heart of the SBU concept. This is the 'shared resource problem'. What happens if a dog and a star, or a cash cow, share key productive resources or technologies? Killing the dog can butcher the economics of the cash cow.

The concept of 'synergy', the economics of one business in a symbiotically beneficial relationship with those of another, is based on precisely these shared resources. If a foundry makes two products, both using molten metal, they can share the benefit from the learning effects; economies of scale; technical R&D; and capacity utilization. If one starts to separate them into disparate SBUs it can damage these synergies. A fundamental law of business is that SBUs tend to drive out synergies. The SBU concept is often used to put a fence around a business. This is done to achieve the following benefits:

- focused and motivated management;
- clarity of recording where profit and losses are made and therefore improved decision making on where to put investment;
- savings in overheads, as they are paid for directly by the users who demand value/service for their money.

The SBU concept has, however, the following drawbacks:

- It can duplicate effort in what could be shared resource areas and thus drive out synergy.
- It can lead to gaps developing between SBUs, which can be targeted and exploited by competitors.
- It can lead to damaging competition between SBUs in the same firm.

Once synergy has been driven out, the corporation becomes, in effect, a conglomerate.

MEASURING SYNERGY

A vital piece of analysis is, therefore, how to measure synergy. We have found that, by analysing the corporate business into four portfolios, profound insights into the relative capacity for synergy can be achieved. This in turn enables us to gain a clearer picture of strategic opportunities and to obtain a deeper understanding of the appropriate organizational structure for a given mix of business. The four portfolios are:

- product market portfolio (one type of which has already been discussed);
- resource portfolio;
- customer portfolio;
- technology portfolio.

The resource portfolio

The resource portfolio, shown in Figure 8.3, identifies the key productive activities in the firm and evaluates how cost effective each is in relation to its competitors. A resource can be described at various levels of aggregation. Examples might include: a plant (or a machine centre), a warehouse, a salesforce, a computer system, a marketing activity or an administrative department. The growth in capacity of each type of activity is shown on the horizontal axis. Resources with a competitive advantage are shown to the left. This advantage can be measured either in cost per unit of throughput or in terms of its impact in differentiation. The area of the circles are proportional to the percentage of the firm's total costs accounted for by each resource.

It is vital to avoid the dangers of static analysis.[4] First, a very wide geographic net should be cast in seeking current and potential competitors. There are a number of approaches for identifying the 'over horizon competitor' which is often the most dangerous type. Whilst Ford, GM and Chrysler were fighting each other for US market share in the 1960s, Toyota and Nissan were consolidating their grip on third markets prior to invading the US. Second, we have found it invariably fruitful to study the small 'maverick' competitors, those with unusually high growth, profitability or innovative strategies. Third, in looking at the growth in the use of specific types of resources, it is vital to project this into the future to avoid snapshot analysis. This dynamic imperative applies equally to all four portfolios in our framework.

As a stand-alone analysis the resource portfolio can be used to identify competitive strengths and weaknesses in a company's operating activities. In Figure 8.3 the double glazing company clearly needs to strengthen its position in making aluminium profiles, selling and glazing.

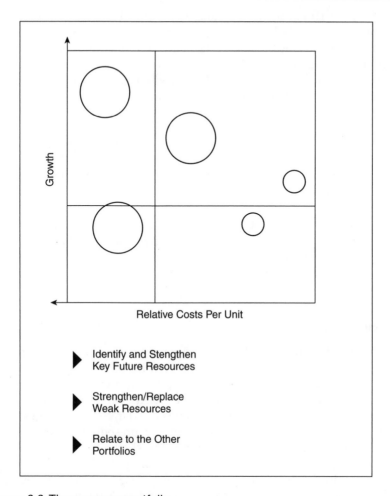

Figure 8.3 The resource portfolio

There are a variety of strategic options which we normally consider in strengthening a resource portfolio. These include:

- consolidating plants to reduce overheads and spare capacity;
- new production technology such as FMS;
- acquisition of lower cost resources, e.g. by buying a company which has them;
- outsourcing the activity in question, with a supplier which has lower costs;
- relocating the activity in a place with lower cost characteristics, e.g. cheaper energy or labour.

A more powerful and dynamic analysis is possible from examining the interplay between the product and the resource portfolios. Changing the sales levels of various products affects the fundamental economics of the individual resources. Equally, changes in resource economics unleash major potential benefits for product economies. Moves which impact both portfolios simultaneously often include:

- New product launches, acquisitions of products, price reductions or advertising campaigns, to life volume throughput of a product which uses a specific resource, where spare capacity can be unlocked.
- Using a strategic alliance, based on a resource area, to allow sufficient volume to enable economies of scale to be generated.

In contrast, improvement in a resource area, for example replacing production machinery, may raise the quality of a product, or the scope for product variety, while altering the fundamental economics of production so that a differentiation is enhanced.

The customer portfolio

By adding a third portfolio to our analysis, the customer portfolio, shown in Figure 8.4, a deeper level of insight can be achieved. The customer portfolio has on its vertical axis the projected growth of the customer's business (groups of customers can also be used). On the horizontal axis is the customer's market share of his business, relative to his biggest competitor. The size of circles, in this instance, represents the value of purchases in the products we are studying. The shaded segments illustrate the volume purchased from the company doing the analysis.

Once again the customer portfolio can be used to identify strengths and weaknesses as a stand-alone analytical tool. Customers which are growing can be characterized as tomorrow's customers and those declining, as yesterday's customers. Companies should plan for strong positions in the portfolio in terms of growing customers which are making major purchases of relevant products. This can lead to a refocusing of sales and marketing strategy.

By relating the customer portfolio to the resource portfolio, further opportunities and synergies can be identified. For example, some important resources may be customer specific. A sales force, warehouse or system might be dedicated to a particular class of customer. By identifying those customers sharing economics in the resource portfolio, the impact on cash flows of changes in the resource portfolio on customers and vice versa can be evaluated. Similarly, the interrelationship of the product portfolio and the customer portfolio can be considered.

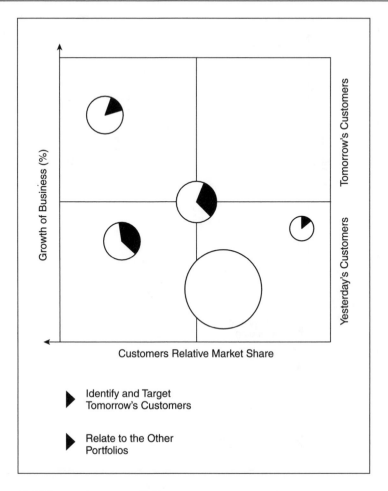

Figure 8.4 The customer portfolio

The technology portfolio

The addition of a technology portfolio, shown as Figure 8.5, identifies further dimensions of synergy. The vertical axis shows the future importance of the product or process technology, the horizontal axis shows the performance of the firm, relative to its competitors in the technology. The circle size illustrates the proportion of expenditure being devoted to each technology. It is vital to use external technology expertise to identify a firm's relative positioning. On a stand-alone basis the technology portfolio can be strengthened by:

• balancing expenditure towards technologies growing in importance;

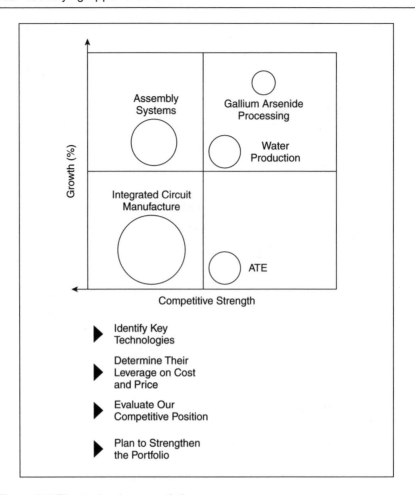

Figure 8.5 The technology portfolio

• acquiring patents or licences to support areas of weakness;
• buying businesses with vital technology skills.

THE FOUR PORTFOLIOS APPROACH

By relating the technology portfolio to the other three (see Figure 8.6) a very rich analysis of synergies is possible. Technology projects in R&D can stand behind products, resources and customer groups. An example would be many of the systems developed by banks.

The four portfolios approach enables the synergies within a corporation to be viewed simultaneously in many dimensions. Thus the company can build layers of competitive advantage and core competences. The

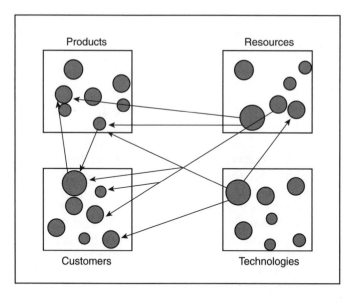

Figure 8.6 Relationships between the portfolios

portfolios themselves are an effective, visual way of illustrating competitive positioning to senior management. The more complex and supporting computer modelling of the impact of various portfolio moves on the net present value of the firm is the basis for quality strategic decision making. It allows the board to identify the key areas of synergy against a dynamic competitive environment. It enables the best elements of each existing and potential competitor to be targeted for improvement.

From our analysis of the behaviour of several large consumer electronics firms in Japan on behalf of a Western competitor, it became obvious that they were actively engaged in building layers of competitive competence. New product developments, technologies, productive resources and target customer groups were all closely interrelated and focused. By building on areas of synergy and strengthening them, the economics of the whole concern prospered.

The four portfolios analysis needs to be repeated regularly because competitors react. In this way new levels of competitive advantage can then be strived for.

The four portfolios approach can also be used to evaluate potential diversification moves. A vital safety rule in climbing cliffs is to always have three limbs in contact with the surface, moving only one at a time to avoid falling. In like manner, by anchoring diversification moves around the synergies available from technologies, customers, resources and products, a robust diversification strategy can be developed. This should feed off strong competences within the business and in turn further strengthen those competencies.

USING THE SBU CONCEPT

It is hardly surprising, in the light of the above discussion, that the SBU concept needs to be questioned. The key issue is how to organize, to safeguard and exploit synergy opportunities across the four portfolios. In their book *Strategies and Styles*[6] Goold and Campbell identified firms like BP, which plan for the long term and have large integrating, co-ordinating, corporate centres. Others, like Hanson Trust, have lean and mean corporate centres with planning activity pushed to the operating units and mainly financial management from the centre.

Our analytical approach would suggest that this reflects Hanson's position as an SBU type company, where the disparate businesses have no synergy. Indeed, it can be argued that the Hanson way is the best way to run unrelated products companies. It is for this type of firm that the SBU concept has value. As there is no synergy between businesses there is nothing to be gained by having centralized departments, such as R&D, or co-ordinating marketing and detailed planning activities. The corporate centre becomes a small, financially driven, control and portfolio management function. Several other successful, unrelated product firms operate in this way, BTR being another example. On the other hand, a vertically and horizontally diversified company like Shell or BP needs to maximize the synergies between its operating subsidiaries.

MANAGING SYNERGIES

To manage synergies there are several commonly used structural, cultural and systems approaches. Structurally, certain shared resources, technology development programmes or customer management activities, can be conducted through specific organization elements, such as central marketing or R&D departments. Co-ordinator roles in the structure are another alternative. From frequent meetings with Japanese firms, many senior and crucial contacts are titled 'co-ordinator' without an apparent line role, but with a key impact on decision making.

3M allows product champions to develop new products and potentially new divisions. This is done by allowing them informal access to resources elsewhere in the organization, primarily dedicated to other uses. One example of this is the 'Post-It', a successful gum-backed note-let for office use. The champion of the Post-It product built a bond with the R&D function which was dedicated to a completely different range of adhesive work. Once the prototype was ready, informal bonds were then established with other divisions and functions. Only once the product was 'proved' were the bonds formalized.

Culturally, collective involvement in decisions between departments becomes important. The development of career paths in the corporation rather than within one division, the rotation of personnel and the development of a one company spirit rather than an SBU one, are all vital. The use of IT to ensure free flows of information on all aspects of company affairs enables decisions to be influenced in favour of synergies on a firmwide basis. Informal communications are equally important. Physically locating key interfaces together helps in this process.

Hence, Shell has massive corporate centres in London and Amsterdam. This is the opposite of an SBU company, which tends to demolish the corporate centre in a cost cutting drive and to relocate in provincially scattered locations. An overriding issue is whether the cost of the corporate centre exceeds or is less than the synergy gains.

The level at which synergy bonding takes place can vary. For example, it is at a single business unit level for a Hanson Trust. It is at a corporate level for British Gas. Firms like Shell have co-ordinating structures and systems at intermediate levels too, for example, within Shell Chemicals as well as in Shell Transport and Trading.

SUMMARY

We have argued that some analytical approaches have oversimplified complex relationships and that this can lead to risky diversification and the establishing of SBUs which may or may not be appropriate to corporate needs. By their nature SBUs can drive out synergy opportunities. Our approach is to analyse the relationships within a corporation through four portfolios, one for each of products, resources, customers and technology. These enable the synergies within a business to be identified and managed through the cultural and systems building process which should focus around these. Appropriate organization structures for companies with synergy potential will recognize the need for co-ordinating and planning functions which encourage the realization of the shared economics.

REFERENCES

1 Peters, T. J. and Waterman, R. H., *In Search of Excellence*, Harper and Row, 1982.
2 Porter, M. E., 'From competitive advantage to corporate strategy', *Harvard Business Review*, May/June, 1987.
3 Hamel, G. and Prahalad, C. K., 'Strategic intent', *Harvard Business Review*, May/June 1989.
4 Henderson, B., *Henderson on Corporate Strategy*, ABT Books, 1989.

5 Wind, Y., Mahajan, B. and Swire, D. J., 'An empirical compassion of standardised portfolio models', *Journal of Marketing*, 47, Spring 1983.
6 Goold, M. and Campbell, A., *Strategies & Styles*, Basil Blackwell, Oxford, 1987.

Part III

Creating synergy benefits

Chapter 9

Introduction to creating synergy benefits

The business press is full of reports of the expected synergy benefits from mergers, acquisitions and restructurings, alongside other reports of companies divesting businesses because they have failed to gain synergies in their past acquisitions or restructuring efforts. It is not surprising, with examples of failure so readily available, that synergy is frequently described as 'elusive'. Sometimes the problem is that managers seek synergy benefits that just do not exist. They attempt to join activities, or share skills that are not a source of competitive advantage. In these cases, the cause of the failure stems from faulty analysis, or from poor implementation. In other instances, though, the potential benefits seem real enough and are even widely recognized within the organization – but they still remain out of reach.

For example, in the introduction we cited a case study on BOK Chemicals, a disguised European company. BOK had businesses in several European countries in similar product areas after a series of acquisitions and mergers during the 1970s. The company made numerous efforts to co-ordinate product development, marketing and manufacturing across these businesses, but it confronted many obstacles. The general managers of two businesses in the decorative/do-it-yourself markets could not reach agreement on product policy or pricing, or other issues of common interest. The businesses failed to achieve any scale economies in manufacturing, and the different sales forces did not support each others' products. BOK tried to encourage co-operation through cross-cultural training, but most people considered it a waste of time and meetings among managers of the different companies were dropped because nothing much came of them.[1] Just why do companies find it so difficult to gain synergies? The authors in this part explore the barriers that managers confront and suggest different approaches to creating synergy benefits.

The first chapter is by Rosabeth Moss Kanter, a professor at Harvard Business School. 'Seeking and achieving synergies' is taken from Kanter's book *When Giants Learn to Dance.*[2] In this book, Kanter discusses the complex changes occurring in corporations, with a focus on American companies. Global competition, declining performance, the need for continuous innovation and renewal, and changing social expectations all put severe pressure on large corporations and Kanter explores how they must adapt. She describes how companies are seeking to combine the discipline and purpose of traditional corporations with the creativity and nimbleness of entrepreneurial organizations. These efforts, in her view, amount to a revolution in management and will lead to new kinds of organizations that she calls 'post-entrepreneurial'. One of the key tasks of the post-entrepreneurial company is to achieve synergies and in this reading Kanter explores how companies can go about doing so.

Synergy, Kanter argues, is the only way multibusiness companies can create value and the post-entrepreneurial corporation therefore has to ensure that nothing stands in the way of this value creation. First, the corporate portfolio of businesses has to be sufficiently related so that each business can contribute to the whole. This sometimes demands restructuring, or redefining the focus of the company and Kanter observes that many companies are in the process of doing just this. It also means creating the right conditions so that cross-business co-operation can flourish and lead to synergy benefits.

Kanter identifies three prerequisites for gaining synergies. First, there must be top management commitment to uncovering synergy opportunities and promoting them. Second, incentives and rewards must encourage team work and co-operation rather than be based solely on individual or unit performance. Finally, people in the organization have to know and communicate with each other. Dense communication networks foster the exchange of ideas and facilitate the co-operation required to achieve synergies.

Kanter's argument can be tested against the BOK example. At BOK there was top-level corporate commitment to identifying synergy opportunities and establishing committees to make them work. But, there were few incentives, beyond encouragement, and few networks of relationships. Kanter's views would suggest that BOK management failed because they did not put in place the appropriate incentives and because they did not commit enough effort for long enough to develop the needed relationships and dense communication networks. For BOK managers, this advice might seem unhelpful. It suggests that they should have kept on even in the face of mounting evidence that they were not getting anywhere. Kanter's view would be that BOK cannot get these synergies until management have transformed the company into a 'post-entrepreneurial organisation'. But she can point to very few who have achieved this synergistic state.

The next chapter, 'The transnational solution', is by Christopher Bartlett of Harvard Business School and Sumantra Ghoshal of INSEAD. It is based on the authors' research in Japanese, American and European multi-national companies, and Bartlett and Ghoshal's full findings are reported in their book, *Managing Across Borders: The Transnational Solution*.[3] In this chapter they discuss some of their research findings and present their concept of the emerging transnational organization.

Bartlett and Ghoshal begin by describing the opportunities available to companies with world-wide operations. Multinational companies able to co-ordinate their global operations gain significant scale economies, overtaking their competitors because of their lower costs and more efficient operations. Other multinational companies prosper through being responsive to local needs, with their autonomous national sub-sidiaries adept at seizing opportunities in their local or regional markets. Changing patterns of international competition, the authors argue, are putting increased pressures on multinationals to exploit many different kinds of opportunities in their globally spread businesses. They have to leverage their resources, their skills, their know-how both locally and globally to remain competitive.

What prevents a company from making the most of its opportunities, according to Bartlett and Ghoshal, is its administrative heritage, or the norms, values and management styles of the company, and its config-uration of assets. Philips's national organizations, for example, were historically highly autonomous and its cadre of expatriate managers prized their independence and control over resources. Whilst this encouraged Philips's subsidiaries to be innovative, it has also made it difficult to co-ordinate operations and efforts across different subsid-iaries. BOK's administrative heritage also fits this pattern. The task facing multinationals, as the authors see it, is for companies first to improve their current capabilities, and then go on to develop new ones. Companies like Philips needed to strengthen their central management. Companies such as Matsushita, which already have strong central management, must improve the flexibility of their local operations. In these efforts, the different multinationals have much to learn from each other.

But this is only the first step. To exploit all the strategic opportunities available to them, multinational companies also have to create strong links across units, making them interdependent on each other and the centre. This is done by allocating resources and responsibilities in a way that promotes interdependence. Such 'transnational' organizations will allow resources, people, skills and know-how to flow freely around the organization, enabling the company to make the best use of them.

There are many similarities in the arguments of Bartlett and Ghoshal and Kanter. These authors argue that corporations have numerous oppor-tunities to create more value through sharing across their units. They urge companies to pursue many different kinds of interrelationships, sharing activities, skills, information, and know-how. They also point to many barriers to such sharing, which can only be overcome by creating new kinds of organizations, with new capabilities. Yet, since organizational capabilities can take years to build, the implication is that synergy will remain elusive for many companies for some time.

In the next chapter, Joseph Badaracco of Harvard Business School focuses on another synergy issue: how alliances can help firms learn new capabilities and expand their skills. Increasing global competition and technological change can make it difficult for a firm to build all its necessary capabilities on its own, and joint ventures with other organizations can help a firm to acquire new capabilities and learn new skills. Badaracco has written about General Motors' and IBM's joint ventures and alliances in *The Knowledge Link*,[4] and the reading 'Managing Alliances' is taken from his book.

In common with authorities such as Hiroyuki Itami and resource-based theorists, Badaracco argues that a firm's critical resources are its knowledge and capabilities rather than its physical assets. The challenge for managers is to expand their firm's capabilities to ensure it remains competitive in the future. As with General Motors and IBM, a firm may have to seek outside partners who have the specialized skills or knowledge it needs to acquire. Such partners may be suppliers, government agencies, component manufacturers or even direct competitors. The benefits of such external relationships can be substantial, such as access to new markets, a broader R&D programme than the firm could finance on its own, and the learning of new capabilities. Alliances, however, also involve considerable risks. Exchanging knowledge or building new skills with a partner may weaken a firm's competitive position, especially if the alliance involves sharing critical capabilities or knowledge. Partners may be able to exploit the information and skills they gain from an alliance in other markets, or even become competitors in the same market. In considering an alliance, managers need to weigh the costs as well as the benefits, in much the same way as they must assess internal synergy issues. Badaracco advises managers not to see alliances as substitutes for internal development of new capabilities and to be chary of sharing core skills with potential competitors. At the same time, the pace of change and the constant need to develop new capabilities often mean that alliances can provide a firm with the best opportunities to expand its skills and know-how.

The obstacles managers face in making alliances work are similar to the barriers to creating synergies within a single organization. Even when partners agree on the mutual benefits of co-operation, it may be difficult to capture benefits from alliances. Each organization has its own approaches, decision-making processes and accepted patterns of behaviour, and it can take time for partners to get to know how the other works. Often, managers see their firms as 'citadels', making it difficult for them to share knowledge or information with outsiders, or to recognize the value of another organization's know-how, and the 'not-invented-here' syndrome can undermine an alliance. Another difficulty is that the transfer of know-how and capabilities is not straightforward, whether it is within or across organizations. Such knowledge is not captured in manuals or computer programs, but is embedded in an organization's processes, its administrative networks and even in its values. To share or exchange such knowledge requires mutual trust and commitment among individuals on both sides of the alliance, and individuals need time to learn to work together and to resolve inevitable differences. Badaracco suggests that small-scale or trial projects can be a good way for partners to see if they can work together before committing to a broader alliance.

The three readings on creating synergy within large corporations, across multinationals and through alliances have a common theme: capturing benefits often requires considerable, even fundamental, changes in organizational culture and in managers themselves. According to Kanter, Bartlett and Ghoshal and Badaracco, managers have to invest the time, effort and resources necessary to change their organizations if they are to gain the considerable and even critical advantages which come from sharing skills and capabilities across units.

The final chapter in this section, 'Building core skills' by Andrew Campbell, is based on a research project on skill sharing in decentralized companies at Ashridge Strategic Management Centre. In this chapter, Campbell explores how decentralized companies manage core skills, and in particular the role of the centre in transferring critical know-how across different businesses. Although Campbell examines only a particular kind of synergy, his article has broader implications for how companies can manage synergies successfully.

Campbell first suggests ways of identifying core skills, based on different methodologies such as successes and failures analysis, benchmarking and skill components analysis. Campbell argues that the analysis of core skills has to break down the skill into its components and sub-components, to ensure that it is a core skill that is relevant and important across several units. Unless this is done at a sufficient level of detail, it is easy to misidentify what the skill is, or to transfer irrelevant skills. Another reason to analyse the skill in detail is because managers have to be clear about what it is they are attempting to manage and to transfer across units.

Campbell goes on to explore the ways in which companies both build and transfer core skills. A core skill may be developed centrally or in one of the units, but since it can potentially be exploited in many areas of the company, the centre's responsibility is to decide how best to transfer the skill to other units. Campbell suggests that the key decision is the amount of pressure used by the centre to ensure that transfer actually takes place. This ranges from simply informing other units of know-how developed elsewhere in the company to imposing a 'company way' or standardization across all units. Campbell suggests that managers have to take a contingency approach in deciding on how to transfer the skill, taking into account organizational realities and commercial imperatives. Sometimes, these come into direct conflict and it is Campbell's suggestions for managing these conflicts that have relevance to other types of synergy.

A conflict between commercial imperatives and organizational realities occurred at BOK, the example cited above. Commercial realities demanded rationalization of manufacturing and joint marketing, but the organizational reality of highly independent unit managers undermined efforts at co-operation. It is the existence of these kinds of conflicts that lead authorities such as Kanter, Bartlett and Ghoshal to argue that we need new kinds of organization, with new capabilities. Campbell, however, reminds managers that fundamental organizational changes are difficult and risky, and he explores the reasonable alternatives available. These include possible withdrawal from businesses requiring complex global linkages if organizational realities throw up too many barriers, or incremental change if commercial imperatives permit. At BOK, for example, the centre's very commitment to achieving synergies across the businesses led it to establish many mechanisms to encourage co-operation, but local managers saw these efforts as heavy handed and resisted them. In Campbell's view, overcoming barriers gradually, or even avoiding them altogether, can be as effective as tackling them head-on. Moreover, Campbell argues for managers to focus on the detailed know-how components rather than the broad organizational or policy issues. If the centre focuses on the detail it will achieve more immediate transfer and start the process of change.

Campbell's latest book on the subject of synergy takes these ideas even further. In *Synergy: Why Links between Business Units Often Fail and How to Make Them Work*,[5] he and his Ashridge colleague Michael Goold argue that the main cause of managerial failure in this area comes from biases in the way corporate-level managers think about synergy. Moreover some of these biases are, he believes, the result of the ideas promoted by authors such as Ansoff, Kanter and Bartlett.

The biases cause corporate-level managers to pursue mirages (synergy opportunities that turn out not to offer any additional value); presume that they need to knock heads together (when business managers are often better left to make their own relationships); assume that they can help oil the wheels (whereas they are often too ignorant of the issues or insufficiently skilled at facilitation); and overlook downside risks. In other words the problem most companies have with synergy stems from the behaviour of corporate-level managers.

Campbell encourages corporate-level managers to see the synergy challenge as a series of targeted interventions aimed at releasing specific synergies. He recognizes that corporate managers need to, on occasion, review their organization's attitude to synergy and its degree of success against the potential. But he sees synergy success being built up from many specific, carefully thought through and targeted initiatives, rather than from sweeping organizational changes, broad reductions in SBU autonomy or intense appeals to 'support the family'.

Campbell's approach is in stark contrast to that of authorities such as Kanter and Bartlett who urge managers to develop new organizational capabilities in order to manage many different kinds of interrelationships. Campbell is wary of opportunities that require capabilities an organization does not possess and that are likely to take a long time to build. In his chapter he focuses, first, on how managers can get benefits from sharing skills without changing the organization and then, if there are opportunities to gain further advantages, he examines the centre's role in leading a process of gradual change.

REFERENCES

1 Cook, D. Smith and de la Torre, J., 'BOK Finishes – Decorative/Do-It-Yourself Markets', in Davidson, W. H. and de la Torre, J., *Managing the Global Corporation: Case Studies in Strategy and Management*, McGraw-Hill Inc., New York, 1989.
2 Kanter, R. Moss, *When Giants Learn to Dance*, Simon & Schuster, New York, 1989.
3 Bartlett, C. A. and Ghoshal, S., *Managing Across Borders: The Transnational Solution*, Harvard Business School Press, Boston, 1989.
4 Badaracco, J. L., Jr., *The Knowledge Link*, Harvard Business School Press, Cambridge, MA, 1990.
5 Campbell, A. and Goold, M., *Synergy: Why Links Between Business Units Often Fail and How to Make Them Work*, Forthcoming, Capstone, London, 1998.

Chapter 10

Seeking and achieving synergies

Rosabeth Moss Kanter

Build a better mousetrap, the old saying goes, and the world will beat a path to your door. Build a better mousetrap in the traditional corporate bureaucracy, however, and the story might unfold a little differently. Here's how I imagine it:

You're very excited about your mousetrap and eager to get it to consumers. But first, the Mousetrap Department manager, her boss, and her boss's boss insist upon thorough reviews, each one asking for some changes before taking it to the others, and then the whole thing goes to the vice-president of the Mouse, Mole, and Skunk Traps Division (MMSTD). The price is marked up way over costs to cover the charge for the company volleyball court, executive dining rooms, middle manager training in how to conduct downward and upward reviews, newspaper subscriptions and lounge chairs for the internal press clipping group, and other overhead charges.

At last, the Better Mousetrap brand is ready to go to market, so an elaborate research project is begun in three rodent-rich cities in three different countries. Unbeknownst to you, the Chemicals and Pesticide Division (CPD) has already collected extensive market data for the launching of its new Mouse Repellent, which is being sold through exactly the same channels. (You learn this from reading the accident report filed by one of your MMSTD truck drivers who almost ran over one of CPD's truck drivers.) And Animal Services, the company's innovative new lease-a-pet acquisition, has completed a psychological profile of the mouse-averse for its Kittycat product line, which points out the desirable features for mousetraps, a profile they are careful not to show you.

Meanwhile, costs have mounted, there has been no way to build on what the other divisions have already done, and the Better Mousetrap gets to market later and at a higher price than the offering of a spiffy new mousetrap specialty start-up. Wall Street, which had once praised your parent corporation, Unrelated Holdings, Inc. for its smart move toward synergy by acquiring three companies with a common interest in rodent control, reacts unfavourably to the news. The stock drops precipitously. Raiders see that the break-up value of UHI is higher than its current stock price; after all, the three mouse-oriented divisions are gaining nothing by being together anyway, and 'corporate' requirements are a drag on their performance.

Then your boss calls you in for a heart-to-heart. 'Sad news, Better Mousetrap Builder,' she says. 'The company has to cut its losses to avoid a takeover, and since your product isn't doing too well, we're letting you go.'

Post-entrepreneurial corporations, in contrast, make the search for synergies a central part of their strategies. Slowly but surely, they are learning how to accomplish more (exploiting new opportunities quickly) while using less (keeping expenses down). They clear the 'clutter' out of the way, such as unnecessary oversight loops that delay action. They get rid of extraneous activities. They make sure each area contributes something to the others. The leaner, more focused, more co-operative and integrated organizations that result help each unit add value to the others. The 'whole' contributes something above and beyond the value of the parts.

This sounds straightforward, yet the implications of taking these steps are revolutionizing corporate structure.

VALUE ADDED: RETHINKING 'ADMINISTRATION' AND 'CORPORATE SERVICES'

At the same time that post-entrepreneurial companies are restructuring their lines of business in the search for focused combinations that build synergies, they are also re-examining their internal structure to make sure that all activities, all departments, 'add value'. For example:

- Interested in cutting costs as well as improving delegation downward, a telephone company – once among the most intricately graded of organizations – has almost eliminated an entire managerial level (promotions now jump people from level three to level five just below the officer ranks) and has doubled supervisory spans of control in its largest unit, which covers 75 per cent of all employees.
- An auto giant took its first step toward streamlining by banning all one-to-one reporting relationships (a boss responsible for only one subordinate).
- A widely respected household products manufacturer has gradually thinned its line management ranks by creating 'high-commitment work systems' in which employee teams take full responsibility for production, without requiring managers.

- A pharmaceutical company is 'delayering', as they put it, to reduce unnecessary levels that were indeed 'delayers' of decisions and actions; it has distributed to all departments a kit of instructions for rearranging the organization chart to work without at least two levels of management.
- An oil company, calling itself an 'elephant learning to dance', is trying to become more agile by collapsing several levels of the management hierarchy.

The principal targets of this kind of reorganization are corporate staffs and middle managers. But restructuring to ensure that every management layer and every corporate service adds value to the organization also raises profound questions about what it means to be a corporation. How much management from the top is really needed? What activities should be under the company's hierarchical umbrella, as opposed to being purchased on the market?

There are two kinds of roles included in the 'corporate' category: supporters and interveners. The questions about supporters are the more easily resolved. Some supporters, whether financial planners or management trainers, are indeed facilitators and integrators who add value by improving the way business units operate or transferring knowledge and expertise among them. Supporters also include the vast armies of clerks and quasiprofessionals whose role is to handle the paperwork and the documentation involved in business transactions. But the ranks of supporters are being thinned anyway by two intertwined forces: information technology and the growth of specialist firms taking over corporate support functions. A leading electronics company, for example, anticipates that computer networks will reduce a purchasing staff of three thousand, doing largely routine work, to a mere hundred professionals negotiating contracts and establishing systems. 'Eighty per cent of our transactions could be ordered directly through the requisition system on terminals, and bank-to-bank funds transfer could support them', a purchasing executive reported. For other companies, the road to smaller internal staffs is to turn over routine transaction processing to the specialist firms that do nothing but handle the payroll or manage accounts receivable or keep the records.

Interveners are a different matter; their role and contributions are more controversial. To some companies, they are the necessary links in a chain of control. To others, they are the principal source of 'fat' to be reduced to get in shape for the corporate Olympics. Over the years, corporate bureaucracies have come to include large numbers of people whose primary task is to check up on others, to ensure that 'standards' are being met. These range from middle managers that oversee other managers who direct the work, to staffs that establish procedures and then monitor how well other managers carry them out. As the same purchasing executive put it, 'Controlling the number of purchase orders checking up on how many parts were ordered, and nitpicking over which day we want it to come in ends up being intervention rather than value added.' In short, interveners serve to slow the work process by adding loops in the decision-making chain or hurdles to cross. The rationale for interveners is that they improve results. Some do. But the growing conviction is that most of them add costs without adding clear perceived value.

'Value-added analysis' is now used in many companies to determine if each step in a work process or decision sequence augments the preceding steps. If it does not, perhaps it should be eliminated. It is this kind of reasoning that cuts out middle-management positions of the traditional kind. If we look at the traditional managerial responsibility, it is clear why the position cannot always withstand this kind of scrutiny. The traditional manager was a link in a reporting chain – a gatekeeper to ensure that things stayed within bounds, an interpreter to the troops below of the sentiments of those above, and a message-carrier to high levels. Did middle managers add value? In too many cases, as administrators they subtracted value rather than adding it, by taking extra time, by telling eager subordinates that the upper echelons would never approve their proposals, by dampening enthusiasm and preventing direct access.

There are delicious ironies in the term 'overhead' for administration and other corporate services. The original meaning of the word clearly involved the physical surroundings in which work took place – the roof over workers' heads. As corporations grew fat and complex, however, 'overhead' began to signify something else to employees: 'the people who can go over my head to second-guess my decisions'. And looming first and foremost among those second-guessers, 'I'm from corporate and I'm here to help you' is considered as fraudulent a statement as 'I'm from the IRS and I'm here to help you'. In both cases, they feel they'll be taxed.

In fact, in many companies I deal with, those running business units wonder whether they would do better if they were independent – and in some cases, the evidence supports them (for example, leveraged buyouts by managers of their own units that produce dramatic increases in performance). In the traditional corporation, a business unit would often have to justify itself to the parent corporation, to explain why the corporation would want to keep owning it. Now, in an interesting reversal, the onus is often on the corporate entity itself – the entity that exists above and beyond the business unit – to, in effect, justify itself to the business unit, to explain why the business should bother to belong to it.

In theory, there should be benefits to business units from their corporate affiliation; post-entrepreneurial corporations can find the following sources of added 'corporate' value:

- scale economies from sharing certain functions or facilities;
- management competence, including a larger talent pool for business units to draw on and sources of expertise to help the unit make better decisions;
- broader career opportunities, to help attract and retain the best people;
- staff services dedicated to the specific needs of the corporation's business units;
- information exchange about technology or markets, broadening the intelligence base available to each business;
- the capacity to look ahead and consider the future across an array of businesses, while business units are immersed in daily operating pressures;
- common values and standards that raise performance.

Johnson & Johnson, for example, is widely praised for its form of corporate organization. Well over one hundred decentralized companies pursue specific product-market charters as part of the corporate family; new companies are spun off from old ones when separable products reach critical mass; and each has an internal board of directors. Value-added by the corporate level comes not only from the cultivation of a managerial talent pool and career opportunities across companies but also from the J & J credo, a statement of values that builds a common cultural focus on serving customers.

While post-entrepreneurial corporations seek ways to add value to their business units, many traditional corpocracies wind up taking more from the business units than they give to them. If they are to compete in the global Olympics, companies can no longer afford to support anything that does not add value to their central business focus. Corporate services must be either restructured to add value or eliminated. Companies have a choice of methods.

Decentralizing and redeploying

Putting more responsibility in the hands of business unit managers and reducing the need for approvals or checkpoints make it possible to operate without so many layers of hierarchy and, by extension, with fewer people. Andrew Grove of Intel, for example, wants his company to be an 'agile giant' – big enough to win global wars of products, technology and trade while moving like a small company. To achieve this, he has decentralized approval and eliminated middle-management layers. Other companies have cut the number of corporate service personnel while increasing the effectiveness of their activities by breaking up large central departments, relying instead on business unit staffs to do the work. This eliminates redundancies and tends to replace a watchdog orientation with a service orientation; instead of 'controlling' from the top, these staffs are now linked closely to the needs of particular businesses. What remains at the corporate level are minimal staffs carrying out future-oriented tasks such as environmental scanning, professional development, and facilitation of cross-business-unit information exchange.

An alternative to cutting staff, then, is to redeploy them. Offering new jobs in a more vital sector (along with attractive early retirement options) can, of course, encourage people to leave voluntarily to ply their trades elsewhere. But it also puts those who remain to better use, making them a source of added value. IBM, for example, embarked on an enormous retraining effort after a 1985 business downturn, enabling a whopping twenty thousand or so employees to change jobs – engineers moving into sales, plant workers into systems engineering and, as in other companies rethinking staff, corporate services providers into the field.[1]

Contracting out

Of course, companies can decide not to manage certain activities themselves at all, and many are doing so in the name of 'focus'. For a widget company to be running a cafeteria and a print shop and a law firm, the reasoning goes, is not the best use of widget managers' time. It increases staff, which adds complexity and hierarchy, and anyway there are specialist firms out there concentrating on running superior cafeterias and print shops and law firms. The company should use their services and concentrate on widgets. The strategy here is to divest all but the solid core. Cut staff to the bone, do without some amenities altogether (who needs to manage a fleet of jet planes?) and contract out for everything else.

The extreme of the contracting-out strategy is represented by companies that are essentially marketing and financial shells working through vast networks of suppliers and dealers. Examples are found in publishing, apparel and other fashion businesses that have long needed the flexibility to make changes quickly, effected by lean core organizations using external specialist organizations for particular tasks. For example, Benetton, an Italian apparel producer, owns outright very few of the assets involved in bringing Benetton clothes to consumers; manufacturing is contracted out to numerous small factories, and retail outlets are licensees. Indeed, Benetton is part of a surge of entrepreneurship in Northern Italy based on networks of small firms allying with one another. In 1982 Benetton contracted out work to 220 production units, which employed ten thousand people; many were partially owned by Benetton managers as individuals, but Benetton itself owned only nine facilities as a company.[2] In another sector, Lews Galoob Toys, maker of 'micromachines', board games and Star Trek toys, contracts out almost everything, including accounts receivable, running a thirty-one-year-old company with almost $70 million in sales with only about one hundred employees.

Berkeley Business School Dean Raymond Miles calls this managerial style the 'corporation as switchboard', the company acting as central information centre and command point for a network of other organizations.[3] This is clearly one strategy small companies can use to grow 'big' in market scope and power very quickly. But it is also on the increase for much larger companies, as post-entrepreneurial strategies take hold. It is not a long leap for companies that consider their manufacturing and sales functions to be 'staffs' for business units that are essentially marketing arms to begin to think about whether they should continue to own so many plants and employ so many salespeople when working through contractors would give them more flexibility.

To put it another way, the *corporation-as-department-store*, a gigantic entity with every conceivable aspect of the production chain and every service it uses under its own roof, is being replaced by the *corporation-as-boutique*. *Focus* is the key word.

Turning services into businesses

In some cases, rather than divesting themselves of staff services, companies are converting them into profit centres, which sell their services on the outside as well as the inside. This is the ultimate post-entrepreneurial, market-oriented response. Let those staff bureaucrats be entrepreneurs and let the market decide if they add value or not. Among the companies thus deriving revenues from their own corporate services are Control Data, selling personnel services; Xerox, logistics and distribution services to customers; General Motors, employee-training programmes; and Security Pacific Bank, data-processing and information systems.

Even when corporate staffs are not set loose in the outside market, companies are still starting to treat them as internal vendors who must compete with outside vendors to get their services purchased. General Foods recently put on a pay-as-you-use basis the 'overhead' charges for corporate staff services, which were formerly assigned uniformly to users and non-users. Of course, under the old system use was mandatory; for example, product managers in the past had to go through up to eight layers of management, including corporate staff, to get business plans approved.[4] But now, those same staffs must prove to their internal customer's satisfaction that they add value. There are sometimes thorny questions of managing internal transfer payments and whether to set rates at market levels, but the principle is clear: Staffs are no longer considered 'overhead' but potential sources of value; they are not watchdogs and interveners but suppliers serving customers.

In short, to use the language of prominent economist Oliver Williamson,[5] companies are dismantling the very management layers and service staffs that helped create the corporate hierarchy in the first place and gradually replacing some of them with marketlike relationships. Many employees are either being replaced with 'outside' contractors or becoming contractors themselves.

THOUGHTFUL RESTRUCTURING VERSUS MINDLESS DOWNSIZING

There are two principal mistakes some companies make in staff restructuring.

First, they exhibit strategic blindness, turning the quest to ensure value added into mindless downsizing and delayering, on the assumption that leanness automatically equals effectiveness. They focus only on the 'less' of the 'doing more with less' imperative, as if the only good staff were a small staff. They fail to differentiate departments and business units in terms of their future contributions and resource needs; while some can be reduced or stabilized, others might profitably grow. Or their goals are cost-driven instead of effectiveness-driven – get the expenses down instead of the performance up. Or they view employees primarily as costs rather than valuing them as assets and they fail to see the value (in skills or experience) that walks out the door with terminated staff. At a machine tool company that has become the subject of a popular Harvard Business School case, a new president from outside was so incensed by high wages in Cleveland that he downsized there and moved the bulk of production to a new plant in the South, only to find productivity lowered because of inexperienced employees. Manufacturing costs were ultimately higher in the South than in the 'high-wage plant' where employee experience raised productivity.[6]

Second, some companies assume that if a little cutting is a good thing, a lot must be even better. They starve themselves into a state of organizational anorexia, the disease that occurs when companies actually increase some costs, such as the hidden costs of overload – tasks haven't disappeared, just the people to do them. It would have been better to review the tasks to see what unnecessary or outmoded work could be eliminated – as Exxon USA did when it conducted its 'hog law' review (a Texas expression for rules and procedures) to see what red tape could be cut forever.

Furthermore, an organization that is too thin risks numerous implementation failures and dropped balls because of lack of follow-up and follow-through – from the inability to return phone calls to customers to making plans without communicating them to all the departments that will have to change something as a result. In general, when anorexic companies starve themselves, they also starve innovation. The pressure of activities the company is already committed to drives out the ability to think about preparing for the future; there is insufficient preparation for tomorrow. If an organization gets too thin, it tends to lack depth in people for backup if a crisis hits, or for development and succession. One company boasted of the money saved by eliminating all but the most experienced middle managers; seasoned people, they reasoned, would save training costs and be able to manage larger groups. But then some of the experienced managers left for better opportunities (after all, they were the most marketable) and the company found itself with no internal successors. Recruitment and training costs shot up. The 'leanness' strategy backfired.

Finally, companies that are lean because they substitute outside contracting for internal employment find themselves engaged in another set of difficult management tasks: they must work with other organizations to make sure the work is done to their specifications on their schedule, and they are vulnerable to the whims of other companies on which they rely.

Even managers who push downsizing and delayering as the best assurance of value added are aware that they are walking a tightrope. In a publishing company that had, in an executive's view, 'built up fat during the good years', over a thousand people who 'added no discernible value' were cut during a time of profit pressures. Now, he said:

There is no money for good people who are being asked to do more with less. We need to keep this core. After two years of cutting, we could either boom or fall flat. A move of our headquarters will be the last straw. We are running the risk of hitting the bone. First one layoff, then another, then shrinkage, then relocations. All of this equals risk to the division.

To counter the risk, he must increase the effort to create teamwork among the remaining staff – teamwork that will help each contribute to the work of the others.

The challenge, then, is not simply to get lean for the sake of doing so, but to build the kind of co-operation that helps the more-focused corporation get maximum value from all of its remaining resources.

VALUE MULTIPLIED: THE PAYOFF FROM SYNERGIES

The structure that is 'right' in theory, the 'right' combination of parts, is still not enough to produce synergy. A business mix that is good from a strategic analysis standpoint brings benefits in practice only if the relationships and processes are established to ensure co-operation and communication – with managers of every area committed to contributing value to one another.

The only real justification for a multibusiness corporation, in my view, is the achievement of synergy – that magical mix of business activities that are stronger and more profitable together than they would be separately. The 'portfolio' or 'holding company' approach – in which each part stands alone and needs to be different in order to compensate for the weakness of other parts – has been increasingly discredited. For example, strategy expert Michael Porter's longitudinal data on a set of Fortune 500 companies showed that most could not digest acquisitions unrelated to their core business; over 70 per cent of the firms divested such unrelated units after about five years.[7]

Sometimes companies have moved away from a portfolio strategy for defensive reasons: the costs of administering diversity or the vulnerability to takeovers engendered by the ease with which the pieces could be unbundled and sold at a premium. But more often, the quest for value multipliers comes from growth goals. There is a growing conviction that doing-more-with-less is possible when the right combination of parts, working together in the right way, can actively contribute to one another's success.

Nowhere do synergies seem more important than in global technology companies, which face brutal, fast-paced competition. PPG Industries, for example, knew this when it launched a Biomedical Products Division out of diverse world-wide acquisitions. Edward Voboril, the group executive, put 'teamwork' number one on his priority list, and he convened the first management conference of the group to build the foundation for it.

From the noncommittal expressions on the faces of the audience as he opened the conference, I could see that he had a hard sell ahead of him. On paper, the fit between the parts was excellent. But he had to cajole suspicious managers from different nations and different businesses out of their territoriality. 'The eggs have gotten scrambled, and we can't unscramble them,' he said, to remind listeners that they had better accept the situation. 'But now we've got the raw materials to succeed on a bigger scale than any of us have seen,' he continued, to appeal to their ambition. And then the real pitch: 'We must turn our attention to the goals we have in common. We can pool our strengths instead of dissipating them.' He had a few carrots to offer them: higher R&D funding than any of the businesses separately had ever known, a world-wide marketing and sales organization to expand the sales of what had been geographically localized products. But still, the formal programmes and structures would not be enough unless heads of different business units from different parts of the world agreed to co-operate.

In the global Olympics, this is indeed what differentiates winners from losers. As international management researchers Christopher Bartlett and Sumantra Ghoshal show, the best competitors in the world markets know how to build co-operation at the business unit level.[8] Instead of either dictating everything from headquarters (the 'centralized' strategy) or allowing every country and every business to go its own way (the ultimate 'decentralized' strategy), multiproduct transnational companies like Proctor and Gamble, Philips, NEC and, increasingly, Colgate have created a balanced organizational strategy. Such a balanced approach helps the separate parts see shared goals, develop common values and standards, communicate among themselves (Colgate uses, among other things, a creative video magazine), pool resources for some activities, create joint ventures and projects, build career paths flowing across their borders, and divide responsibility for innovation.

PPG Biomedical Division's goal was to be among those world-class companies. For the next three days, the assembled managers talked about their businesses, identified areas of overlap with potential for co-operation, found solutions in another corner of the world to the problems plaguing them at home, and built the foundation for continuing communication. By the end of the conference, some teams had formed to explore matters of mutual interest, and there was an agreement to divide the innovation labours – for example, one country taking the lead in development technology that many countries and many divisions could use. 'The work has just begun,' Voboril commented afterward. 'My job will be to keep pushing those synergies, to help each division take advantage of the knowledge and the marketing inroads that their peers develop. We'll keep sliding back, and I'll keep pushing.'

Cross-selling, product links, combining expertise, improved market intelligence, and leaps in efficiency are some of the outcomes of synergy. For example:

- *Cross-selling*. By 1986 Prudential expected over $30 million in commissions from sales shared by stockbrokers and insurance agents, up from $4 million two years earlier.[9]
- *Product links*. General Foods, after restructuring to decentralize, wanted to keep the benefits of a whole company identity. Chairman Philip Smith set up a task force of marketing executives to work on integrative programmes aimed at retailers that would get more shelf space for all products. This led to a programme, Team Up for Kids, tying in a number of products.[10]
- *Combining expertise*. Pillsbury applied the expertise of its packaged food researchers to help revitalize its Godfather's Pizza chain, developing new food products for sale in the restaurants. (Individually

packaged slices of pizza was the first such product.) Similarly, Pillsbury used the expertise and resources of the restaurant group in
finding sources of, storing, and distributing fresh vegetables to open
the possibility of a Green Giant line of branded fresh vegetables for
supermarket sales. Similarly, co-ordinating research and development
on a world-wide basis allowed Procter & Gamble to take advantage of
the varieties of expertise found in different countries to speed new
product development.

- *Market intelligence.* A technology company got its multinational product divisions to alert one another to market signals, a practice that
helped make product launchings in new countries more effective than
ever in the company's history. Each product division served a different
array of countries. Combining experience and data through communication across divisions, the company saw immediate payoffs in
world market share growth.

- *Leaps in efficiency.* Combining operations of several divisions allowed
Shenandoah Life Insurance to increase productivity and quality dramatically. Before: one form was routed to 32 people, across nine sec-
tions and three departments, taking 27 days. After: the job was done
by one self-managing clerical team of six people handling 13 per cent
more work faster, with fewer errors and 80 per cent less supervision.[11]

Such benefits have led companies with a cowboylike tradition to
develop new structures aimed at achieving synergies. For example,
Procter & Gamble's traditional emphasis on internal competition grew
out of a respected organizational innovation by Neil McElroy, later
chairman, over 50 years ago: the assignment of a single marketing
manager, a 'brand manager', to each product. The rationale back then
was that each product should receive distinctive treatment, treatment
more likely to produce creative ideas, and that the company would grow
faster by competing intensely against itself. In the early 1980s, in light of
a changing market-place and a proliferation of categories and brands,
Procter & Gamble moved away from this cowboylike stance to a greater
reliance on business teams. Now, as an observer put it, Procter &
Gamble's brand managers 'no longer operate like mini-czars but are
assigned to teams with manufacturing, sales and research managers,
people they once outranked'. CEO John Smale explained the business
team to the *Harvard Business Review* as a concept that says, 'When
you're going to address a problem, get the people who have something
to contribute in the way of creativity if not direct responsibility. Get
them together.' Teams are credited with turning around the sales of a
losing product (Pringles potato chips), with packaging inventions, and
with speeding the process of getting a new product to market.[12] A

network of 'organizational effectiveness consultants' trained in skills for facilitating team formation supports the search for synergies.

One especially comprehensive and successful case of a concerted effort to build value multipliers is American Express. In 1986, roughly 10 per cent of American Express's net income came from cross-selling and other synergies. The one big success was selling life insurance, but there were also many 'singles and doubles instead of home runs', as CEO James Robinson put it. Robinson made achieving synergies a priority in 1982, emphasizing that American Express was 'one enterprise' united by common overall goals and asking senior executives to identify two or three promising 'One Enterprise' synergy products in their annual plans. A manager of corporate strategy watched over this, issuing a One Enterprise report among 100 top executives, giving visibility to those engaged in collaboration. Evaluations and incentives were tied to this programme: the Chairman of American Express Bank received one of two 1985 bonuses for efforts such as selling traveller's cheques for the card division and introducing brokerage services to its overseas clients. And by 1987 the company had sifted through about 260 ideas for collaboration between businesses, about 70 per cent of which have worked. Among these ideas were sharing of office space, data processing capabilities, and marketing expertise among departments and also cross-marketing of products.[13]

American Express's search for synergies rests on an entrepreneurial foundation – a set of rather autonomous and focused business units concentrating on their own businesses, with a corporate staff of about 800 auditors, lawyers, and public relations experts. The One Enterprise programme is an attempt to convey that American Express is 'one big family' of entrepreneurial companies. Each unit or division is trying to maximize its profit and if its leaders see that help from someone else in another unit is going to aid them, they will seek it out and try to convince the others that it is in their best interest also. This approach is based on decentralization with voluntary co-operation, not centralization with top-down commands. The synergies the company finds tend to be ways of augmenting what one unit wants to do rather than forcing all units to rely on a single method or a single corporate function. American Express never thought that one sales force could cross-sell life insurance, annuities, stocks and bonds, and credit cards, but the One Enterprise approach means that each company can find occasional marketing leads for the others.

There are nice cash bonuses and recognition for the people who work on One Enterprise projects – something they often have to do after hours and in their spare time. These were among the winning One Enterprise projects for 1987:

- A ten-person team representing all four major business units (Travel Related Services, IDS, Shearson Lehman Hutton, the American Express Bank) and a data processing unit (First Data Resources) negotiated a deal with AT&T for major price reductions. The team discussed the telecommunication needs of their respective companies, pulled the information into a coherent plan, and then worked at AT&T, saving tens of millions of dollars.
- Jim and Malcolm of TRS expanded business opportunities for the whole company by introducing other units to key TRS contacts – for example, a large airline that might be able to use SLH financing for the purchase of new planes.
- Katie, Pete, and Julie of IDS developed a new investment service for Trade Development Bank customers in Luxembourg.
- Gustavo of TRS supported SLH in developing a Financial Management Account product for Latin America, after SLH requested the help of TRS people who were familiar with the cultural differences and business expectations of the area.
- Craig and Ramesh of TRS and Jack of IDS assisted in the development of an Investment Management Account for American Express credit card holders, using IDS expertise to find ways to sell mutual funds to TRS customers.

Two forms of synergy seem most common at American Express, one externally oriented (marketing leads) and one internally oriented (efficiencies from using another company's 'back-office' information-processing capacity). For example, the TRS marketing organization that places traveller's cheques with banks and other institutions to sell them helps IDS market financial planning on a mass basis through those banks. Similarly, TRS or Shearson professionals who have relationships with the chief financial officer or controller of companies planning large restructurings can pave the way for IDS to offer financial counselling to employees deciding whether to take early-retirement options. 'When they help IDS, they sort of expect that the favour will be returned,' Harry Freeman, executive vice president, observed. 'This starts a cycle of internal synergies that build on each other and create a companywide spirit of co-operation.'

Back-office collaborations might take the following form: IDS may want to create a new mutual fund which will require an information processing capacity; by going to Shearson to see about using its Boston Safe subsidiary, a very efficient back office for mutual funds, IDS can save a substantial amount in setup expenses while compensating Shearson for use of the system; Shearson gets a source of additional return on its investment.

But even when synergy is a stated goal, there are many roadblocks. In other financial services companies, for example, synergies such as cross-marketing and the development of financial supermarkets seem limited by territoriality – the unwillingness of salesmen representing different products to work together. When Prudential first experimented with joint sales programmes involving insurance agents and stockbrokers, the efforts were 'crashing failures', according to George Ball, head of the brokerage unit. Or the attempt to achieve synergy is hurt by the unwillingness of executives to share customer lists, as with American Express's charge card people's initial reluctance to share their lists with the brokerage. Or internal co-operation and cross-marketing can threaten external relationships. Sears wondered whether to give its merchandise group access to the Discover credit card customer list because other merchants who have accepted the card could be upset.[14] All of these roadblocks were internal, having nothing to do with any unwillingness of customers to change their habits.

Similar problems are by-products of the very decentralization that also gives some companies their entrepreneurial strength. But without the ability to co-operate across areas, the units might as well be split up into independent businesses. This was the dilemma faced by the $200 million technology development company I will call 'Firestar'. In 1986, a new president put the issue of internal competition high on his list of things to change:

There are natural competitive forces in a technology business. With the breadth of technology we have, it is easy to look at one area, e.g. electronics, and say that that group might do work in electronic materials, while the materials group might feel like that business is part of its scope and mission in life. Another example is the Computer Integrated Manufacturing Systems (CIMS) market. Our manufacturing technology and information systems groups have the technical knowledge to compete against each other for business in that market – or they could work jointly.

In his view, each of the six sectors of Firestar saw itself in competition with the others. Compensation to senior managers had been based on the performance of their sectors *vis-à-vis* the others. There was no incentive to co-operate internally and as a result, the business sectors didn't 'see the whole company' when making decisions. The groups acted independently rather than with a shared interest in the division. The president remarked that 'I didn't see everyone's oar in the water at the same time.' Some co-operation did exist from time to time, but it was not encouraged enough; if it happened, it happened by chance more than by design. 'We don't have a bunch of Machiavellian types running around screwing their buddies,' he said, 'but we also are not getting enough synergies.'

'Turf battles' had clearly arisen between business sectors in this company. For example, two groups separately approached the same customer, without a co-ordinated effort – 'the left hand didn't know what the right was doing.' As the president put it:

Group A had studied the problem, decided it wasn't a good opportunity for us and did not bid on the contract. Group A was the main line technology group for the type of problem involved here, the next best suited to evaluate the project. Unbeknownst to Group A, though, Group B looked at the same project and made a bid. The bid is still pending, but it probably won't be accepted. When Group A found out what Group B had done, they were livid, outraged. You may ask, 'How could a group feel a charter to make a bid like that?' Well, Group B could see it as part of its mission.

Another example was even more vivid:

Last year we established a new Aerospace office to be closer to an air force base, one of our biggest customers. This new office appeared to me to be in direct competition with several business sectors here at headquarters. In fact, they could have been in competition with all of the other divisions, that is how broad their mission statement was. This has set up a 'we/they' mentality. As it was, we had three other groups in competition for aerospace business: the materials and electronics groups and the business development staff. This had to be changed. The new office staff are supposed to be our point people on the scene, not to compete with us but rather to use all the company resources to solve the customers' problems.

Then there were the minor instances of rivalry – minor, but no less irritating and costly, such as two different groups investing in the same piece of equipment, each purchasing one when instead they could have shared one.

Seeing these barriers to synergy, the president made the search for value multipliers in Firestar his major priority, shaping his approach to every aspect of the business, from strategic planning to compensation.

Successful efforts to increase synergy generally have three components: a focus from the top and the development of methods and managers to find value multipliers; shifts in incentives and rewards and a culture of communication and co-operation resting on a foundation of personal relationships.

Providing leadership and vehicles to identify opportunities

The first ingredient in the search for synergies is a familiar one: leadership from the top. American Express's Jim Robinson made identification of synergies a priority in 1982, when he asked senior executives to define two or three One Enterprise projects in their annual plans. Executives are quick to point out that One Enterprise is not *forced* on anyone; projects must be in the best interests of the business unit. But Robinson's leadership is also clear. Consider Harry Freeman's view:

Over the years we have managed to achieve a lot of useful synergies. Useful synergy does not come from directives from the top. It really comes when somebody in one of the business units thinks he can do a hell of a lot better, or make more money, or introduce a much better product and really needs somebody or sees that some unit in another business unit can be really helpful. He then tries to convince the other guy that it is in his or her interest. What you try to do is create an environment of entrepreneurship about the whole place. One Enterprise was never meant to be the total programme. The main driver of synergy does not come from directives. It comes from shared self-interest.

Jim Robinson is a great One Enterprise guy. If you go outside the company and were using someone else's system, you'd better have a very good answer ready for him. Now if your answer is good, he'll say, 'Terrific,' or he may call up those other guys and say, 'Hey, why don't you get more reasonable?' There is a certain amount of executive pressure to co-operate. But if you do go outside and find it cheaper for the same quality, Jim Robinson is going to say, 'Go outside. We are in business for the profit of the shareholders.'

Once top management identifies synergy goals, a 'synergy czar' may then swing into action, serving as chief cheerleader and recorder of the efforts to find value multipliers. Sometimes the corporate strategy office plays this role, nudging cross-area projects into strategic plans, suggesting areas of overlap offering joint possibilities, convening task forces and councils to hammer out ways to maximize the payoffs from joint resource use and encouraging collaborative efforts. This alone represents a striking shift of mind-set for many strategic planners, who are more accustomed to identifying the value of assets before an acquisition or diversiture than to finding ways to gain the benefit of internal collaboration.

At Pillsbury, the appointment of a synergy czar was a valiant attempt to shore up some ailing businesses by bringing the resources of various units together to create value multiplier effects. Then-CEO John Stafford realized that segmentation of the food industry required giving each division great autonomy; at the same time, someone was needed at the top to pull things together in order to capitalize on new opportunities that might cut across division lines. In March 1986, Stafford assigned James Behnke to the new position of senior vice-president for Growth and Technology – or, as Behnke put it on business cards he had printed, 'Senior Vice-President, Blurring'.

Behnke's business development group worked with the divisions to marshal all of Pillsbury's resources, which in practice meant getting restaurant divisions to help food divisions and vice versa. As a result of Behnke's efforts, new business opportunities opened up. For example, when Green Giant (specialists in canned vegetables) decided to develop branded fresh vegetables, they lacked three critical resources, which Burger King helped provide: year-round supply, a distribution system and food service customers. Behnke extracted three lessons from Pillsbury's experience:

First, it must be a win/win situation. If company A wins 10 points, and company B loses 5 points, Pillsbury gains 5 points, but it will never work. Both companies A and B must gain points, even if it is only 2.5 points each.

Second, if you go too low down an organization, then it gets tougher and tougher to cross disciplines. At the lower levels, people are more provincial, more guarded, more defensive. If the effort is important enough – you should tackle only the big projects – then the negotiations need to go on between the top levels of the organization. More senior people must be involved.

What makes it work is the chemistry of the people. There can be no systems, no rules, no manuals – people hate that stuff. There can be no pressure, only suction.

Unfortunately for Pillsbury and Stafford, the search for multipliers came too late to dilute the effects of other business problems. Mounting losses led to the return of the former chairman, Stafford's resignation in 1988 and frequent mention of Pillsbury as a takeover target. The search for value multipliers is a long process that cannot guarantee the quick rescue of failing businesses.

Realizing the importance of a concerted long-term effort to build synergy, the president of Firestar, the technology development company, built a number of strategic planning exercise from a near-term outlook (which leads to pressures to 'beat your buddy in competition') to more long-term goals. They reviewed the standard business plan questions – Where are you now? Where do you want to be? How are you going to get there? But they added a twist of their own, approaching planning on two levels. Each sector came up with its own business plan; then, working together, the groups wrote strategic plans for different market areas, such as the industrial market and the defence business.

The president also created an investment council, comprising Firestar's senior business sector leaders and the business development staff. The council was guided by the strategic direction of each sector and of Firestar as a whole. It evaluated investment in R&D, capital equipment and human resources (hiring needs). The goal was to change the past practice of tactical investing to a more strategic, holistic approach; for example, instead of having the manufacturing sector tactically purchase a piece of equipment, that purchase would now be considered a more general investment, an item with potential utility for other sectors as well.

Both components of the strategic planning were part of an effort to struggle against the forces that make a diverse technological company's sectors compete single technology with single technology. Instead, Firestar wanted to become a more fully integrated company, gaining power from a multidisciplinary approach. The company's strength was always its broad technological offerings; to capitalize on this required cross-business-unit co-operation. As the president put it, 'A good materials company is limited to only materials. We can do materials, but also do process design, environmental impact – we can provide our customers with many ancillary support services. We take a systems approach to the problem.' His goal was to 'foster a culture in which everyone gravitates toward working together to create synergy'.

Incentives and rewards

The approaches necessary to build synergy could not be more different from the shootouts of cowboy management. Destructive competition is set up so that the losers lose as much as the winners gain. There's a single prize, which the winner takes; but in addition to missing the prize, the losers also incur costs. What drives the competition in a negative direction, then, is largely fear of losing. The destructive side of the battle stems as much from avoiding punishment as from seeking rewards. Co-operation is likely, however, when there are incentives for performing well, regardless of who comes in first. If one of the goals of competition is to develop options, then it is important to reward the generating of alternatives, not just getting the right answer. Some rewards come from playing the game well, even if the ultimate prize goes to someone else. Joint incentives, which give everyone something if anyone reaches high levels of performance, make co-operation even more likely.

The creation of an inter-business-sector development fund was one of Firestar's new president's first moves. He held a reserve of funds for use in projects that spanned the boundaries of two or more sectors. Previously, if a sector was going to work with another sector, it had to invest by itself – only one sector put up the money, though the other would also get some benefits. This situation did not encourage co-operation; why help support a competitor? The president found these new funds to be an immediate incentive for joint projects. The atmosphere at the company soon began to reflect this emphasis. As he said:

In an environment where team play gets rewarded, we now openly discuss the pros and cons of major bidding decisions. The decision making is more holistic. If two separate groups think they should both bid on a contract, they'll put together a joint proposal. The problems in the past have arisen when one group thinks bidding is a good idea and another does not. Then I bring the two groups together for a meeting to discuss both sides of the decision. When sectors can't agree, I help them resolve the problems by making the ultimate decision.

Although some of this crossing of lines did happen before, there was no necessity or drive to do so. Now there was *incentive*, as opposed to just a hope that co-operation would happen.

A second approach is to add team incentives to senior managers' evaluation and compensation. American Express has a variety of ways to reward achievement of synergy goals, starting with special awards, bonuses, and publicity for specific One Enterprise projects, available to contributors at any organizational level. Synergy goals are also built into top management incentives. Incentive compensation awards (called portfolio awards) for senior managers in one of the businesses are determined primarily by the performance of their business unit, but a significant chunk of each award is determined by the performance of all the business units. For senior corporate managers, the portfolio award is divided into quarters, and 25 per cent is determined by the performance of each of the major business units. Furthermore, a large number of employees own shares in the company and a large number of officers have stock options. This package of incentives and rewards directs people's attention to the performance of the whole company, not just the performance of their own business.

Firestar's new president had to revise both incentive and evaluation systems. He began to ask the question, 'How much business did you develop for the rest of the company, not just for yourself?' Sector leaders were asked to develop inter-sector markets and programmes. In the past, managers hadn't been evaluated on the combined results of two or three sectors together. Now that was part of the evaluation. This provided an incentive for sector leaders to work together and avoid one-to-one competition; they could be rewarded for working together and across sectors. Managers were now encouraged to bring back leads for others, to market for the entire division. 'Instead of dangling the carrot in front of each sector manager, I've put the carrot between the organizations,' the president said.

Similarly, at Bankers Trust, the heads of corporate banking and corporate finance review the proposed bonuses for each other's officers and can influence the amount if an officer has been uncooperative. If trends toward synergy incentives and rewards continue, there is also a need for new measurement systems that can permit attribution of the benefits from collaboration.[15]

Communication, relationships, and the foundation for co-operation

Communications is the third key to achieving synergies. Many opportunities for synergy come in the form of information sharing; thus, the channels need to be established to enable managers and professionals from different business units and different parts of the world to communicate. Post-entrepreneurial companies tend to be characterized by more frequent events that draw people together across areas – executive conferences, meetings of professionals assigned to different businesses, boards and councils that oversee efforts in diverse places and transmit learning from them. Training centres and educational events are a potent means for increasing communication. General Electric's facility in Crotonville, New York, is much more than a corporate college; it is in effect a synergy centre that helps people identify shared interests across businesses and tackle common problems together.

Computer networks and other information systems can enhance the communication that knits a company together in pursuit of synergies. But systems – no matter how easy to use – do not necessarily guarantee co-operative communication without the knowledge of one another that people develop through face-to-face relationships. For this reason, Digital Equipment Corporation runs a helicopter service to and from major New England facilities to permit people to get together to transmit information and pursue joint projects. People develop relationships with one another this way faster than they do through electronic mail, as important as systems like that are for making communication easy and instantaneous; and those relationships make co-operation possible.

It is harder to get the benefits of co-operation and easier for rivalry to get out of hand when there is no history of past relationships to draw on to give the rivals understanding of one another, when there are no shared experiences to prevent mistrust and hostility – or worse, when past experiences have been negative. Co-operation flourishes on a foundation of shared experience. Even in encounters involving strangers, relationships make a difference. For example, players in laboratory games like 'prisoners' dilemma' do better when given the chance to talk with one another beforehand.[16] Friendships help. After first encountering resistance to joint sales programmes involving stockbrokers and insurance agents, Prudential made the programmes work by encouraging joint efforts where there seemed to be natural affinities on the basis of friendship.[17]

Synergy is also difficult to achieve when there is a clear and apparently unbridgeable structural separation between areas. Their activities are not intertwined, they seem to need nothing from one another, and their apparent independence is reinforced by separate career paths or communication patterns or reporting relationships. Co-operation, in contrast, is engendered by structural links that make the parties inter-dependent. Awareness of mutual needs reduces rivalries to a friendlier level. So do integration mechanisms that remind the parties of joint interests – for example, liaisons between groups or people with a foot in each camp.

Expectations also help. The anticipation of a shared future dampens the killer instinct. Even in competition, there will be more co-operative relationships among rivals when the competition is viewed as tempor-ary, when the composition of the opposing team is known to change regularly, when today's losers can join winners in another effort toward another goal. Robert Axelrod's computer simulations of prisoners' dilemma games found the most successful strategy to be TIT for TAT, a strategy that began by co-operating and then simply reciprocated the opponent's last move. He argued that co-operating was most likely when people or groups knew they would have to deal with one another again in the future.[18]

In short, co-operation is encouraged when people perceive a shared fate. They see that they and other rivals have a joint stake in a larger outcome – advancing their joint enterprise as a whole. This idea was behind James Robinson's One Enterprise programme at American Express. Another CEO stressed 'dual citizenship' to all his managers, making them members, simultaneously, of both their business unit and a corporate project team, with 'citizenship responsibilities, rights and rewards' stemming from each.

We have come full circle in the search for synergies. To get value multiplied requires removing the sources of value subtracted. Tilting the balance toward co-operation offers the possibility of tackling new business opportunities as well as eliminating the costs of in-fighting. Encouraging co-operation even among nominal rivals helps organiza-tions gain the synergies that come with the transfer of good ideas from one unit to another. It makes it easier to focus on standards for quality performance and to concentrate organizational energy where it should be concentrated, on achieving the goal, not on eliminating rivals. And it offers flexibility; today's friends can more easily be tomorrow's collaborators.

There is so much competition already inherent in most organizations – from the 'pyramid squeeze' that means that not all of the talented people can rise to top positions, to the natural pride that one department takes in doing better than another – that the task of managers is often not to fuel the fires but to dampen them.

The real danger of performance shootouts is that someone you need may die of the wounds.

THE CORPORATION'S NEW SHAPE

Striving for synergies is essential to managing the do-more-with-less imperative of the corporate Olympics. Fewer resources, intelligently combined, can work together to bring greater payoffs and to pursue new opportunities with greater speed. A stress on synergies can help companies save on fixed costs and tackle new opportunities at the same time.

Getting there, however, requires the corporation to take on a new shape. The company that achieves synergies looks and operates very differently from the swollen, lethargic 'corpocracy' that many large American businesses allowed themselves to become. No longer does the typical corporate organization chart resemble the Eiffel Tower – a broad pyramid of productive activities on the bottom and a tall, narrow hierarchy of many levels of managers piled upon managers, stretching all the way to the top. The model for the post-entrepreneurial corporation is a leaner organization, one that has fewer 'extraneous' staff and is thus more focused on doing only those things in which it has competence. In the post-entrepreneurial company, there are fewer and fewer people or departments that are purely 'corporate' in nature; more responsibilities are delegated to the business units, and more services are provided by outside suppliers. And fewer layers of management mean that the hierarchy itself is flatter. Thus, the 'vertical' dimension of the corporation is much less important. At the same time, the 'horizontal' dimension – the process by which all the divisions and departments and business units communicate and co-operate – is the key to getting the benefits of collaboration.

The post-entrepreneurial corporation represents a triumph of process over structure. That is, relationships and communication and the flexibility to temporarily combine resources are more important than the 'formal' channels and reporting relationships represented on an organizational chart. *In Olympic contests requiring speed and dexterity, what is important is not how responsibilities are divided but how people can pull together to pursue new opportunities.*

Management sage Peter Drucker recently used the image of a symphony orchestra to describe the new model of the leaner, flatter corporation.[19] In the orchestra, performers with different skills concentrate on perfecting their professional competence, while a single conductor co-ordinates the overall performance; performers with similar specialties form self-managed work teams, operating without a bureaucratic hierarchy above them. The image is useful and evocative as far as it goes. But for corporate players to make beautiful music together they must achieve a balance between concentrating on their own areas of skill and responsibility and working together with others. They need to do their own jobs well while keeping one eye on what might be useful for someone else. They need to understand enough about the company's other areas to identify possibilities for joint action and mutual enhancement. They need to simultaneously focus and collaborate. They must function in many roles: as soloist, ensemble players and members of the orchestra.

REFERENCES

1 Quinn Mills, D., *The IBM Lesson*, Times Books, New York, 1988.
2 Heskett, J. L. and Signorelli, S., 'Benetton', Harvard Business School case study, 1984.
3 For more extended discussion of this concept, see Raymond E. Miles and Charles C. Snow, 'Fit, Failure, and the Hall of Fame', *California Management Review*, vol. 26, no. 3 (Spring 1984), pp. 10–28; and 'Organizations: A New Concept for New Forms', *California Management Review*, vol. 28, no. 3, Spring 1986, pp. 62–73. Miles has used the switchboard metaphor only in working papers, but the press picked up on it, most notably in a 1985 *Business Week* cover story on the 'hollow corporation'. So the image is now established. Tom Peters is pushing a similar concept; see Tom Peters, *Thriving on Chaos: Handbook for a Management Revolution*, New York, Knopf, 1987.
4 Stern, A. L., 'General Foods Tries the Old Restructure Ploy', *Business Month*, November 1987, pp. 37–9.
5 Williamson, O. E., *Markets and Hierarchies: Analysis and Antitrust Implications: A Study in the Economics of Internal Organization*, Free Press, New York, 1975.
6 Hammermesh, R. G. and Dossabhoy, N., 'Cleveland Twist Drill', Harvard Business School case study 1984.
7 Porter, M., 'From Competitive Advantage to Corporate Strategy', *Harvard Business Review*, vol. 65, no. 3, May–June 1987, pp. 43–59.
8 Bartlett, C., and Ghoshal, S., *Managing Across Borders: The Transnational Solution*, Harvard Business School Press, Boston, 1989.
9 Swartz, S., and Weiner, S., 'Stalled Synergy: Many Firms Back Off from Offering Arrays of Financial Services', *Wall Street Journal*, November 12, 1986.
10 Stern, *op. cit.*
11 Sherwood, J. J., 'Creating Work Cultures with Competitive Advantage', *Organizational Dynamics*, 16, Winter 1988, pp. 5–27.
12 Solomon, J., and Hymovitz, C., 'Team Strategy: P&G Makes Changes in the Way It Develops and Sells Its Products', *Wall Street Journal*, August 11, 1987.
13 Williams, M. J., 'Synergy Works at American Express', *Fortune*, February 16, 1987, pp. 79–80.
14 Swartz and Weiner, *op. cit.*
15 Crane, D. B. and Eccles, R. G., 'Commercial Banks: Taking Shape for Turbulent Times', *Harvard Business Review*, vol. 62, no. 6, November–December 1987, pp. 94–100. See also Robert Eccles and Dwight Crane, *Doing Deals* Boston: Harvard Business School Press, 1988.
16 Kohn, A., *No Contest*, Houghton Mifflin, 1986, Boston, 1986, p. 69.
17 Swartz and Weiner, *op. cit.*

18 Axelrod, R., *The Evolution of Cooperation*, Basic Books, New York, 1984.
19 Drucker, P. F., 'The Coming of the New Organization', *Harvard Business Review*, vol. 66, no. 1 January–February 1988, pp. 45–53.

Chapter 11

Transnational solution

Christopher Bartlett and Sumantra Ghoshal

The enormous success of Japanese companies that burst into the international competitive arena in the 1960s and 1970s has triggered a barrage of analysis and advice in the Western business press. Most of this analysis highlighted the convergence of consumer preferences worldwide, the impact of changing technologies and scale economies on international industry structures, and the emergence of increasingly sophisticated competitive strategies that have led to a rapid process of globalization in a large number of world-wide businesses.[1]

As Western companies have searched for the source of the newcomers' incredible ability to sell everything from automobiles to zippers, one conclusion has gained increasing credibility: companies that are unable to gain firm strategic control of their world-wide operations and manage them in a globally co-ordinated manner will not succeed in the emerging international economy. There are few senior managers in the West who are unaffected by the implications of this message.

The concerns of top managers in Japan, however, have been quite different and have focused on the forces of localization that have also been gathering strength in the recent past. Like their Western counterparts, they have been sensitized not only by their own experiences, but also by stories in the Japanese business press, which have been focused on the growing barriers to trade and, most recently, the impact of a strengthening yen in offsetting the efficiencies of global-scale Japanese plants. These managers are much more sensitive to the flip side of globalization – the growing demand of host governments for local investments, the building resistance of consumers to standardized homogenized global products, and the changing economics of emerging flexible manufacturing technologies that are making smaller-scale production and more tailored products feasible.

In the course of a study of some of the world's leading Japanese, European, and American multinationals, we found that these globalizing and localizing forces are working simultaneously to transform many industries.[2] But for historical reasons, few companies have built the organizational capabilities to respond equally to both of these forces.

Many of the European- and American-based companies had well-established networks of fairly independent and self-sufficient national subsidiaries – 'decentralized federations' we call them. Those with such organizations had little difficulty in responding to the increased demands from their host governments or adapting to shifts in consumer preferences world-wide, and their strategic posture was often literally multinational – multiple national positions, each highly sensitive to its local market. The problem with this strategy and the organizational structure that supported it was that it was difficult to co-ordinate and control these world-wide operations in order to respond to the global forces.

Most of the Japanese companies we studied had the opposite problem. Their operations tended to be concentrated in the home country – we term them 'centralized hubs' – and this gave them the ability to capture the opportunities presented by the global forces. Indeed, the strategic posture of these companies was literally global – the world was considered as an integrated whole. Such an approach made these companies less successful in building world-wide operating units that were sensitive and responsive to the countervailing forces of localization.[3]

THE CONSTRAINT OF A COMPANY'S HERITAGE

As the international operating environment became more complex over the past decade or so, the great temptation for companies was to try to imitate the organizational characteristics and strategic postures of their competitors. For example, in the United States, multinational managers are being advised to 'rein in far-flung autonomous subsidiaries, produce standardized global products, and pull decision-making power back to the home office', with the reminder that 'this is a formula that, not coincidentally, many Japanese companies have used for years'.[4]

But the appropriate response to the developing international demands cannot be captured in a formula – and certainly not one that is imitative of companies in totally different situations. The problem is that while a company's tasks are shaped by its external environment, its ability to perform those tasks is constrained by what we term its 'administrative heritage' – the company's existing configuration of assets, its traditional distribution of responsibility, and its historical norms, values and management style.[5] This internal organizational capability is something that cannot be changed overnight or by decree, and one of the important lessons for management is to shift its attention from a search for the ideal organization structure to a quest for ways in which to build and leverage the company's existing capabilities to make them more responsive to the ever-changing external demands.

That is not to deny that there are lessons to be learned from other companies – indeed our research indicates quite the opposite. However, the important lesson is that either blind imitation simply to eliminate obvious differences or wholesale adoption of another company's organizational approach or strategic posture is likely to end in failure. In the first part of this chapter, we distill some of the important transferable lessons that *can* be learned from companies that manage global co-ordination effectively and from those that have been most successful in developing and managing a responsive and flexible localized approach. Although the lessons are drawn from a broader study, we will emphasize the importance of a company's administrative heritage by comparing and contrasting the approaches of two leading consumer electronics companies and suggesting ways in which they can learn from each other.

But while such lessons are helpful, they do not provide the full solution. Today's operating environment in many world-wide businesses demands more than efficient central management and flexible local operations – it requires companies to link their diverse organizational perspectives and resources in a way that would allow them to leverage their capabilities for achieving global co-ordination and national flexibility simultaneously. In response to this need, a few companies have evolved beyond the simpler multinational or global approach to international business and developed what we term a *transnational* capability – an ability to manage across boundaries.[6] In the final part of the article, we will describe some of the characteristics of such an organization, and will suggest some steps that can be taken to build these capabilities.

MAKING CENTRAL MANAGEMENT FLEXIBLE: LESSONS FROM MATSUSHITA

For companies that expanded internationally by establishing fairly independent and self-sufficient subsidiary companies around the world, the task of imposing some kind of global direction or achieving some measure of co-ordination of activity is often a Herculean challenge. The problem that has confronted successive generations of top management at Philips is typical. The Dutch-based electronics giant has built a justifiable reputation as one of the world's most innovative companies, yet has continually been frustrated in its attempt to deliver its brilliant inventions to the world's markets. The recent failure of its VCR system is a classic example.

Despite the fact that it was generally acknowledged to be technologically superior to the competitive VHS and Beta formats, the Philips V2000 system failed because the company was unable to commercialize it. Within the company there is no shortage of theories to explain the failure: some suggest that those who developed the product and its competitive strategy were too distant from the market; others feel the barriers between research, development, manufacturing and marketing led to delays and cost overruns; and another group points to the fact that world-wide subsidiaries were uninvolved in the project and therefore uncommitted to its success. All these explanations reflect organizational difficulties and have some element of truth.

On the other hand, Matsushita Electric Company, Philips' archrival in consumer electronics, has built the global leadership position of its well-known Panasonic and National brands on its ability to control its global strategy from the centre in Japan – yet it has been able to implement it in a flexible and responsive manner throughout its world-wide operations. As we tried to identify the organizational mechanisms that were key to Matsushita's ability to provide strong central direction and control without becoming inflexible or isolated, three factors stood out as the most important explanations of its outstanding success:

- gaining the input of subsidiaries into its management processes;
- ensuring that development efforts were linked to market needs;
- managing responsibility transfers from development to manufacturing to marketing.

By examining how these core mechanisms work in Matsushita, managers in other companies may see ways in which they can gain more global co-ordination without compromising local market sensitivity.

Gaining subsidiary input: multiple linkages

The two most important problems facing a centrally managed multinational company are that those developing the new product or strategy may not understand market needs or that those required to implement the new direction are not committed to it. Matsushita managers are very conscious of these problems and spend much time building multiple linkages between headquarters and overseas subsidiaries to minimize their impacts. These linkages are designed not only to give headquarters managers a better understanding of country level needs and opportunities, but also to give subsidiary managers greater access to and involvement in headquarters decision-making processes.

Matsushita recognizes the importance of market sensing as a stimulus to innovation and does not want its centrally driven management process to reduce its environmental sensitivity. Rather than trying to limit the number of linkages between headquarters and subsidiaries or to focus them through a single point (as many companies do for the sake of efficiency), Matsushita tries to preserve the different perspectives,

priorities and even prejudices of its diverse groups world-wide and tries
to ensure that they have linkages to those in the headquarters who can
represent and defend their views.

The organizational systems and processes that connect different parts
of the Matsushita organization in Japan with the video department of
MESA, the US subsidiary of the company, illustrate these multifaceted
interlinkages. The vice-president in charge of this department has his
career roots in Matsushita Electric Trading Company (METC), the organization with overall responsibility for Matsushita's overseas business.
Although formally posted to the United States, he continues to be a
member of the senior management committee of METC and spends
about a third of his time in Japan. This allows him to be a full member
of METC's top management team that approves the overall strategy for
the US market. In his role as the VP of MESA, he ensures that the local
operation effectively implements the agreed video strategy.

At the next level, the general manager of MESA's video department is
a company veteran who had worked for 14 years in the video product
division of Matsushita Electric, the central production and domestic
marketing company in Japan. He maintains strong connections with
the parent company's product division and is its link to the local American market. Two levels below him, the assistant product manager in the
video department (one of the more junior-level expatriates in the American organization) links the local organization to the central VCR factory
in Japan. Having spent five years in the factory, he acts as the local
representative of the factory and handles all day-to-day communication
with factory personnel.

None of these linkages is accidental. They are deliberately created and
maintained and they reflect the company's open acknowledgement that
the parent company is not one homogeneous entity, but a collectivity of
different constituencies and interests, each of which is legitimate and
necessary. Together, these multiple linkages enhance the subsidiary's
ability to influence key headquarters decisions relating to its market,
particularly decisions about product specifications and design. The multiple links not only allow local management to reflect its local market
needs, they also give headquarters managers the ability to co-ordinate
and control implementation of their strategies and plans.

Linking direction to needs: market mechanisms

Matsushita's efforts to ensure that its products and strategies are linked
to market needs does not stop at the input stage. The company has
created an integrative process that ensures that the top managers and
central staff groups are not sheltered from the pressures, constraints and
demands felt by managers on the front line of the operations. One of the

key elements in achieving this difficult organizational task is the company's willingness to employ 'market mechanisms' for directing and regulating the activities located at the centre. Because the system is unique, we will describe some of its major characteristics.

Research projects undertaken by the Central Research Laboratories (CRL) of Matsushita fall into two broad groups. The first group consists of 'company total projects' which involve developing technologies important for Matsushita's long-term strategic position and that may be applicable across many different product divisions. Such projects are decided jointly by the research laboratories, the product divisions, and top management of the company and are funded directly by the corporate board. The second group of CRL research projects consists of relatively smaller projects which are relevant to the activities of particular product divisions. The budget for such research activities, approximately half of the company's total research budget, is allocated not to the research laboratories but to the product divisions. This creates an interesting situation in which technology-driven and market-led ideas can compete for attention.

Each year, the product division suggests research projects that they would like to sponsor and which would incorporate their knowledge of world-wide market needs developed through their routine multiple linkages to subsidiaries. At the same time, the various research laboratories hold annual internal exhibitions and meetings and also write proposals to highlight research projects that they would like to undertake. The engineering and development groups of the product divisions mediate the subsequent contracting and negotiation process through which the expertise and interests of the laboratories and the needs of the product divisions are finally matched. Specific projects are sponsored by the divisions and are allocated to the laboratories or research groups of their choice, along with requisite funds and other resources.

The system creates intense competition for projects (and the budgets that go with them) among the research groups, and it is this mechanism that forces researchers to keep a close market orientation. At the same time, the product divisions are conscious that it is their money that is being spent on product development and they become less inclined to make unreasonable or uneconomical demands on R&D.[7]

The market mechanism also works to determine annual product styling and features. Each year the company holds what it calls merchandising meetings which are, in effect, large internal trade shows. Senior marketing managers from Matsushita's sales companies world-wide visit their supplying divisions and see on display the proposed product lines for the new model year. Relying on their understanding of their individual markets, these managers pick and choose among proposed models, order specific modifications for their local markets, or simply refuse to take products they feel are unsuitable. Individual products or even entire lines might have to be redesigned as a result of input from the hundreds of managers at the merchandising meeting.

Managing responsibility transfer: personnel flows

Within a national subsidiary, the task of transferring responsibility from research to manufacturing and finally marketing is facilitated by the smaller size and closer proximity of the units responsible for each stage of activity. This is not so where large central units usually take the lead role, and Matsushita has built some creative means for managing these transitions. The systems rely heavily on the transfer of people, as is illustrated by the company's management of new product development.

First, careers of research engineers are structured so as to ensure that most of them spend about five to eight years in the central research laboratories engaged in pure research, then they spend another five years in the product divisions in applied product and process development, and finally they spend the rest of their working lives in a direct operational function, usually production, wherein they take up line management positions. More important, each engineer usually makes the transition from one department to the next along with the transfer of the major product on which he has been working.

The research project that began Matsushita's development of its enormously successful VCR product was launched in the late 1950s under the leadership of Dr Hiroshi Sugaya, a young physicist in the company's Central Research Laboratory. As the product evolved into its development stage, the core members of Dr Sugaya's team were kept together as they transferred from CRL to the product development and applications laboratory located in the product division. After a long and difficult development process, the product was finally ready for commercial production in 1977, as many of the team moved with the project out into the Okanyama plant.[8]

In other companies we surveyed, it was not uncommon for research engineers to move to development, but not with their projects, thereby depriving the companies of one of the most important and immediate benefits of such moves. We also saw no other examples of engineers routinely taking the next step of actually moving to the production function. This last step, however, is perhaps the most critical in integrating research and production both in terms of building a network that connects managers across these two functions, and also for transferring a set of common values that facilitates implementation of central innovations.

Another mechanism that integrates production and research in Matsushita works in the opposite direction. Wherever possible, the company tries to identify the manager who will head the production task for a new product under development and makes him a full-time member of the research team from the initial stage of the development process. This system not only injects direct production expertise into the development team, but also facilitates transfer of the innovation once the design is completed. Matsushita also uses this mechanism as a way of transferring product expertise from headquarters to its world-wide sales subsidiaries. Although this is a common practice among many multinationals, in Matsushita it has additional significance because of the importance of internationalizing management as well as its products.

As with the multiple linkages and the internal market mechanisms, this organizational practice was a simple, yet powerful tool that seemed to be central to Matsushita's ability to make its centrally driven management processes flexible, sensitive, and responsive to the world-wide opportunities and needs. More important, these three organizational mechanisms are simple enough to be adopted, probably in some modified form, by other companies. They meet the needs of those trying to build an organization process that allows management at the centre more influence and control over world-wide operations, without compromising the motivation or operating effectiveness of the national units.

MAKING LOCAL MANAGEMENT EFFECTIVE: LESSONS FROM PHILIPS

If Matsushita is the champion of efficient centrally co-ordinated management, its Netherlands-based competitor, Philips, is the master of building effective national operations world-wide. And as surely as Philips' managers envy their Japanese rival's ability to develop products and strategies in Osaka that appear to be implemented effortlessly around the globe, their counterparts in Matsushita are extremely jealous of Philips' national organizations that are not only sensitive and responsive to their local environments, but are also highly innovative and entrepreneurial.

For example, the company's first colour TV set was built and sold not in Europe, where the parent company is located, but in Canada, where the market had closely followed the US lead in introducing colour transmission; Philips' first stereo colour TV set was developed by the Australian subsidiary; teletext TV sets were created by its British subsidiary; 'smart cards' by its French subsidiary; a programmed word processing typewriter by North American Philips – the list of local innovations and entrepreneurial initiatives in the company is endless.

Whilst Matsushita has had no difficulty in establishing effective sales organizations and assembly operations around the world, top management has often been frustrated that its overseas subsidiaries do not exhibit more initiative and entrepreneurial spark. Despite pleas to its overseas management to become more self-sufficient and less dependent on headquarters for direction, the company has found that the decentralization of assets that accompanies its 'localization' programme has not always triggered the kind of independence and initiative that had been hoped for.

Out of the many factors that drive Philips' international organization, we were able to identify three that not only appear central to the development and maintenance of its effective local management system, but also may be adaptable to other organizations that are trying to promote national innovativeness and responsiveness within a globally integrated organization:

- Philips' use of a cadre of entrepreneurial expatriates;
- an organization that forces tight functional integration within a subsidiary;
- a dispersion of responsibilities along with the decentralized assets.

A cadre of entrepreneurial expatriates

Expatriate positions, particularly in the larger subsidiaries, have been very attractive for Philips' managers for several reasons. With only seven or eight per cent of its total sales coming from Holland, many different national subsidiaries of the company have contributed much larger shares of total revenues than the parent company. As a result, foreign operations have enjoyed relatively high organizational status compared to most companies of similar size with headquarters in the United States, Japan, or even the larger countries of Europe. Further, because of the importance of its foreign operations, Philips' formal management development system has always required considerable international experience as a prerequisite for top corporate positions. Finally, Eindhoven, the small rural town in which corporate headquarters is located, is far from the sophisticated and cosmopolitan world centres that host many of its foreign subsidiaries. After living in London, New York, Sydney or Paris, many managers find it hard to return to Eindhoven.

Collectively, all these factors have led to the best and the brightest of Philips' managers spending much of their careers in different national operations. This cadre of entrepreneurial expatriate managers has been an important agent in developing capabilities of local units, yet keeping them linked to the parent company's overall objectives. Further, unlike Matsushita where an expatriate manager typically spends a tour of duty of three to six years in a particular national subsidiary and then returns to the headquarters, expatriate managers in Philips spend a large part of their careers abroad continuously working for two or three years each in a number of different subsidiaries.

This difference in the career system results in very different attitudes. In Philips, the expatriate managers follow each other into assignments and build close relations among themselves. They tend to identify strongly with the national organization's point of view and this shared identity makes them part of a distinct subculture within the company. In companies like Matsushita, on the other hand, there is very little interaction among the expatriate managers in the different subsidiaries, and most tend to see themselves as part of the parent company temporarily on assignment in a foreign country.

One result of these differences is that expatriate managers in Matsushita are far more likely to take a custodial approach which resists any local changes to standard products and policies. In contrast, expatriate managers in Philips, despite being just as socialized into the overall corporate culture of the company, are much more willing to be advocates of local views and to defend against the imposition of inappropriate corporate ideas on national organizations. This willingness to 'rock the boat' and openness to experimentation and change is the fuel that ignites local initiative and entrepreneurship.[9]

Further, by creating this kind of environment in the national organization, Philips has had little difficulty in attracting very capable local management. In contrast to the experience in many Japanese companies where local managers have felt excluded from a decision-making process that centres around headquarters management and the local expatriates only, local managers in Philips feel their ideas are listened to and defended in headquarters.[10] This too, creates a supportive environment for local innovation and creativity.

Integration of technical and marketing functions within each subsidiary

Historically, the top management in all Philips' national subsidiaries consisted not of an individual CEO but a committee made up of the heads of the technical, commercial, and finance functions. This system of three-headed management had a long history in Philips, stemming from the functional backgrounds of the founding Philips brothers, one an engineer and the other a salesman. Although this management philosophy has recently been modified to a system which emphasizes individual authority and accountability, the long tradition of shared responsibilities and joint decision making has left a legacy of many different mechanisms for functional integration at multiple levels. These integrative mechanisms within each subsidiary in Philips enhance the efficiency and effectiveness of local decision making and action in the same way that various means of cross-functional integration within Matsushita's corporate headquarters facilitates its central management processes.

In most subsidiaries, integration mechanisms exist at three organizational levels. First, for each product, there is an article team that consists of relatively junior managers belonging to the commercial and technical functions. This team evolves product policies and prepares annual sales plans and budgets. At times, subarticle teams may be formed to supervise day-to-day working and to carry out special projects, such as preparing capital investment plans, should major new investments be felt necessary for effectively manufacturing and marketing a new product.

A second tier of cross-functional co-ordination takes place at the product group level, through the group management team, which again consists of both technical and commercial representatives. This team meets monthly to review results, suggest corrective actions and resolve any interfunctional differences. Keeping control and conflict resolution at this low level facilitates sensitive and rapid responses to initiatives and ideas generated at the local level.

The highest level co-ordination forum within the subsidiary is the senior management committee (SMC) consisting of the top commercial, technical, and financial managers in the subsidiary. Acting essentially as a local board, the SMC provides an overall unity of effort among the different functional groups within the local unit and assures that the national unit retains primary responsibility for its own strategies and priorities. Again, the effect is to provide local management with a forum in which actions can be decided and issues resolved without escalation for approval or arbitration.

Decentralized authority and dispersed responsibility

While Matsushita's localization programme was triggered by political pressures to increase local value added in various host countries, the company has also hoped that the decentralization of assets would help its overseas units achieve a greater measure of local responsiveness, self-sufficiency, and initiative. To management's frustration, such changes were slow in coming.

Philips, on the other hand, had created such national organizations seemingly without effort. The difference lay in the degree to which responsibility and authority were dispersed along with the assets. Expanding internationally in the earliest decades of the century, Philips' managers were confronted by transport and communications barriers that forced them to delegate substantial local autonomy to its decentralized operating units. The need for local units to develop a sense of self-sufficiency was reinforced by the protectionist pressures of the 1930s that made cross-shipments of products or components practically impossible. During World War II, even R&D capability was dispersed to prevent it from falling into enemy hands, and the departure of many corporate managers from Holland reduced the parent company's control over its national operations abroad.

In the post-war boom, while corporate managers focused on rebuilding the war-ravaged home operations, managers in foreign units were able to capitalize on their well-developed autonomy. Most applied their local resources and capabilities to build highly successful national businesses, sensitive and responsive to the local needs and opportunities. In doing so, they achieved a degree of local entrepreneurship and self-sufficiency rare among companies of Philips' size and complexity.

Although it would be impossible for another company to replicate the historical events that resulted in this valuable organizational capability, the main characteristics of their development are clear. First, it must be feasible for offshore units to develop local capabilities and initiative, and this requires the decentralization of appropriate managerial and technological resources along with the reconfiguration of physical assets.

While this is necessary, it is not sufficient, however, as Matsushita and many other companies have begun to recognize. Local initiatives and entrepreneurial action must not only be feasible, they must also be desirable for local managers. This requires the legitimate delegation of responsibilities and authority that not only gives them control over the decentralized resources, but rewards them for using them to develop creative and innovative solutions to their problems. Only when the decentralization of assets is accompanied by a dispersion of responsibilities can local management develop into a legitimate corporate contributor rather than simple implementers of central direction.

BUILDING TRANSNATIONAL CAPABILITIES: LESSONS FROM L.M. ERICSSON

In multinational corporations, the location of an opportunity (or threat) is often different from where the company's appropriate response resources are situated. This is so because environmental opportunities and threats are footloose, shifting from location to location, while organizational resources, contrary to the assumptions of many economists, are not easily transferable even within the same company. Further, the location of a company's strategic resources – plants and research centres are good examples – is related not only to actual organizational needs and intentions, but also to the idiosyncrasies of the firm's administrative history. The result is a situation of environment-resource mismatches: the organization has excessive resources in environments that are relatively non-critical, and very limited or even no resources in critical markets that offer the greatest opportunities and challenges.

Such environment–resource mismatches are pervasive in MNCs. For many historical reasons, Ericsson has significant technological and managerial capabilities in Australia and Italy, even though these markets are relatively unimportant in the global telecommunications business. At the same time, the company has almost no presence in the United States, which not only represents almost 40 per cent of world telecommunications demand but is also the source of much of the new technology. Procter & Gamble is strong in the United States and Europe, but not in Japan where important consumer product innovations have occurred recently and where a major global competitor is emerging. Matsushita has appropriate technological and managerial resources in Japan and the US, but not in Europe, a huge market and home of archrival Philips.

Rectifying these imbalances in the configuration of their organization resources is taking these companies a long time and, since the relative importance of different environments will continue to change, the problem will never be fully overcome. The need, therefore, is not simply to make adjustments to the geographic configuration or resources, but also to create organizational systems that allow the spare capacity and slack resources in strong operating units to be redirected to environments in which they are weak.

Simply creating effective central and local management does not solve this mismatch problem, and to succeed in today's demanding international environment, companies must develop their organizational capabilities beyond the stages described in the first part of this article. The limitation of companies with even the most well-developed local and central capabilities is that the location of resources also tends to determine the locus of control over those resources. Whether organizationally mandated or not, local management develops strong influence on how resources available locally are to be used. Further, organizational commitments are usually hierarchical, with local needs taking precedence over global needs. Consequently, at the core of resolving the problem of environment–resource mismatches is the major organizational challenge of loosening the bonds between ownership and control of resources within the company.

Among the companies we studied, there were several that were in the process of developing such organizational capabilities. They had surpassed the classic capabilities of the *multinational* company that operates as decentralized federation of units able to sense and respond to diverse international needs and opportunities; and they had evolved beyond the abilities of the global company with its facility for managing operations on a tightly controlled world-wide basis through its centralized hub structure. They had developed what we termed *transnational* capabilities

– the ability to manage across national boundaries, retaining local flexibility while achieving global integration. More than anything else this involved the ability to link local operations to each other and to the centre in a flexible way and, in so doing, to leverage those local and central capabilities.

Ericsson, the Swedish telecommunications company, was among those that had become most effective in managing the required linkages and processes, and we were able to identify three organizational characteristics that seemed most helpful in facilitating its developing transnational management capabilities:

- an interdependence of resources and responsibilities among organizational units;
- a set of strong cross-unit integrating devices;
- a strong corporate identification and a well-developed world-wide management perspective.

Interdependence of resources and responsibilities

Perhaps the most important requirement of the transnational organization is a need for the organizational configuration to be based on a principle of reciprocal dependence among units. Such an interdependence of resources and responsibilities breaks down the hierarchy between local and global interests by making the sharing of resources, ideas and opportunities a self-enforcing norm. To illustrate how such a basic characteristic of organizational configuration can influence a company's management of capabilities, let us contrast the way in which ITT, NEC and Ericsson developed the electronic digital switch that would be the core product for each company's telecommunications business in the 1980s and beyond.

From its beginnings in 1920 as a Puerto Rican telephone company, ITT built its world-wide operation on an objective described in the 1924 annual report as being 'to develop truly national systems operated by the nationals of each company'. For half a century ITT's national 'systems houses' as they were called within the company, committed themselves to integrating into their local environments and becoming attuned to national interests and market needs. All but the smallest systems houses were established as fully integrated, self-sufficient units with responsibility for developing, manufacturing, marketing, installing and servicing their own products.

With the emergence of the new digital electronic technology in the 1970s, however, this highly successful strategic posture was threatened by the huge cost of developing a digital switch. Since no single systems house would be able to muster the required technological and financial resources on its own or recoup the investment from its local market, the obvious solution was for ITT to make the System 12 digital switch project a corporate responsibility. However, given their decade of operating independence, the powerful country unit managers were unwilling to yield the task of developing the new switch to the corporate R&D group – and indeed, little expertise had been gathered at the centre to undertake such a task.

By exercising their considerable influence, the European systems houses were able to capture the strategic initiative on System 12, but then began disagreeing about who should take what role in this vital project. Many of the large systems houses simply refused to rely on others for the development of critical parts of the system; others rejected standards that did not fit with their view of local needs. As a result, duplication of effort and divergence of specifications began to emerge and the cost of developing the switch ballooned to over $1 billion.

The biggest problems appeared when the company decided to enter the battle for a share of the deregulated US market. Asserting its independence, the US business launched a major new R&D effort, despite appeals from the chief technological officer that they risked developing what he sceptically termed 'System 13'. After further years of effort and additional hundreds of millions of dollars in costs, ITT acknowledged in 1986 that it was withdrawing from the US central switching market. The largest and most successful international telecommunications company in the world was blocked from its home country by the inability to transfer and apply its leading edge technology in a timely fashion. It was a failure that eventually led to ITT's sale of its European operations and its gradual withdrawal from direct involvement in telecommunications world-wide.

If effective global innovation was blocked by the extreme independence of the organizational units in ITT, it was impeded in NEC by the strong dependence of national subsidiaries on the parent company. The first person in NEC to detect the trend toward digital switching was the Japanese manager in charge of the company's small US operation. However, his role was one of selling corporate products and developing a beachhead for the company in the US market. Because of this role, he had a hard time convincing technical managers in Japan of a supposed trend to digitalization that they saw nowhere else in the world.

When the US managers finally were able to elicit sufficient support, the new NEAC 61 digital switch was developed almost entirely by headquarters personnel. Even in deciding which features to design into the new product, the central engineering group tended to discount the requests of the North American sales company and rely on data gathered in their own staff's field trips to US customers. Although the

NEAC 61 was regarded as having good hardware, customers felt its software was unadapted to US needs. Sales did not meet expectations.

Both ITT and NEC recognized the limitations of their independent and dependent organizations systems and worked hard to adapt them. But the process of building organizational interdependence is a slow and difficult one that must be constantly monitored and adjusted. In our sample of companies, Ericsson seemed to be the most consistent and experienced practitioner of creating and managing a delicate balance of interunit interdependency. The way in which it did so suggests the value of a constant readjustment of responsibilities and relationships as a way of adapting to changing strategic needs while maintaining a dynamic system of mutual dependence.

Like ITT, Ericsson had built, during the 1920s and 1930s, a substantial world-wide network of operations sensitive and responsive to local national environments; but like NEC, it had a strong home market base and a parent company with technological, manufacturing and marketing capability to support those companies. Keeping the balance between and among those units has required constant adjustment of organizational responsibilities and relationships.

In the late 1930s, management became concerned that the growing independence of its offshore companies was causing divergence in technology, duplication of effort, and inefficiency in the sourcing patterns. To remedy the problem they pulled sales and distribution control to headquarters and began consolidating responsibilities under product divisions. While world-wide control improved, the divisions eventually began to show signs of isolation and short-term focus. Thus, in the early 1950s the corporate staff functions were given more of a leadership role. It was in this period that the central R&D group developed a crossbar switch that became an industry leader. As the product design and manufacturing technology for this product became well-understood and fully documented, however, Ericsson management was able to respond to the increasing demands of host governments to transfer more manufacturing capacity and technological know-how abroad. Once again, the role of the offshore subsidiaries increased.

This half a century of constant ebb and flow in the roles and responsibilities of various geographic, product and functional groups allowed Ericsson to build an organization in which all these diverse perspectives were seen as legitimate and the multiple capabilities were kept viable. This multidimensional organization gave the company the ability to quickly sense and respond to the coming of electronic switching in the 1970s. Once it had prevented the emergence of strong dependent or independent relationships, product development efforts and manufacturing responsibilities could be pulled back to Sweden, without great difficulty. Where national capabilities, expertise, or experience could be useful in the corporate effort, the appropriate local personnel were seconded to headquarters. Having established overall strategic and operational control of the digital switching strategy, however, corporate management at Ericsson was then willing to delegate substantial design, development and manufacturing responsibilities to its international subsidiaries, resulting in a reinforcement of the interdependence of world-wide operations.

Sourcing of products and components from specialized plants have long provided a base of interdependence, but recently that has been extended to product development and marketing. For example, Italy is the company's centre for global development of transmission system development. Finland has the leading role for mobile telephones and Australia develops the company's rural switch. Further, headquarters has given some of these units responsibility for handling certain export markets (e.g. Italy's responsibility for developing markets in Africa). Increasingly, the company is moving even advanced core system software development offshore to subsidiary companies with access to more software engineers than it has in Stockholm.[12]

By changing responsibilities, shifting assets and modifying relationships in response to evolving environmental demands and strategic priorities, Ericsson has maintained a dynamic interdependence among its operating units that has allowed it to develop entrepreneurial and innovative subsidiary companies that work within a corporate framework defined by knowledge and creative headquarters product and functional groups. This kind of interdependence is the basis of a transnational company – one that can think globally and act locally.

Interunit integrating devices

Although the interdependence of resources and responsibilities provides a structural framework for the extensive use of interunit co-operation, there is a need for effective organizational integrating mechanisms to link operations in a way that taps the full potential of the interdependent configuration.

Compared to some companies in our study where relationships among national companies were competitive and where headquarter-subsidiary interactions were often of an adversarial nature, the organizational climate in Ericsson appeared more co-operative and collaborative. The establishment and maintenance of such attitudes was important since it allowed the company's diverse units to work together in a way that maximized the potential of the interdependent operations. We identified three important pillars to Ericsson's success in interunit integration:

- a clearly defined and tightly controlled set of operating systems;
- a people-linking process employing such devices as temporary assignments and joint teams;
- interunit decision forums, particularly subsidiary boards, where views could be exchanged and differences resolved.

Ericsson management feels strongly that its most effective integrating device is strong central control over key elements of its strategic operation. Unlike ITT, Ericsson has not had strong or sophisticated administrative systems (it introduced strategic plans only in 1983), but its operating systems have long been structured to provide strong worldwide co-ordination. Knowing that local modifications would be necessary, the company designed its digital switch as a modular system with very clear specifications. National units could custom-tailor elements of the design to meet local needs without compromising the integrity of the total design system. Similarly, Ericsson's global computer-aided design and manufacturing system allowed the parent company to delegate responsibility for component production and even design without fear of losing the ability to control and co-ordinate the entire manufacturing system.

Rather than causing a centralization of decision making, management argues that these strong yet flexible operating systems allow them to delegate much more freely, knowing that local decisions will not be inconsistent or detrimental to the overall interests. Rather than managing the decisions centrally, they point out they are managing the parameters of decisions that can be made by local units, thereby retaining the flexibility and entrepreneurship of those units.

But in addition to strong systems, interunit co-operation requires good interpersonal relations, and Ericsson has developed these with a long-standing policy of transferring large numbers of people back and forth between headquarters and subsidiaries. It differs from the more common transfer patterns in both direction and intensity, as a comparison with NEC's transfer process will demonstrate. Where NEC may transfer a new technology through a few key managers, Ericsson will send a team of 50 or 100 engineers and managers from one unit to another for a year or two; while NEC's flow is primarily from headquarters to subsidiary; Ericsson's is a balanced two-way flow with people coming to the parent not only to learn, but also to bring their expertise; and while NEC's transfers are predominantly Japanese, Ericsson's multidirectional process involves all nationalities.[13]

Australian technicians seconded to Stockholm in the mid-1970s to bring their experience with digital switching into the corporate development effort established enduring relationships that helped in the subsequent joint development of a rural switch in Australia a decade later. Confidences built when a 40-man Italian team spent 18 months in Sweden in the early 1970s to learn about electronic switching, provided the basis for the subsequent decentralization of AXE software development and the delegation of responsibility for developing the corporate transmission systems to the Italian company.

But any organization in which there are shared tasks and joint responsibilities will require additional decision-making and conflict-resolving forums. In Ericsson, often divergent objectives and interests of the parent company and the local subsidiary are exchanged in the national company's board meetings. Unlike many companies whose local boards are pro forma bodies whose activities are designed solely to satisfy national legal requirements, Ericsson uses its local boards as legitimate forums for communicating objectives, resolving differences and making decisions. At least one, and often several senior corporate managers are members of each board, and subsidiary board meetings become an important means for co-ordinating activities and channelling local ideas and innovations across national lines.

National competence, world-wide perspective

If there is one clear lesson from ITT's experience, it is that a company cannot manage globally if its managers identify primarily with local parochial interests and objectives. But as NEC has learned, when management has no ability to defend national perspectives and respond to local opportunities, penetration of world markets is equally difficult. One of the important organizational characteristics Ericsson has been able to develop over the years has been a management attitude that is simultaneously locally sensitive and globally conscious.

At the Stockholm headquarters, managers emphasize the importance of developing strong country operations, not only to capture sales that require responsiveness to national needs, but also to tap into the resources that are available through world-wide operation. Coming from a small home country where it already hires over a third of the graduating electrical and electronics engineers, Ericsson is very conscious of the need to develop skills and capture ideas wherever they operate in the world. But, at the same time, local managers see themselves as part of the world-wide Ericsson group rather than as independent autonomous units. Constant transfers and working on joint teams over the years has helped broaden many managers' perspectives from local to global, but giving local units systemwide mandates for products has confirmed their identity with the company's global operations. It is this ability for headquarters and subsidiary managers to view the issues from each other's perspective that distinguishes the company that can think globally yet act locally.

CONCLUSION: ORGANIZATIONAL CAPABILITY IS KEY

There are few companies that have not recognized the nature of the main strategic tasks facing them in today's complex international business environment. Philips' managers have understood for years that they need to build global scale, rationalize their diverse product lines and establish a more integrated world-wide strategy. And whilst their counterparts at Matsushita have recently made localization a company watchword, this is just the culmination of years of effort to build more self-sufficient and responsive national subsidiaries which the company recognizes it will need to remain globally competitive. If changes have been slow in coming in both companies, it is not for the lack of strategic clarity about the need for change but for want of the organizational ability to implement the desired change.

In the course of our study, we found that managers engaged in a great deal of cross-company comparison of organizational capabilities. And the managerial grass inevitably looked greener on the other side of the corporate fence. Philips' managers envied their Japanese competitors' ability to develop global products, manufacture them centrally, and have them launched into markets world-wide on a time cycle that would be virtually impossible in their own organization. On the other hand, as Matsushita's managers face growing pressure from host governments world-wide, and as they feel the vulnerabilities of their central sourcing plants in an era of the strong yen, they view Philips' world-wide network of self-sufficient, well-connected and innovative national organizations as an asset they would dearly love to have. But the apparently small step from admiration to emulation of another company's strategic capabilities usually turns out to be a long and dangerous voyage.

What we suggest is that managers ignore battle cries calling for 'standardization, rationalization, and centralization' or any other such simplistic quick-fix formulas. What is needed is a more gradual approach that, rather than undermining a company's administrative heritage, both protects and builds on it. Having built flexible central and local management capabilities, the next challenge is to link them in an organization that allows the company to do what it must to survive in today's international environment – think globally and act locally. For most world-wide companies it is the development of this transnational organizational capability that is key to long-term success.

REFERENCES

1 See for example, Theodore Levitt, 'The Globalization of Markets', *Harvard Business Review*, May/June 1983, pp. 92–102; Michael Porter, 'Changing Patterns of International Competition', *California Management Review*, 28/2 Winter

1986, pp. 9–10; and Gary Hamel and C. K. Prahalad, 'Do You Really Have a Global Strategy?' *Harvard Business Review*, July–August 1985, pp. 139–48.

2 The research on which this article is based consisted of a three-year-long in-depth study of nine leading American, Japanese and European multinational companies in three diverse industries. We interviewed over 235 managers in the headquarters and a number of different national subsidiaries of these companies to uncover how these companies with their diverse national backgrounds and international histories were adapting their organizational structures and management processes to cope with the new strategic demands of their operating environments. The companies studied were Philips, Matsushita and General Electric in the consumer electronics industry; Ericsson, NEC and ITT in the telecommunications switching industry; and Unilever, Kao and Procter & Gamble in the branded packaged products business. The complete findings of this study will be reported in our book *Managing Across Borders: The Transnational Solution*, Harvard Business School Press, 1989.

3 For a more detailed explication of the decentralized federation and centralized hub forms of multinational organizations, see Christopher A. Bartlett, 'Building and Managing the Transnational: The New Organizational Challenge', in Porter, M. E. ed., *Competition in the Global Industries*, Harvard Business School Press, Boston, MA, 1986.

4 'Rebuilding Corporate Empires – New Global Formula', *Newsweek*, April 14, 1986, p. 40.

5 The concept of administrative heritage is explained more fully in Christopher Bartlett *op. cit.* and also in Bartlett, C. and Ghoshal, S. 'Managing Across Borders: New Strategic Requirements', *Sloan Management Review*, Summer 1987, pp. 7–17.

6 The organization we describe as the transnational has a long but discontinuous history in the internal management literature. The concept of such an organizational form was manifest in Howard Perlmutter's celebrated paper, 'The Torturous Evolution of the Multinational Corporation', *Columbia Journal of World Business*, January–February 1969, pp. 9–19. Similarly, C. K. Prahalad and Yves Doz's idea of a multifocal organization is described in *The Multinational Mission: Balancing Local Demands and Global Vision*, New York, NY: The Free Press, 1987; Gunnar Hedlund's definition of the heterarchy in 'The Hypermodern MNC – A Heterarchy?' *Human Resource Management*, Spring 1986, pp. 9–35; and Roderick White and Thomas Poyneter's description of the horizontal organization in 'Organizing for Worldwide Advantage', presented at the seminar on Management of the MNC at the European Institute for Advanced Studies in Management, Brussels, on June 9–10, 1987, are conceptually similar to what we describe as the transnational organization though the models differ significantly in their details.

7 Westney and Sakakibara have observed a similar system of internal quasi-markets governing the interface between R&D operating units in a number of Japanese computer companies. See Eleanor Westney and K. Sakakibara 'The Role of Japan-Based R&D in Global Technology Strategy', *Technology in Society*, no. 7, 1985.

8 See Rosenbloom, R. and Cusumano, M., 'Technological Pioneering and Competitive Advantage: Birth of the VCR Industry', *California Management Review*, 29/4, Summer 1987 pp. 51–76, for a full description of this interesting development process.

9 See John Van Mannen and Edgar H Schein, 'Towards a Theory of Organiza-

tional Socialization', in Staw, B. ed., *Research in Organizational Behaviour*, Greenwich, CT: JAI Press, 1979 for a rich and theory-grounded discussion on how such differences in socialization processes and career systems can influence managers' attitudes towards change and innovation.

10 See Bartlett, C. and Yoshihara, H., 'New Challenges for Japanese Multinationals: Is Organizational Adaptation Their Achilles' Heel?', *Human Resource Management*, 27/1, Spring 1988 pp. 1–25, for a fuller discussion of some of the personnel management implications of managing local nationals in a classic centralized hub Japanese organization.

11 The need for both feasibility and desirability for facilitating innovativeness of organizations has been suggested by Lawrence Mohr, 'Determinants of Innovation in Organizations', *American Political Science Review*, 63 (1969).

12 For a detailed discussion on how managers make such choices and how new responsibilities and relationships are developed, See Bartlett, C. and Ghoshal, S., 'Tap Your Subsidiaries for Global Reach', *Harvard Business Review*, November–December 1986, pp. 87–94.

13 The effectiveness of personnel transfers as an integrative mechanism in multinational companies has been highlighted by many authors, most notably by Edstrom, E. and Galbraith, J. R., 'Transfer of Managers as a Coordination and Control Strategy in Multinational Organizations', *Administrative Science Quarterly*, June 1977.

Reproduced from Bartlett, C. and Ghoshal, S., 'Organizing for Worldwide Effectiveness', *California Management Review*, 31(1), Fall 1988 by permission of The Regents. © The Regents of the University of California 1983.

Chapter 12

Managing alliances

Joseph L. Badaracco, Jr.

Peter Drucker has observed that strategy must ultimately degenerate into work. A strategy that utilizes alliances is, like any other, no better than its implementation.[1] Its success depends, in part, on how well the alliances are managed. But what does management consist of? Managing alliances, particularly knowledge links, is at bottom a process of learning, creating, sharing and controlling knowledge. As executives manage the boundaries of their firms, they are determining when and how knowledge and skills will move into and out of their organizations. To succeed, they frequently must break down the walls around their firms and teach their organization to learn in new, often uncomfortable and threatening ways.

Creating and managing alliances is an unnatural act for many American managers. Intellectually and intuitively, they believe that firms are best run as citadels. For decades, powerful forces have led them to strip-mine knowledge and skills from many of their crucial ongoing relationships. Workers' tasks were deskilled, often to the point of mind-numbing repetition; labour unions were treated as adversaries with whom it was dangerous to share in-depth knowledge about a business; government was seen as another antagonist, whose regulators, antitrust enforcers, and other meddlers were best kept at arm's-length; and suppliers and buyers often communicated little more to each other than price specifications and delivery dates. Yet American executives did become adept at managing knowledge within their firms' boundaries. Companies are repositories of embedded knowledge. Inside them, information, technology, rumours, cost data, plans, judgements about personnel, trial balloons, and other sorts of knowledge move within complex social and administrative networks.

Indeed, the best starting point for understanding how to manage alliances is an examination of the factors that encourage or impede the acquisition, communication, and creation of knowledge within an organization. These factors do not fit neatly together in a formula, and their relative weight varies from situation to situation. They include: a clear sense of a project's objectives; incentives to share and build knowledge and skills; the right basic resources and capabilities; a champion or leadership team with strong personal commitment to the endeavour's success; a sense of teamwork and purpose among participants at all levels; encouragement, albeit within limits, to experiment, fail, and try again; a sense of trust among the individuals and groups expected to contribute knowledge, skills, and resources; and support from senior management.

In short, what matter are leadership, trust, and commitment. These commodities are often scarce inside companies, because of politics, bureaucracy and other impediments. In alliances, the challenges are even greater. Over time, partners may come to disagree on an alliance's purpose and objectives; in a world of fluctuating exchange rates and proliferating knowledge, this can happen quickly. Even if the partners have complementary capabilities, they may be reluctant to share them, particularly if the companies are or could become competitors. The 'not-invented-here' mentality can lead each partner to undervalue the capabilities the other brings to an alliance. Trust and commitment are imperilled when organizations with different cultures must communicate and work together. This problem is especially serious when the allies have a long history of antagonism, which is the case for many American companies and their suppliers, workers, labour unions, dealers and the government. Partners may also need to reconcile different management systems – for accounting, compensation, promotions, and reporting. Finally, strong leadership may be less likely to emerge in a joint enterprise for which two or more bosses are ultimately responsible; such arrangements violate Napoleon's maxim that one bad general does better than two good ones.

Alliances that overcome these challenges can help companies prosper in a world of knowledge-intensive competition. But under what conditions is this likely to happen? The experiences, either successful or disappointing, of the firms examined in this book, as well as experiences reported in other studies of joint ventures and co-operative R&D suggest what these conditions are. They can be created by managers with different skills and styles – as long as, ultimately, the basic conditions are met. When this happens, the dice are loaded in favour of success.

The first condition is that managers considering an alliance must have a clear, strategic understanding of their company's current capabilities and the capabilities it will need in the future. In their haste to consummate a deal that fills an urgent need, managers can easily leave this condition unmet. As a result, they may commit their company to an alliance that makes sense as a discrete deal but causes strategic damage. A product link might, for example, provide a company with a product it needs at a very low cost. Yet the partnership may take the pressure off managers and engineers to build the capabilities to develop similar products. The deal could also open new markets and teach crucial skills to the partner, thereby spawning a competitor.

In a world of knowledge-driven competition and fleeting product-based advantages, firms must be understood as pools of embedded knowledge and capabilities. This, not plants or cash or even patented technology, is their fundamental asset. A firm's core knowledge, cap-abilities and skills can be identified through questions like these: Which individuals have the craftsman-like knowledge, born of special talent and particular experience, that sets them apart from their counterparts in competing firms? Which teams and groups 'know' how to do things or make things better, faster, or more efficiently than their competitors? What are the crucial links, formal and informal, through which the company orchestrates these pools of individual and small-group talent? And what relationships with external parties are vital conduits for bring-ing new skills and capabilities into the company?

Looking to the future, the central questions are: What knowledge does a company need to meet its long-term strategic goals? Which capabilities – not necessarily which products – will give it an advantage over its competitors three to five years hence?[2] In a world of globalized knowl-edge, few firms are permanently powerful. Risks to a firm's capabilities can be uncovered by asking: What is the half-life of the core capabilities of a company? Which competitors – tiny startup firms, established firms, even nations – are aiming to replicate or improve on these capabilities and the products or services that they make possible?

Sustained strength is strength continually renewed. It rests upon the ability to create and replenish knowledge and capabilities – through a unique combination of internal efforts, market transactions, mergers and acquisitions, and product and knowledge links. Embedded knowledge is especially useful to firms, since it buys them time in which they can further build skills and reap profits for reinvestment in better technol-ogy, customer support, new products, and so forth. Embedded knowl-edge also gives firms more bargaining chips for negotiating alliances, and it helps attract a wider set of prospective partners. GM's North American distribution network, the bundle of skills and capabilities that Toyota has perfected in its Toyota City operations, and Fanuc's prowess at designing and manufacturing robots have opened doors to many possible relationships for each firm and have strengthened their hands in bargaining.

The second condition is that managers must consider a wide range of possible alliances. Alliances can greatly expand the opportunities managers have to build their companies' core capabilities. When managers consider possible alliances, they have three pivotal decisions to make. The first is the choice of a partner. As this study has shown, a firm may choose any type of organization, at home or overseas, as a partner. GM's and IBM's remarkable collections of partners link them with competitors, suppliers of parts and components, the UAW, the Media Lab at MIT, and government bodies here and abroad.

The second choice is deciding which activities the co-operative endeavour will undertake. IBM's and GM's new relationships show that all of the classical business functions can be performed collaboratively – including marketing, manufacturing, R&D and finance, as well as decisions about pricing, capacity, product lines, and even strategy. The third choice establishes the form of the relationship. Both IBM and GM have relied upon joint ventures, licensing agreements, minority equity investments and forums for technical collaboration, as well as less formal, more flexible arrangements based on long-standing relationships and mutual trust.

Just as DNA, the biochemical building block of life, combines into myriad forms, so these three deceptively simple decisions can be made in an unlimited variety of ways, creating relationships between organizations that range from loose and tenuous links to close, intricate, time-honoured ties. In making these decisions, managers can act boldly. One example is the multiplicity of alliances that IBM Japan has created. These transformed it quickly and dramatically from a large IBM overseas subsidiary into a true Japanese enterprise group. GM's alliances in Korea are another example. They are not simply tie-ups with companies in the Daewoo Group. Like Japan in the 1950s and 1960s, Korea in the 1980s pursued a strategy of international development orchestrated by government planners, its Ministry of Finance, major banks, and the heads of the conglomerate groups that dominate the Korean economy. Daewoo was among the most important of these groups, and its businesses competed in all the strategic sectors of the Korean economy. Through the Daewoo relationship, GM had, in effect, a loose partnership with 'Korea Incorporated'.

The third condition is that before committing their company to an alliance, managers must scrutinize the values, commitment and capabilities of prospective partners. In order to assess a possible partner's values and culture, a manager must be aware of many varied and often subtle factors. Companies, like other social communities, develop norms of behaviour, symbols and ways of interpreting the environment. They resemble villages, which seem similar to a traveller passing quickly through, but which are idiosyncratic and sometimes even inexplicable to those who stop and stay a while. Complex cultural differences distinguish firms, not only in the same country, but even in the same city and the same industry. Some crucial questions that managers must ask are: Does the company (or university laboratory or government body or labour union) make decisions in a centralized or decentralized way? What vision of the future are its leaders pursuing? Do its managers seem open or secretive? How do they treat each other? Does the prospective partner seem to value internal co-operation? What relative values does it place on technology, marketing, product quality and financial results? What attitude toward risk do its past actions imply? What kind of company do its customers, suppliers, and competitors think it is? There is no checklist that guarantees coverage of all relevant factors, but the answers to questions like these help managers to sketch a composite picture of a potential ally. The more closely the two companies' values match, the better a partnership's prospects.

Assessment of a possible ally's capabilities also requires a strategic perspective. An attractive partner for a knowledge link has a combination of products, knowledge, technology, capabilities, financial strength, and talent. Moreover, its strategy commits it to use or develop these capabilities in an alliance, rather than through independent efforts, mergers, or market transactions. By determining the prospective partner's strategic intent, managers can find out how serious the partner is about the alliance and what calibre of personnel and resources it is likely to commit; with this information, they will be better able to protect their firm's interests. Working with a prospective partner on a small preliminary project is often a safe way to get a clearer sense of the other party's culture and capabilities before creating a full-scale alliance. In the end, a promising ally should show depth of capabilities and commitment, not just capital or the capacity to produce a single product cheaply today. Such an ally will be able to adapt and persevere when technology, exchange rates, markets and government policies change, as they surely will.

The fourth condition is that managers must understand the risks of opportunism, knowledge leaks and obsolescence. The question of opportunism and self-interest is especially pressing when partners want to create new knowledge and capabilities. Dealings between companies engaged in knowledge-intensive competition are unlikely to be guided solely by harmony and goodwill. The race to develop knowledge and capabilities is just as intense, conflict-ridden and plagued by opportunism as were past battles for crucial resources, or the trade routes connecting Renaissance city-states. Often, the partners are competing with each other – for profits, market share, resources and knowledge – at the same time as they co-operate. In other cases, they may become competitors in the future.

When a firm forms a partnership with a strong, successful competitor – as GM did with Toyota – this problem can become acute. How much will a powerful partner be willing to commit to an alliance if it is competing against its ally in other markets? Common sense and business experience both suggest that the general answer is, 'No more than necessary.' Toyota did not join forces with GM out of an altruistic desire to aid the firm that was among its most dangerous adversaries. Rather, Toyota joined NUMMI at a moment of vulnerability. Rising protectionist barriers in the United States were threatening its strategy of exporting aggressively from its Japanese production base. Toyota's competitors, Nissan and Honda, had much more experience than Toyota in managing overseas operations – because of Honda's experience in the motorcycle business and because both Nissan and Honda had been forced overseas by Toyota's strength in the domestic market. But in the early 1980s, Toyota had no experience with US workers and labour unions, US suppliers and truckers, or managing a large overseas operation, and its efforts to form an alliance with Ford had failed. NUMMI provided Toyota with the opportunity to learn about American business, and consequently it agreed to a joint venture with GM, even though it knew it was providing GM with a badly needed apprenticeship in Toyota's skills and management practices.

Toyota drove a hard bargain. The car that NUMMI first assembled was neither new nor stylish nor technologically sophisticated, but a vehicle Toyota had already been making and selling in Japan for several years. In the jargon of Detroit, the Chevrolet Nova was a 'econobox,' a small, fuel-efficient, well-made, unobtrusive vehicle. Also, Toyota permitted GM to sell only a four-door vehicle, keeping the two-door hatchback for itself. The latter car, the Corolla FX, sold successfully through Toyota dealerships without the financial incentives of several hundred dollars per car that GM offered with the Nova by 1987. In addition, the major components of the car, including the drive train, were made in Toyota City, so Toyota captured the margins and scale economies of their manufacture and kept their engineering and production away from GM's gaze.

Alliances, especially knowledge links, create the risk that knowledge and capabilities will flow to partners in unintended and harmful ways, through the actions of technicians or managers who are several levels below the executives responsible for an operation. In most cases, knowledge and capabilities do not migrate because a firm's partners are devious or predatory.[3] Rather, many of the relationships described in this book have been created expressly to combine the capabilities and knowledge of two firms. This means that each partner is expected to learn a certain amount about the other's capabilities and that channels of communication have been opened by them.

Knowledge links, managed carelessly, can become knowledge leaks. Over the years, the little brother in an alliance can outgrow and even dominate the older sibling. For example, in the 1960s, Honeywell relied on NEC to sell simple computers in Japan and to supply basic components. The relationship provided easy profits for Honeywell and an opportunity to fully exploit the sales potential of its older technology. As time passed, however, NEC's capabilities grew – by dint of its own efforts and through what it learned from its partners, including Honeywell. Ultimately, NEC became the dominant partner in its relationship with Honeywell. Its computer division was by far the larger of the two, and some of its technology was among the most advanced in the world. NEC became the principal hardware suppliers to a three-way joint venture in which the other partners were Honeywell and France's Group Bull – an arrangement that most industry analysts regarded as a Honeywell retreat from the computer business.

Risks such as these are not reasons to shun alliances. Inevitably, a company will strengthen its partner – the ally would not have decided to join a partnership without the prospect of gain. GM strengthened Isuzu, Suzuki and Daewoo by selling their cars through its North American dealer network. As with any business risk, the key questions are whether the risks have been assessed accurately, whether they are justified by the possible benefits and whether they can be managed, or better still, reduced. For years, the Big Three US auto firms underestimated the risks posed by their Japanese adversaries. GM may have underestimated the risks that Toyota would learn more from NUMMI than it would learn – because it was run by Toyota managers who were forced to learn to work with American workers, suppliers, and labour unions – and the risk that Toyota would deploy what it learned more quickly than GM by transferring its new skills to its Greenfield, Kentucky plant. Hence, an important part of assessing a partnership's risks is asking how dangerous and how likely the worst-case scenario is. What are the chances that a partner will garner key knowledge and rapidly exploit it? How much damage would this cause?

The fifth condition is avoiding undue dependence on alliances. Alliances, in general, should be ways of supplementing and improving a firm's embedded knowledge, not substitutes for internal development. GM limited its dependence on its Asian allies through its Saturn project, which was an attempt to independently replenish the knowledge and capabilities crucial to its business.

Companies can also reduce dependence by being extremely cautious about alliances with competitors or alliances involving its core capabilities. British Prime Minister Palmerston said that Britain had no permanent friends or permanent enemies, only permanent interests. A firm's foremost interest must be in safeguarding and strengthening its core knowledge and skills.[4] (Sometimes a weak firm has no choice but to enter a perilous relationship. Its executives should at least have their eyes open as they do so.) Both GM and IBM have followed this guideline in forming their new relationships. None of IBM's partnerships involved the manufacture, design, or sale of mainframe computers, which were its core skills. Furthermore, when IBM sought to link its personal computers with other computers and mainframes in large networks, it reduced its dependence on outside suppliers of parts and components. The PS/2 System is dramatically different – except for its software, which is designed by Microsoft, IBM's long-time ally, the system is proprietary. IBM designs and manufactures its crucial components in highly auto-mated, wholly owned and carefully guarded facilities.

GM considered but ultimately rejected a joint venture with EDS. If a joint effort with EDS had produced a breakthrough – new knowledge about automating automotive design, for example – then EDS, an extre-mely aggressive, market-oriented company, could have moved quickly to commercialize its new knowledge, possibly taking it to Ford, Chrysler, and other GM competitors. 'Not-to-compete' clauses and other legal arrangements might have contained the problem, but enforcing such agreements if often costly and time-consuming and it is ultimately frustrating when the knowledge at issue has already escaped. By owning EDS and Hughes Aircraft, GM could control the pace and direction of the flow of new knowledge. It secured ultimate control of both firms by owning them, thereby gaining assurance that the skills and knowledge it created through its joint efforts with each would be sold to other firms at a time and in a manner of GM's choosing.

When alliances do involve core capabilities, whether directly or indir-ectly, executives must guard against shifts in the balance of power, manoeuvres by other parties, and the expropriation of vital knowledge or capabilities. Managing a firm's boundaries involves carefully moni-toring all of a company's relationships for such dangers. A firm that has large-scale, complex relationships with another organization should assign a single executive to be 'gatekeeper'. The gatekeeper is responsible for overseeing all dealings between the organizations.[5]

Finally and paradoxically, a company can sometimes reduce its depen-dence on an alliance either by creating several similar alliances or by seeking to be the senior partner in the relationship. Toyota and Daewoo provided GM with different versions of the same product: high-quality, low-cost small cars. Toyota exercises hegemonic influence over its family of suppliers. It usually buys a large fraction of their output, often helps finance them, provides equipment and managerial advice and some-times lends its executives to them. Above all, it has integrated their production operations, intricately and intimately, with its assembly operations through JIT.

The sixth condition is that a company's alliances must be structured and managed like separate companies. Even if managers deal successfully with opportunistic partners, excessive dependence and knowledge leaks, they face another set of challenges once an alliance has been established.

These are the challenges of managing the myriad day-by-day and month-by-month details of successful co-operation.

The list of these challenges is lengthy.[6] Partners' accounting systems, compensation practices, management styles and culture sometimes differ significantly. The fact that a joint activity inevitably has two bosses – or more, depending on how many parents it has – can complicate and slow decision making. Even if one of the partners is given full responsibility for the day-to-day management of the operation, the parents must agree on major decisions. Special circumstances can add other difficulties. GM's dealings with its Asian partners were also complicated by antitrust scrutiny in the United States. The FTC required that Toyota and GM keep detailed logs describing discussions and transactions between the two companies. None of GM's other relationships were subject to this degree of scrutiny, but several of them required lengthy meetings with the FTC or the Antitrust Division of the Justice Department, as well as continuing reports on the ventures.

In order to overcome these challenges, managers should design an alliance as if they were establishing a separate company. An alliance should be a sphere of activity with an explicit mission and specific performance objectives, a timetable for their achievement, its own resources and control systems, and personnel with a sense of loyalty and commitment to the alliance's success. It should have clear guidance on what technology and know-how will be contributed to the alliance, what will remain proprietary and what administrative mechanisms will resolve questionable cases. Through such arrangements managers can work closely with personnel from other organizations without risking the loss of knowledge and capabilities that would imperil the firm's strategic interests. In the creation of these unique, often fragile, mini-companies, painstaking attention to detail is crucial. In the phrase of architect Mies van der Rohe, 'God resides in the details.'

The managers of an alliance and the executives of their parent companies need to know what technological, financial and competitive aims the alliance is intended to achieve. They should set clear milestones and performance measures so that everyone can assess its progress. The mission statement should also set clear limits on the partnership's activities. Can some of its activities overlap with those of a parent? Can it compete with its parent organizations? If so, in what markets? Of course, changes in market conditions and in the strategies of the parent companies, along with the trial-and-error approach inevitable in new endeavours and the constant proliferation of knowledge, preclude absolute clarity about an alliance's mission. As a result, some important details will have to be 'filled in later'. Hence, an alliance should include mechanisms – some formally specified in the initial contracts and others emerging only as the endeavour progresses – for resolving these issues as they arise. Moreover, the basic mission will have to be reviewed and updated by its parents, perhaps every three to five years. These reviews also provide occasions for firms to consider whether to expand their collaboration further. IBM Japan and NTT have gradually added joint ventures and other collaborative efforts to their initial alliance. Since 1971, GM and Isuzu have added partnerships in Great Britain and several developing countries.

Like an independent business, an alliance should be managed in a way that gives its personnel strong incentives to work for the success of the partnership, not merely of the parents. Successful relationships specify authority and roles. The parties involved know who is responsible for what and measurement systems assess the performance of the joint effort. Moreover, one partner should, in most cases, have day-to-day operating responsibility for managing an alliance. Studies of one common form of collaboration, joint ventures, have found that this approach raises the chances of success. A recent managerially oriented study concluded that 'the more "shared" the management of a venture promises to be, the more difficult it will be to manage . . . joint ventures in which both parents are heavily involved managerially have a much higher failure rate than those in which one or the other dominates.'[7]

Each party should assign managers, engineers and other personnel who are committed to making the venture work. And, beyond good intentions, they need the right skills. Each party tends to judge the other's commitment by the calibre of personnel assigned to the joint endeavour. Once assigned, crucial personnel should not be quickly rotated out of the alliance and back to the parent company. Fledgling enterprises need stability and the sharing or creation of embedded knowledge requires close, long-term, apprentice-like efforts.

If possible, a partnership should begin with small trial efforts at collaboration, so the parties can see whether their two cultures are sufficiently compatible and whether 'champions' emerge on both sides – that is, managers with appropriate skills who are personally committed to making the venture work. At bottom, co-operative arrangements are not fundamentally links between one firm and another, nor do they connect firms and labour unions or firms and government agencies. Such abstractions do not exist, and they cannot have relationships with each other. Only individuals and small groups can. Hence, the success of a collaboration depends on whether specific individuals in separate organizations can work together and accomplish joint tasks.

The seventh condition is that the partners must come to trust each other. When managers are asked what matters most to successful alliances, they say consistently and with conviction that trust and open communication are indispensable.[8] Openness is paramount in knowledge links because much of what the parties are trying to learn from each other or create together is so difficult to communicate. It is often embedded in a firm's practices and culture, and it can only be learned through working relationships that are not hampered by constraints.

When two competitors join forces, as in the case of GM and Toyota, the problem of trust becomes even more troublesome. Managers on each side know how to treat competitors: with caution and suspicion. Employees are naturally inclined to hold their cards close to their chest, limiting collaboration with their partner. Every alliance is a unique, sometimes fragile, managerial and economic enterprise, with inescapable difficulties, errors and surprises that can fester and swell into divisive issues. If an alliance encounters difficulty, partners can easily make scapegoats of each other. Mistrust, whatever its origins, breeds inflexibility. Studies have confirmed that when the parents of a joint venture trust each other, they are more inclined to grant substantial autonomy to managers, enabling them to respond more quickly to problems and opportunities and thereby raising the venture's chances of success.[9] The parties in a collaborative relationship are dependent on each other. Hence, the promotions, bonuses and careers of the managers involved depend on the performance of the outside parties, with whom they have no prior experience and whose values and culture may differ radically from their own. In such situations, parties that do not trust each other are likely to create elaborate systems for running the joint endeavour, monitoring each other, and adjudicating disputes. Bureaucracy is a costly substitute for trust.

After an alliance is created, managers on both sides should expect to spend a great deal of time trying to make the relationship flourish. Ideally, the parties will begin working together on tasks at which they are likely to succeed. Then, rather than blame each other for frustrations and failures that often occur when initial tasks prove too difficult, both sides will grow more confident about the future. Moreover, the learning process, in organizations as in the world at large, usually takes place through a long series of small steps. The accumulation of small successes will reinforce this process.

The eighth condition is that managers must change their core operations and traditional organizations so that they will be open to learning from alliances. Successful alliances also depend upon the right relationship between the partnership and the organizations that create it. Consider, for example, a company that wants to create a knowledge link with a supplier so that the firms can work jointly to develop and test components for a new generation of products. The relationship will probably fail if the buyer does not change its procurement practices. The classic clerk with a green eyeshade who sends out purchase orders twice a year and chooses the lowest bidder cannot be the focal point of a knowledge-driven relationship with suppliers. Instead there must be collaboration among research, engineering and marketing people from both the buyer and the supplier.

GM and its Asian partners created several organizational structures to manage their relationships.[10] For Isuzu and Suzuki, GM stationed personnel in Tokyo to facilitate their dealings with Chevrolet. These included marketing, manufacturing and engineering consultants, as well as planners, procurement and distribution managers, and industry analysts. At the Daewoo Motor Company, GM was represented by a career executive who lived in Korea and served as executive president of the Daewoo Motor Company and its joint representative director. Roughly two-thirds of GM's Japanese suppliers had sales offices in the United States. Their representatives called on individual GM divisions and could summon engineering support, either from the United States or from Japan. At the same time, GM units like Delco and Harrison Radiator based managers in Japan to help co-ordinate relationships. GM also created a separate organization called Overseas Components Activities (OCA) that served as a bridge between divisions and its Japanese suppliers.

Even with such administrative arrangements firmly in place, a company can face difficulty in getting its own organization to take new, affiliated companies and their products seriously. Often, the cause is the 'not-invented-here' syndrome. In other cases, functional personnel on both sides of a relationship complain about the division of labour and opportunities, saying that activities or investment funds were being diverted to a partner or to a joint venture rather than being given to them. The creation of a partnership is often viewed as evidence that some members of an organization have failed to perform as they should. Even when there are no clearly defined losers, collaboration may nevertheless bear the aura of failure or defeat. When GM linked itself with Toyota, it was conceding that Toyota – which two decades earlier had been mocked in Detroit for making tiny vehicles called Toyopets – could now teach it important lessons.

How seriously each partner views a relationship also depends upon the market conditions it faces. When demand for a company's products is strong, its alliances are not given high priority, since they do not seem to fill an urgent need. When demand is weak, personnel and managers tend to concentrate almost exclusively on fixing their own company's problems, and they pay less attention to distant overseas relationships. Only when demand falls into some intermediate zone are these relations taken completely seriously.

Companies must sometimes be willing to modify initial arrangements if they are to get the full benefit of the knowledge and capabilities of their partner. To its credit, IBM modified its relationship with Rolm several times – from partial equity ownership to full ownership of an independent subsidiary to integration in IBM's operations – before abandoning the effort. In contrast, GM has been criticized for failing to create organizational arrangements that would help it learn from NUMMI. In 1986, an MIT report concluded that the plant tours, videotapes and manuals GM relied upon had conveyed only 'a very partial understanding of NUMMI's procedures'.[11] This suggested GM had failed to appreciate that learning and communicating embedded knowledge is far more difficult than passing along migratory knowledge.

GM's experience with efforts to transfer knowledge and capabilities led one of its executives to specify ten steps crucial for success. They were:

1 Involve prospective users up front.
2 Encourage users to participate in the development of the technology.
3 Apply the new technology to a few critical problems before attempting to transfer it.
4 Package the technology so it is accessible to users.
5 Provide formal training in using the new technology.
6 Follow up to determine the effectiveness of the transfer process.
7 Provide users with the opportunities to meet collectively and share their experiences with the technology.
8 Do not rely solely on written reports to sell technology.
9 Be willing to provide resources such as people, time, and money to sell the technology.
10 Consider transferring people along with the technology.[12]

The final condition is that alliances must be led, not just managed. Even when it is done brilliantly, organizational design and attention to administrative detail alone cannot ensure the success of an alliance. Through words and actions, senior executives must clearly communicate the purpose, importance, and legitimacy of each alliance. They also need to set personal examples of commitment, patience and flexibility, in order to show how concerned they are that the relationship succeed. A sense of urgency about taking advantage of alliances is particularly important in firms that have managed themselves as citadels in the past. Critics of GM's use of its Asian alliances often refer to GM's decades-long tradition of concentrating on building large cars for the North American market in fully owned North American facilities. IBM faces similar difficulties in shifting attention away from its long-established focus on building mainframes and selling them to large corporations.

Flexibility goes hand in hand with patience. Some executives and many middle-level personnel have ideas about strategy that are far too rigid for the fluid, knowledge-driven, competition-driven world of alliances. The alliance strategies of GM and IBM did not spring full-blown from the minds of corporate strategists. Rather, GM's strategy for dealing with the diffusion of small car know-how and IBM's strategy for dealing with the migration of technology for personal computers reflected the turbulence of a time when knowledge was being created at an accelerating pace and was migrating in surprising directions. In what Peter Drucker has called the 'age of discontinuity' strategy cannot be the equivalent of engineering blueprints conceptualized at one point and then cast in bronze forever. Strategy is the evolution of a central idea over a long period of trial and error. It is a pattern of decisions that evolves over time under the aegis of a few broad central objectives.

REFERENCES

1 This chapter draws heavily on more than 30 interviews I conducted with managers involved in the joint activities of GM and IBM. In these, I discussed lessons they had drawn from their experience managing alliances.

  In addition, the chapter draws on Vernon, R., *Sovereignty at Bay*, Basic Books, New York, 1972; Stopford, J. M. and Wells, Jr., L. T., *Managing the Multinational Enterprise: The Organization of the Firm and Ownership of the Subsidiaries*, Basic Books, New York, 1972; Franko, L. G., *Joint Venture Survival in Multinational Corporations*, Praeger, New York, 1973; Contractor, F. J. and Lorange, P. *Cooperative Strategies in International Business*, Lexington Books, Lexington, MA, 1987, pp. 253–369; Harringan, K. Rudie, *Strategies for Joint Ventures*, Lexington Books, Lexington, MA, 1985, pp. 355–75; and Gomes-Casseres, B., 'Multinational Ownership Strategies', unpublished Ph.D. diss., Harvard Business School, Boston, 1985.
2 A comprehensive framework for thinking through these issues appears in Prahalad, C. K. and Hamel, G., 'The Core Competence of the Corporation', *Harvard Business Review*, May–June 1990, pp. 79–91.
3 A persuasive argument that the balance of benefits in relationships often changes, not as a result of perfidy, but because of harder work, better business judgment, and superior strategy by one of the partners, is found in Hamel, G., Doz, Y. L. and Prahalad, C. K., 'Collaborate with Your Competitor – and Win', *Harvard Business Review* January–February 1989, pp. 113–39.
4 For evidence that firms have often followed this precept, see Gomes-Casseres, B., 'Joint Ventures in the Face of Global Competition', *Sloan Management Review*, Spring 1989, pp. 17–26.
5 The role of a gatekeeper is described in detail in Hamel, Doz, and Prahalad, 'Collaborate with Your Competitor – and Win', pp. 136–39.
6 Studies of joint ventures corroborate many of these concerns. For example, two scholars concluded that:

  Long overseas experience on the part of a firm goes hand in hand with the preference for wholly owned subsidiaries over joint ventures (and a preference for any kind of subsidiary over a license) . . . where an effective strategy demands that the firm should be able to exercise a high degree of control over its foreign affiliates, the presence of other parties participating in the direction of the affiliate will be counted as a negative factor.

  See Vernon, R. and Wells, Jr., L. T., *The Manager in the International Economy*, Engleswood Cliffs, NJ: Prentice-Hall, 1986, p. 64. A recent study of 35 North American and Western European joint ventures, in contrasting them with internal efforts, concluded that 'joint ventures are a much more difficult form of organization to manage well'. See Killing, J. P., *Strategies for Joint Venture Success*, New York: Praeger, 1983, pp. 8–12.

Another study, this one of joint ventures between US and Japanese companies in the 1960s and 1970s, led its authors to conclude that 'the joint venture has always been an awkward compromise of conflicting interests'. See Abegglen, J. C. and Stalk, G. C., *Kaisha*, New York: Basic Books, 1985, pp. 226–31. A. McKinsey & Company study concluded that of all the firms that started out with some general intention of creating a partnership with another firm, only about two per cent eventually created an arrangement that proved to be a long-term success. Of course, many of them did not proceed with their initial concept and others, who could not find a suitable partner with whom to do business, were never able to test their concept. But even in the cases where two firms signed a formal agreement, only one in three lasted beyond the lifetime of the product lines involved in the partnerships. See Alster, N., 'Dealbusters: Why Partnerships Fail', *Electronic Business*, April 1, 1986, p. 72. George Taucher, a professor of business administration at IMEDE in Switzerland, has concluded even more pessimistically that 'strategic alliances are doomed'. He gives four basic reasons for his view: firm's shifting strategies, the sheer complexity of many alliances, lack of a clear decision-making focus, and career considerations that create conflicts between the goals of the alliance and the self-interests of the managers involved. See Taucher, G., 'Beyond Alliances', IMEDE: Perspectives for Managers, no. 1, 1988.

7 Killing, J. P. *Strategies for Joint Venture Success*, p. 84.
8 Managers use other terms, such as credibility, a sense of personal obligation, commitment, mutual respect, a capacity for listening and understanding – a family of precepts closely related to trust and open communication. In a similar vein, the author of a recent study of 35 joint ventures in North America and Western Europe observed that:

If you ask parent company personnel about the success of their joint ventures, in nine of ten answers the idea of a trust will figure prominently. The following comment . . . is quite typical: 'So far, we have enjoyed very successful experiences with all our foreign partners. Profits and growth in the environment of trust and mutual respect have been the gold rules of our relationship.'

See Killing, J. P., *Strategies for Joint Venture Success*, p. 82. Evidence for the importance of trust also comes from studies of the factors that contributed to successful co-operative endeavours such as joint ventures. See also Flick, S. E., 'The Human Side of Overseas Joint Ventures', *Management Review* January 1972, p. 29; Zimmerman, M., *How to Do Business with the Japanese*, New York: Random House, 1985; Wright, R. W. 'Joint Venture Problems in Japan', *Columbia Journal of World Business*, Spring 1979, pp. 25–31.

Even in the United States, with its reputation for individualism and litigiousness, there is evidence that many important economic activities are governed mainly by informal, private arrangements based on trust and confidence. See, for example, Macaulay, S., 'Non-Contractual Relations in Business: A Preliminary Study', *American Sociological Review*, Spring 1963, pp. 55–67. Macaulay concluded that 'businessmen often prefer to rely on "a man's word" in a brief letter, a handshake, or "common honesty and decency" – even when the transaction involved exposure to serious risk.' Even when two companies did use a contract to specify formally their relationship, Macaulay found that legal sanctions were rarely used to make adjustments when subsequent events made adjustments necessary. One executive who participated in this study said, 'You can settle any dispute if you keep the lawyers and the accountants out of it. They just do not understand the give and take needed in business.' (*ibid.*, p. 61.)

9 For a detailed analysis of this observation about joint ventures, see Killing, J. P., *Strategies for Joint Venture Success*, pp. 82–5.

10 This description of the organization of GM's activities in Japan is based on interviews with GM personnel at the General Motors Overseas Corporation in Tokyo and in Detroit, and on internal documents they provided.

11 The study, by James P. Wonrock, is cited in Keller, M., *Rude Awakening*, New York: William Morrow, 1989, p. 134.

12 Wolff, M. F., 'Technology Transfer: A GM Manager's Strategy', *Research-Technology Management* (September/October 1989), pp. 9–10.

Reproduced from Badaracco, Joseph L., Jr., *The Knowledge Link*, Harvard Business School Press, Boston, MA, 1991. Chapter 6, pp. 129–146 (plus notes).

Chapter 13

Building core skills

Andrew Campbell

INTRODUCTION

Decentralized companies are currently wrestling with the problem of how to manage skills and competences across their portfolio of businesses. This paper describes how managers at the centre can define which skills they should focus on and what role the centre should take in managing them.

Prior to the 1980s, companies handled skills that were important to more than one business unit through strong central functions. Many companies had large central functions such as marketing, engineering or information technology (IT). British Petroleum, for example, had a central engineering function of more than 1500 people as recently as the mid 1980s. These central functions set policies and standards throughout the corporation. They also controlled most of the recruitment, in particular the graduate intake, organized training and acted as skill reservoirs for their companies.

In the 1980s, companies started to decentralize these central functions and reduce the size of corporate headquarters. Where functions were retained, their policy-making role was reduced and their service role emphasized.[1] At BP, for example, a previously strong IT function was set up as in internal consulting service, selling its expertise to the business units. Over a short period the function shrank by more than half its former size because the business units chose not to use its services.

There were a number of reasons why these changes took place. First, nimble *niche competitors* focused on specific segments of the market and took away market share from the established competitors. In response, the larger companies had to segment their business into market-focused and competitor-focused units, giving the managers of these business units the freedom to take whatever action was necessary to compete in the new environment. The increased competition from focused businesses caused large companies – most recently IBM is an example – to give more autonomy to their business unit managers and reduce the size and influence of central functions.

Second, there was a growing *perception of mismanagement by the centre*. The central functions were frequently seen as bureaucratic and unresponsive to the needs of the businesses. One business unit chief executive told us: 'The problem with central marketing is that they are always right. It is always someone else's fault. You would think we existed to serve them rather than the other way round.'

Often the centre was criticized for imposing inappropriate skills. We were told by the head of a record retailer: 'We have a completely different security problem to that of our sister company, yet we were forced to use the central security service. Their problem is mainly about shrinkage caused by customers. Our problem is staff. You can't use the same security principles to solve both problems.'

In other cases central functions were criticized for using the wrong methods of mechanisms: they imposed central standards in situations where businesses needed flexibility to meet customer needs; they set up co-ordination committees between managers who had few common interests; they ran expensive conferences for managers with little to learn from each other; and they centralized the development resources and budgets in situations where variety of development efforts would have been more suitable.

A third reason for decentralization was that *skills became less scarce*. Historically, central functions had existed in part because of the scarcity of skills. But, over time, the business units were more able to do their own work in areas like engineering and IT, and external suppliers were more available in everything from catering services to corporate strategic planning. The availability of skills and competent external suppliers made central functions less necessary. They could no longer benefit the organization by acting as a skill reservoir.

SKILLS MANAGEMENT NEGLECTED

The decentralization trend has undoubtedly produced net benefits. Greater freedom and accountability have promoted initiative at the business unit level, and this has resulted in increased performance. But decentralization has also had a cost. As companies decentralized and reduced the control exerted by the corporate centre, they have used 'lateral linkages', such as informal networking and corporate-wide projects, to replace the central functions.[2] For example, when Electrolux acquired businesses in the white goods industry with the intention of developing an international strategy, it did not centralize any functions. Instead it set up formal co-ordination in four product areas, networking mechanisms to encourage cross-fertilization, and five corporate-wide projects designed to improve operating performance.

However, for many companies, these lateral linkages have proven harder to operate than expected. 'Horizontal planning', as Michael Porter calls it, has frequently been crowded out by vertical, strategic business unit (SBU) planning.[3] Co-ordinating committees and networking mechanisms have often proved time-consuming and delivered little value.[4] Business unit managers have developed an aversion to corporate projects, which they see as a distraction from their real priorities. And most personnel functions have not taken on the functional training or functional recruitment activities of the old central functions. The result of all these changes is that some important corporate skills are no longer being adequately managed.[5]

In this chapter we attempt to show that companies pursuing decentralization do not need to lose control of the management of these key skills. Based on our interviews with a sample of exemplar companies (Figure 13.1), we describe a systematic approach to the management of skills that involves:

1 identifying the company's 'core skills' in detail;
2 understanding the different roles the centre can play in developing and transferring those core skills across the business units;
3 choosing an approach that makes commercial sense and takes in account the company's capability and natural way of working.

IDENTIFYING CORE SKILLS

The first problem facing managers in decentralized companies is to decide what skills to try to build. At one level this may be a trivial question. If the businesses in the portfolio are mainly consumer packaged goods, as in Unilever, then one of the important core skill areas is marketing. If most of the businesses are connected by common technologies, such as precision coatings and polymers, as in 3M, then a core skill area is the technology itself.

But at the level of detail needed for taking management action the identification of core skills is not straightforward. For example, within the marketing function at Unilever it is necessary to decide which marketing skills are core and which are not. For example, is consumer research a core skill area that needs to be managed? Is new product testing? Is advertising agency selection? Is product positioning? Is product packaging? And, outside of the marketing area, is sales-force management a core skill that Unilever's central management should be focusing on? Is industrial selling? Is the management of multicountry retailers? Central managers need to develop a way of identifying the

---

Sample

A sample of companies were chosen on three criteria. First, companies where management were prepared to give us broad interviewing access. Second, companies where management believed they were good at transferring skills and capabilities across the portfolio. Third, companies we had reason to believe were well managed. The companies in the sample were:

Courtaulds	– Protective Coatings Division
Mars	– Confectionery Division
3M	– Technical Division
Philips	– UK Division
Shell	– Automotive Marketing Division
Unilever	– Personal Products Division
Whitbread	– Restaurants Division

Methods

At each site we focused our interviews on one or two functional areas, choosing, in each case, a function of critical importance to the business.

Interviews aimed to achieve three outputs:

1 Document linkage benefit stories: situations where a business unit had benefited from learning from another part of the group.

2 Record the linkage mechanisms being used by the companies to encourage skill development and transfer.

3 Understanding the commercial and organizational context in which the linkages were happening.

Figure 13.1 Research sample and methods

skill areas that will benefit the most from some central involvement in developing and transferring best practice.

To do this central managers need to understand the connection between skills and competitive advantage and the difference between the centre's role in managing the skills of a single business unit and managing core skills across business units.

Understanding skills

Skills are important to competitive advantage. To succeed against competitors, each business unit needs to have a strategy for gaining advantage in the market-place. Without some kind of advantage in meeting market needs a business unit cannot expect to out-perform its competitors.

Advantage can come from many different sources. Location can be a source of advantage, for example, due to lower labour costs in a particular area. Size can be a source of advantage due to economies of scale. But most sources of advantage are rooted in superior skills: the business makes better quality products, markets them better, has better sales people and looks after the customers better, because of some superior know-how.[6]

Few businesses have superior skills in all functions but successful businesses have a skill advantage in some functions important to the business unit's strategy. If the strategy is about quality, the unit is likely to have an advantage in manufacturing skill or in total quality management. If the strategy is about service, then the business will need to have some advantage in service skills either through designing better systems or easier to service products.

With this understanding of skills, we can draw a 'skill tree' for a business unit that links the 'key business skills' with the needs of the market place (Figure 13.2). A key business skill is an activity the business needs to do particularly well to succeed with its strategy. Most strategies involve a cluster of key business skills. The confectionery business at Mars needs to have strong skills in volume manufacturing, quality management, product branding and new product development to succeed with its strategy of being the brand leader in the mass-market, countline-dominated, snack-food sector of the confectionery market.

Each key business skill in the cluster can be analysed further into 'components' and 'sub-components'.[7] Components are the factors needed to perform the key business skill to a high standard. Components can be broken down into sub-components and to even finer levels of detail. Figure 13.3 is an illustrative 'skill component analysis' of an important skill area in Whitbread Restaurants – delivering delightful service.

Figure 13.2 Skill tree

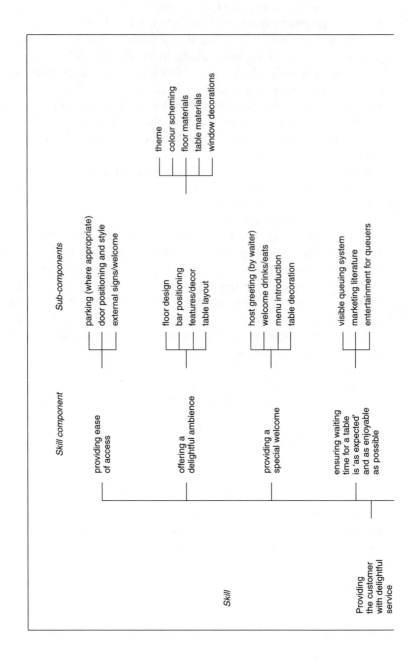

Skill

Providing the customer with delightful service

Skill component

providing ease of access

offering a delightful ambience

providing a special welcome

ensuring waiting time for a table is 'as expected' and as enjoyable as possible

Sub-components

parking (where appropriate)
door positioning and style
external signs/welcome

floor design
bar positioning
features/decor
table layout

host greeting (by waiter)
welcome drinks/eats
menu introduction
table decoration

visible queuing system
marketing literature
entertainment for queuers

theme
colour scheming
floor materials
table materials
window decorations

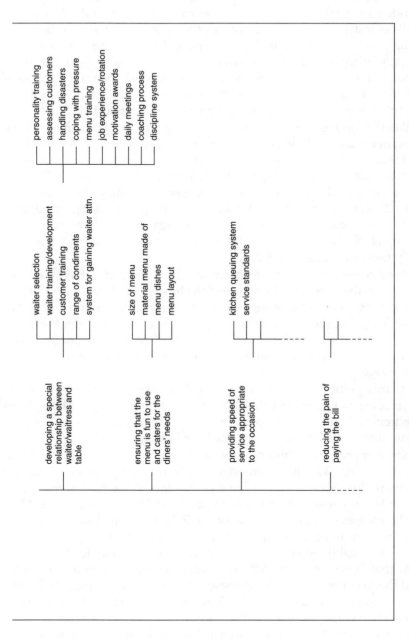

Figure 13.3 Skill components and sub-components

The figure illustrates the broad range of components that make up a business skill. Some components are inanimate, such as the quality of the parking facilities or the quality of the ambience. Others depend on the skills of individuals or teams such as the greeting of guests or the waitering. The way we are using the phrase 'business skill' is, therefore, slightly different from the normal use of the word skill. A business skill is something the business, as a whole, does well whether it is because of the skills of the employees or because of inanimate factors such as the layout of the work floor or the quality of the materials being used.

Each component of a business skill depends on know-how. If the component is a skill such as waitering, the know-how may be embedded in the individual waiters or waitresses. If the component is inanimate like the size of the menu, the know-how is likely to be codified as recorded knowledge (e.g. a menu becomes daunting if it has more than 25 items on it). In any business skill there are a large number of components each of which depends on elements of know-how. It is, therefore, the management of the know-how that is critical to successfully managing business skills.

Some components are more important than others: they have a greater impact on the overall performance of the business skill. We can call these key components: components where the quality of the know-how can have a big impact on the overall performance. It is through these key components that a business can gain competitive advantage. By developing know-how that is superior to competitors a business can gain advantage.

At this point it is worth taking stock of the new language we are developing to understand skills. It consists of 'key business skills', 'skill components and sub-components', 'key components' and 'superior know-how'. The last two terms need further explanation.

Key components are those components that are critical to the building of a superior skill. Key components are the components where the company has or can develop some proprietary know-how, some superior ability or knowledge that is not widely used by its competitors. Most of the components of a business skill will be performed to a reasonable standard by most competitors. For example, most family restaurants serve reasonably good food on clean plates on clean tables in a restaurant that is not overcrowded. The difference between unusual service and the average does not lie in these standard components. It is the key components such as the behaviour of the waiter that distinguish between average and excellent service.

Of course businesses can have weaknesses even in standard components and part of the management task is to reduce the impact of weaknesses. However, as we will make clear later, it is through focusing on key components and on creating superior know-how that a group of businesses can build competitive advantage across its portfolio of businesses.

The thesis that we are presenting is, therefore, that understanding skills at a business level involves defining 'key business skills' and pinpointing the 'key components or sub-components' where 'superior know-how' can give the business a competitive advantage.

Managing skills from the centre

In many companies the strategic planning process is used to clarify the key business skills and to give the centre an opportunity to assess how the business unit is planning to develop its skills. In more advanced companies strategic controls are being developed to measure a business unit's performance in key areas.[8] The centre can, therefore, use a combination of planning processes and control procedures to make sure that the business units are devoting the necessary attention to their key business skills. The centre can audit the business unit's plan to make sure it will keep them ahead of competitors.

The management and building of 'core skills' across the portfolio of business units is a different process which requires a different role from the centre. A 'core skill' is a key business skill that is 'relevant' in a number of businesses in the portfolio (say at least a third) – property development in Whitbread Restaurants, component purchasing in Philips UK, colour mixing of paints in Courtaulds Protective Coatings, site selection in Shell's automotive retailing businesses. These are all key business skills for individual business units.

These skills are 'relevant' to sister companies in the portfolio, because they have 'key components' in common. It is rare that a key business skill is identical across a number of businesses: if the businesses are in different countries the markets and cultures are different; if the businesses are in the same country but in different products, then the technologies and customers will be slightly different. As a result, it is not common for a skill to be relevant in its entirety. A skill is normally relevant because it has key components in common and, in particular, because the superior know-how developed in one business can be used in the other businesses.

Where core skills exist, in other words where the businesses have key components in common, they centre has a role in managing the superior know-how that the businesses share. In these circumstances (Figure 13.4) the centre has a role that goes beyond just making sure that each business has a work plan for keeping ahead of competitors. The centre has a role in helping the businesses work together to speed up the development of know-how and ensure that the benefits are spread to the other business units.

---

1 The strategy of the business units are sufficiently similar that they have some key business skills in common:

- the same business in different countries; or
- similar businesses in different markets in the same country; or
- similar markets being served with different products.

2 The key business skills are sufficiently similar that they have some key components in common:

- superior know-how exists (or the potential for superior know-how) enabling at least one business unit to out perform competitors in the key business skill;
- the proprietary know-how can be used to advantage in the other businesses.

Figure 13.4 When will core skills exist?

The centre's role in building core skills

Building core skills involves managing the development and transfer of best practice in key skill components that are common across business units. Success comes from focusing on transferable best practice and the know-how that lies behind it. Skill trees and skill component analysis, defined in the previous section, are useful tools to help managers identify key skill components that involve transferable know-how.

The management of these key components involves making choices about how to develop proprietary know-how and how to transfer the benefits across the business units. In our field work we observed that companies chose different central roles for different components. These different roles are based on different levels of involvement in both *the development process* and the *transfer process*, and we were able to define *five generic approaches to managing core skills.*

THE DEVELOPMENT PROCESS

Proprietary know-how is the basis of superiority in a business unit's key business skills. It is normal, therefore, for business units to invest in the development of the know-how involved in the key components. With a portfolio of businesses with similar key components development of know-how can be occurring in all of the businesses simultaneously. The centre's role in this development process is to decide whether to interfere with the decentralized decision making of the separate business units.

At one extreme the centre can decide to remain detached from the development process allowing business units to carry out local development work against their local agendas and priorities. At the other extreme the centre can choose to take charge of development to gain from the benefits of economies of scale, to eliminate duplication or to ensure that sufficient money is spent. In between these extremes are many intermediate positionings in which the centre seeks to co-ordinate the work being carried out in different units. For example, in a company with a portfolio of retail businesses, development work on retail operating systems could be carried out centrally through a central systems unit; it could be done separately by each business developing enhancements to their existing systems; it could be done by a lead business with the intention of transferring the developments to other businesses; or it could be done by a combination of businesses working together or working with the centre.

In practice there are many variations and combinations. In some cases the resources are located in the centre, reporting to a central functional manager, yet many of the development projects are commissioned and directed by the business unit managers. In other cases the development work is carried out in the business units, but under the direction of a central development manager. By judging which manager had final authority over both the size and direction of development work we are able to develop a classification of the degree of centralization of the development process.[9]

The transfer process

The way in which the benefits of know-how are transferred across business units depends upon the nature of the know-how. If the know-how is embedded in the innate skills of individuals or teams, then the benefits of the know-how can be transferred by creating a central service built round these innate skills, by developing and transferring skilled individuals or by transferring the know-how involved in selecting, training and developing the skilled individuals. If the know-how is in the form of codified knowledge, it can be transferred by simple communication.

What we have observed is that the main concern of the centre is not so much the choice of mechanisms for transferring the benefit, but rather the choice of the degree of pressure the centre should exert to ensure that the transfer occurs.

The minimum level of pressure is where the centre seeks to make the less competent units aware of the know-how and skills available elsewhere, allowing the business unit managers to decide for themselves which mechanisms of transfer to use and how far to take advantage of the know-how. This can be done by creating networks of managers in different units, by newsletters and face-to-face communication, and even by offering expert help or services from the centre.

The maximum level of pressure is where the centre demands that the business units use the benefits of the available know-how and act quickly to discipline managers who are slow to respond. This can be done by issuing policy instructions, insisting on certain performance standards, removing reluctant managers and setting up central functions to carry out the activities concerned.

In between these two extremes there are many other positionings. The centre can exert pressure to transfer the benefits of know-how by vigorously challenging the managers in business units, applying peer pressure through committees or task forces and supplying performance data and benchmarks to embarrass the poor performers.

Five generic approaches to managing core skills

To simplify the date we collected, we developed a matrix: one axis represents the degree of central control in the development process, the other represents the level of pressure used by the centre in the transfer process (Figure 13.5). As we plotted company examples on this matrix, we identified five generic roles for the centre in managing core skills: 'stimulate the network', 'promote central developments', 'co-ordinate common solutions', 'impose best practice' and 'create a company way'.[10]

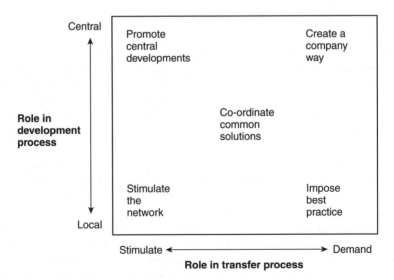

Figure 13.5 The role of the centre in managing core skills

- *Stimulate the network* is the central role that requires least involvement. Development is local and uncoordinated. The centre may stimulate development by encouraging business units to spend money on the area. But it does not attempt to control either the size of expenditure or the direction of development. Know-how is transferred between units through formal and informal networks. The centre will stimulate these networks by sharing information and creating opportunities for managers to meet each other. But the centre will not put pressure on individual businesses to take up know-how or best practice developed in other parts of the group. In decentralized companies the majority of key skill components are managed in this way because stimulating the network is the role that involves the least interference from the centre.
- The centre may decide to *promote central developments* in order to encourage the transfer of know-how that has been developed centrally. Even though the centre will have decided the size of the development budget and directed individual development projects, central managers may prefer to allow business unit managers to make their own decisions about whether to use these developments in their own businesses. It is common for the centre to take on this role for key components that involve scientific research and central laboratory work. For example, 3M has technical centres that are centrally controlled laboratories focusing on a technology with group-wide relevance. These laboratories have responsibility for advancing the technology. But they have no power to pressure divisions to use the technology they develop.
- *Co-ordinate common solutions* is a central role that involves working closely with business units on both development and transfer. Many cases fit this middle ground, where development efforts are jointly conceived and directed and the centre puts pressure on businesses that are slow to take up the new developments. The know-how advances that resulted in the deodorant Axe were developed by the French subsidiary of Unilever Personal Products as a result of a product concept brief defined by the centre. The centre then worked closely with other European countries to roll out the benefits of this know-how and attempted to persuade countries to stick closely to the original Axe concept. The centre and the French subsidiary continue to work together to refine the 'product instructions' based on experience and further know-how developments throughout Europe.

We noted that it is unusual for the centre to attempt to co-ordinate development work without also seeking to pressure businesses to implement the results of the development. It is also unusual for the centre to pressure businesses to accept skills and know-how from other business units without also seeking to influence the development efforts. As a result 'co-ordinate common solutions' is a role that covers all of the central ground in our matrix.

- *Impose best practice* is not a common role. We did however identify a few cases where the centre imposed know-how when it had not directed the development work. Companies adopt this approach when the centre discovers big discrepancies in performance in a skill area that is easily documented. For example, at Whitbread Restaurants, the centre noted that its Pizza Hut subsidiary was benefiting from having clearly defined quality standards for customer service. So it imposed this practice on the other restaurant chains. The centre did not impose particular standards. It imposed the policy that each restaurant should have defined standards. In other words it imposed a management process that was easy to document. We have found that this role – impose best practice – is most common in manufacturing and operating areas, particularly where the know-how is in the form of codified knowledge.
- The final approach, *create a company way*, involves the centre controlling development work and imposing methods and standards on the organization. It is a common role for the management of know-how in the finance and personnel functions and it is also widely used on issues where there is an additional benefit from consistency and standardization – for example in the know-how connected with brand names. The use of the Shell logo is centrally controlled by managers in the marketing division. They issue policy guidelines on what is allowed and what is not allowed and they control development work on how to improve the logo and the way it is used.

  In many skill areas such as marketing or process engineering it is not possible to document policies and standards that can be written down and imposed. Nevertheless, we found many examples in these less easily documented skills areas where the centre had 'created a company way' of doing things. For example, one of 3M's key skill components is the way managers, passionately committed to their ideas, bootleg resources to pursue projects that have not been funded in the development budget. This is not a skill that can be documented in methods and standards. Yet it has become a 3M company way, jealously guarded by central management and symbolized by the 15 per cent rule – managers are allowed 15 per cent of their time to pursue projects of their own choosing. The 'company way' has been created by managing values and cultural norms rather than through policy statements and instructions.

As we documented company examples, we noticed that the centre can take on a different role for different key business skills and even for different key skill components (Figure 13.6). The central role at 3M differs for different skills. New product marketing skills are highly

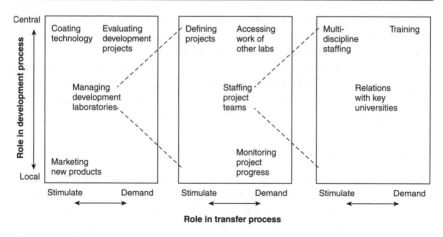

Figure 13.6 The role of the centre

decentralized: the centre 'stimulates the network'. Coating technology is more centralized: the centre 'promotes central developments' in certain areas where it has designated a technology centre. Even within a key business skill such as the management of development laboratories the centre takes on a different role for different components. The way the centre becomes involved in the know-how concerned with the process of defining projects could be to promote central developments. The know-how involved in monitoring projects could be managed by imposing best practice. At each further level of detail the choice of how the centre manages know-how can differ by sub-component.[11]

CHOOSING A CENTRAL ROLE FOR EACH KEY COMPONENT

Having identified the key skill components and understood the different options, the company can set about choosing the most suitable central role for managing each component. During our research we had hoped to be able to specify what central role would be most appropriate for each type of skill component. However, the evidence from our research sample indicated that there was no stable link between the type of skill component and choice of central role. The choice of central role seemed to depend more on the culture of the company than the component. Both Mars and Unilever have brand management skills; yet they manage similar skill components in very different ways with equal effectiveness. In Mars the know-how involved in selecting advertising agencies is managed by stimulating the network. In Unilever Personal Products, on the other hand, it is managed by creating a company way. We realized that each company has an established way of working and an established role for the centre on most issues. It is not that one is better than the other. Both companies have found ways to make their system work well.

We realized, therefore, that companies need to ensure that the approach they choose takes account of the established ways of working – what we have called *cultural constraints*. These constraints need to be balanced with the *commercial needs of the business* and tensions that occur between the two need to be managed sensitively.

Cultural constraints

The centre's established roles are influenced by the policies it has taken in the past on decentralization and involvement. The established roles are mainly informal, based on understandings that have developed between managers over time and precedents that have been set in the past. When taken together, the centre's established roles amount to an informal 'decentralization contract'.[12] If it were possible to write them all down, these established roles would define in detail the way the centre is expected to get involved in or remain detached from all aspects of the business.

We realized that it is this decentralization contract that is the most potent force in the choices managers make about how to manage a particular skill component. Instinctively managers in Mars or Shell or Whitbread ask themselves 'If I interfere on this issue will it contravene the principles of decentralization and autonomy we subscribe to?', or 'What is the usual way that we handle this kind of issue?'.

Moreover, these instincts appear to make sense. From looking at cases of failure, cases where attempts to centralize development or impose know-how had been blocked, we noted that a major cause was resistance by unit managers who believed that the centre was 'interfering'.[13] These decentralization contracts appear to exist in the minds of managers, and unless explicitly renegotiated, the existing contract acts as a barrier to changes in the central role. The current decentralization contract is a 'constraint' of the organization that should be taken into account when choosing the centre's role.

Commercial imperatives

But we also noted other influences on the choice of central role, influences relating to the market-place, technology and competitive dynamics. These influences we have called 'commercial imperatives' – commercial reasons that make it imperative that either the development process or the transfer process is managed in a particular way. For example, the amount of money needed for research to advance know-how is frequently much greater than any one business unit can afford.

By centralizing development work the company can afford bigger projects and gain from economies of scale. Information technology is one area where the need to centralize development is increasing as the costs of writing software rise. Perversely, the pressure to centralize software development is increasing at a time when many IT functions are being decentralized. The tension being created by these two trends is likely to slow down know-how development in one of the functions that has the greatest potential for creating new core skills. For companies where IT is a potential source of advantage, choosing the appropriate development approach is vital to future competitive success.

Commercial imperatives can also exist for the transfer process. In situations where standardization is important to commercial success the transfer of know-how must be imposed by the centre. Accounting firms, for example, need to be able to offer identical services from different country partnerships to large multinational companies. Standardization is particularly important in the audit service. As a result, international accounting firms such as Price Waterhouse have standard audit manuals used by each of the different partnerships, and a central technical function whose role is to approve changes to the manuals and support development initiatives. The central technical function imposes know-how transfer in order to ensure common audit standards in different partnerships.

Figure 13.7 provides a list of the factors that managers should consider when deciding whether there are any commercial imperatives that limit the choice of central role. Thus for each skill component, management must choose a central role based on any commercial imperatives that relate to the component; and any restrictions arising from the cultural constraints. Figure 13.8 is a model designed to help managers focus on these two dimensions – commercial imperatives and cultural constraints.

Managing tensions

In many situations the centre can choose a role that meets the needs of the commercial imperatives and does not clash with its cultural constraints. In these situations the decision about how to manage the skill component is easy to make.

But in some situations the imperatives and the constraints point toward different solutions – there is a tension between the role the centre should take to maximize performance and the role the centre should take to fit in with the established organization rules of behaviour. The trite answer to this tension is for central managers to change the rules. In practice, a much more politically astute solution needs to be found because without the support of business unit managers all efforts to manage skill components will fail.

Development process

1 Rarity of skill/resources needed for development
   - if rare centralization of development effort is likely to be better
2 Economies of scale of tasks needed for development
   - if high then co-operative or central development is likely to be better
3 Importance of market interaction in the development process
   - if it is important then decentralized processes are likely to be better
4 Stage of know-how life cycle
   - in early stages a decentralized approach that encourages diverse developments is likely to be better

Transfer process

1 Degree of further development or application work needed to use the new know-how in the local environment
   - if it is high then imposing know-how is likely to be inappropriate
2 Size of performance gap between the company and its competitors
   - if the company's performance is substantially worse than its competitors then imposition may be necessary to retain competitiveness
3 Degree to which standardization has commercial value
   - if standardization is valuable in its own right then imposition is appropriate
4 Stage of know-how life cycle
   - in the maturer stages of the cycle imposition may be more appropriate

---

Figure 13.7 Factors likely to create commercial imperatives

Tensions between imperatives and constraints occur in a limited number of predictable situations (Figure 13.9). To illustrate the challenge of managing these tensions we will examine one situation in detail – product internationalization. In this situation the product is becoming more international, making product and marketing know-how in one country more relevant to other countries. But in prior years companies in different countries will have operated independently and frequently the companies may not have been part of the same organization. Where independence has been high the established decentralization contract will only allow the centre a minimal role: development will have been decentralized and few networks for transferring know-how will exist.

But the commercial forces of internationalization are making it necessary to centralize development, co-ordinate marketing decisions and standardize some product features. Assuming the trend to internationalization continues, the centre will need to move, over time, into a dominant role, creating a company way for most of the key skill components. The management challenge is to find a way of going from a situation where the centre has been uninvolved in know-how management to a

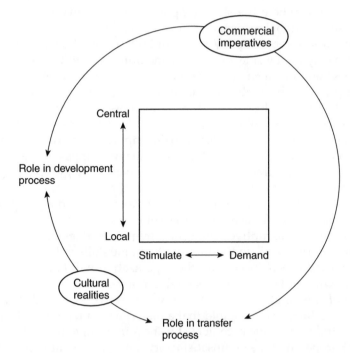

Figure 13.8 Choosing a management approach: imperatives and realities mode

situation where the centre dominates the management of certain critical know-how components.

We have noted three successful responses to this challenge. The first response is to avoid the problem by de-emphasizing or exiting that part

---

- The trend for customer needs or products to become more alike (globalization)

- Know-how developments that affect
  - economies of scale
  - size of development needed
  - availability of skill
  (know-how innovation)

- The process of know-how maturing
  (know-how S-curve)

- Changes to the need for co-ordination from
  - convergence of de-coupling
  - globalization
  - customer demand for one-stop shopping (co-ordination)

Figure 13.9 Forces creating tensions

of the business where the skill components need managing. This is in many cases a rational response. If the dominant organization behaviour in other parts of the company is one of high levels of decentralization, the centre may not be able, even in the medium term, to win the support of business unit managers to a change in behaviour in this product area. The company will be unable to manage the critical skill components well and will be likely to lose ground to competitors over time. Rather than follow a second-best solution which could lead to loss of competitive position the company will do better to de-emphasize or exit the business.

The second response is to seek to make major changes in the existing decentralization contract by formulating a new strategy, changing the organization structure, renegotiating roles and changing managers who resist the new order. When done with determination and a grasp of the detail at the skill component level, this solution can be effective. But it is risky and highly disruptive. The centre frequently does not have sufficient grasp of the detail, individuals with unique skills or knowledge can be sidetracked or sacrificed, and the organization will take some years before it will settle into the new relationships. The track record for changes of this kind is poor.[14] While we were working with Unilever Personal Products, we were told that a major reorganization and change in the central role for the detergents business in Europe under the flag of 'Lever Europe' had been unsatisfactory and a new attempt to co-ordinate the businesses in Europe was being made only 18 months after the first attempt was announced.

The third solution to the challenge is to change gradually. The initial step in gradual change is to identify the key skill components and start managing each component in the best way possible, given the restrictions of the existing decentralization contract. These 'toe-in-the-water' initiatives serve two purposes. They help to clarify the skill component giving managers the opportunity to judge its relevance. They also begin to develop a groundswell of support for more involved management. Because the toe-in-the-water initiatives do not threaten the existing decentralization contract they do not attract political attention.

The next step in gradual change is to increase the involvement of the centre as the support for involvement develops. The centre responds to pressure from the business unit managers rather than the other way round. In Unilever Personal Products, we identified a groundswell of support from younger marketing directors and product managers for greater co-ordination by the centre. The need to transfer know-how quickly, to roll out new product ideas before competitors in as many countries as possible, and to standardize some product attributes to aid international recognition is apparent to these managers. Until recently the forces in favour of decentralization and independence have slowed up the transfer process and encouraged not-invented-here attitudes.

Now many of the old style managers have retired and a new breed of globally aware managers are taking their place. It is now appropriate for the centre to play a stronger co-ordination role in both the development of know-how and the transfer of its benefits.

The final step in gradual change is to pull together the many small changes in a new statement of the centre's role and strategy. In gradual change the definition of the strategy and appropriate working relationships come near the end of the change period rather than at the beginning.[15]

It is apparent that some situations do not allow managers time for gradual change. Major change or an exit from the business are the only choices. However, in many situations there is time: four or five years is not too long a period in which to make the changes. In these cases, an understanding of the existing decentralization contract and a sensitive attitude towards winning support from business unit managers will help to avoid the expensive mistakes made by so many companies.

CONCLUSION

In reality, many recent attempts by decentralized companies at building and sharing know-how have been disappointing. At Philips UK, for example, the Organization and Efficiency (O&E) function set out to build skills in total quality management, just-in-time manufacturing and fast product development. These skill areas were clearly important to many of the business units in the UK. Yet little was actually achieved, despite the vigorous efforts of the O&E managers, and eventually the function was disbanded.

The reasons for this lack of success are instructive and by no means unusual. First, the O&E managers did not break down the skill areas mentioned into enough detail to define the key components or pinpoint the components that were relevant across the businesses. Since Philips UK business units are highly diverse, ranging from consumer products to professional products and from high-tech areas like semi-conductors to mature areas like light bulbs, few skill components were in fact relevant to the majority of business units. Second, Philips's switch from a geographic structure to a product structure during the 1980s made the role of the national organization unclear and sapped the determination of the UK centre to take an active role in managing know-how. Without the determination of the centre the existing decentralization contract was unlikely to change. Finally the O&E managers were unable to win the attention of business unit managers to their initiatives: the business unit managers were reluctant to commit time to working with UK-based functional managers as long as the degree of control likely to be exercised by the Dutch-based division bosses was unknown. Because the business unit managers did not accept what the O&E function was trying to do little could be achieved.

The Philips example illustrates the three conditions necessary for success in building core skills: whichever role it chooses, the centre must be determined; the business unit managers must have accepted the centre's role; and the effort must be focused on key components that are relevant across business units.

At Philips today, faced with a profit crisis, nothing immediate is being done to find another way of building core skills across the UK business units. The danger is that the profit revival about to come from decentralization and increasing accountability may lead managers to believe that the centre does not need to play an active role in building core skills. If this happens, Philips will find it hard to hold its place in the world electronics industry.

Our research suggests, however, that companies pursuing decentralization do not need to lose control of the management of their core skills. To succeed in the task, managers must start by carefully analysing the components that make up core skills and that are relevant across business units. As Eero Lumatjarvi, Senior Marketing Member of Unilever Personal Products Co-ordination, said, 'The key is to decide which elements of the product package know-how are critical and relevant across countries. Should we focus on the colour of the bottle, the shape of the label, the brand name, etc? That is what we are trying to decide.'

Once the skill components have been chosen, the centre needs to decide how much control to retain over the development of know-how and the transfer of best practice. Heavy-handed initiatives can be worse than complete inaction. By examining the commercial forces at work and remaining sensitive to the organization's natural ways of working, the centre can choose a role that will speed up the building of core skills.

In some future cases this role may involve the creation or retention of a central function to set policies and manage development budgets. In other cases it may involve no more than organizing a conference to stimulate the informal network between managers. The choice of mechanism (e.g. central function versus functional conference) is less important than the choice of central role. In fact, for each central role a broad range of mechanisms can be effective.

In short, building core skills in an increasingly decentralized environment demands painfully detailed analysis of skill components as well as full acceptance by both the centre and the business unit managers as to how the skill components are best managed. Companies who are prepared to meet these conditions will be able to build their core skills faster than their competitors and thus maintain their competitive edge.

REFERENCES

1 Rosabeth Moss Kanter has been one of the most prominent recorders of the process of corporate headquarters slimming. In *When Giants Learn to Dance*, Simon and Schuster, 1989, she describes the jargon: 'Inside companies, downsizing (cutting employment), demassing (eliminating middle management positions), and decentralizing corporate staff functions are among the tactics used by companies eager to be seeking and destroying wealth dissipators (improving profits)' (p. 57).

2 Rosabeth Moss Kanter has also been in the forefront of academics studying the new mechanisms that companies are using to replace the old central functions. Chapter 4 in *When Giants Learn to Dance*, titled 'Achieving Synergies: Value Added, Value Multiplied', describes many of the changes taking place.

   Michael Porter's book *Competitive Advantage*, Free Press, 1985, also has a useful chapter on mechanisms – Chapter 11 'Achieving Interrelationships'. The section from p. 393 – organizational mechanisms for achieving interrelationships – provides a useful classification.

   C. K. Prahalad and Yves Doz also describe horizontal mechanisms in *The Multi-National Mission*, Free Press, 1987. In Chapter 11, 'Managing Interdependencies Across Businesses', they show how data management tools, manager management tools and conflict resolution tools can be used to manage without central functions.

   Christopher Bartlett and Sumantra Ghoshal – *Managing Across Borders*, HBS Press, 1989, also describe the new style of management in an excellent chapter titled 'Managing Complexity: Developing Flexible Coordination'.

3 Porter, M., *Competitive Advantage*, Free Press, 1988, Chapter 10.

4 All of the authors in note (2) above also comment on the difficulty management have had in making lateral mechanisms effective. Michael Porter opens his chapter on interrelationships with the sentence 'Achieving interrelationships has in practice proven to be extraordinarily difficult for many firms.'

   In the conclusion to *When Giants Learn to Dance* Moss Kanter describes two 'principal problems' getting in the way of 'synergies'. The first is 'top management typically overestimates the degree of co-operation it will get and underestimates the costs.' (p. 345).

   Bartlett and Ghoshal examine the successes and failures of the companies in their sample and conclude 'perhaps the most difficult task is to co-ordinate the voluminous flow of strategic information and proprietary knowledge required to operate a transnational organization' – p. 170, *Managing Across Borders*.

   In the opening sentences on their chapter on interdependencies Prahalad and Doz comment 'few companies seem to have found an approach to manage the evolving interdependencies across businesses successfully'.

5 Gary Hamel and C. K. Prahalad have made this point eloquently in a famous *Harvard Business Review* article 'The Core Competence of the Corporation', *Harvard Business Review*, May/June1990, no. 3. The point has also been made by Rosabeth Moss Kanter in her criticism of 'mindless downsizing' and 'management cowboys'. The focus on capability, competence and skills is resurfacing under the title 'the resource based view of strategy' (see note 6 below). The reality is that the earliest writings of Chester Barnard and Kenneth Andrews clearly underlined the importance of building capability.

6 There is a growing school of literature called the 'Resource-Based Theory of Competitive Advantage', Grant, R. M., *California Management Review*, Spring 1991. It is also referred to in a number of different articles in the *Strategic*

Management Journal, Summer 1991 special issue on global strategy edited by Christopher Bartlett and Sumantra Ghoshal. David Collis's article 'A Resource-based Analysis of Global Competition' is an excellent example of the research which this school is now spawning.

7 In essence this tool is identical to the value chain tool of Michael Porter, the business system tool of McKinsey & Co and the activity-based analysis tool of Braxton Associates. It differs in being much more detailed than the value chain and focused on skill elements rather than activity elements.

8 Best practice in this area is described by Michael Goold and John Quinn in *Strategic Control*, Hutchinson, 1990.

9 Sumantra Ghoshal develops a categorization of innovation processes within multinational companies that is similar. He identifies central, local and global innovations, p. 47. – 'The Innovative Multinational', unpublished PhD thesis, Harvard University, no. 8617980.

The same categorization is described in *Managing Across Borders*, Bartlett and Ghoshal, HBS Press, 1989.

10 Norman Blackwell, Jean-Pierre Bizet and David Hensely, all of McKinsey & Co, develop a similar categorization in 'Shaping a Pan-European Organisation', *McKinsey Quarterly*, July 1991. McKinsey & Co sponsored the research on which this paper is built and the exchange of thinking helped to bring our view and theirs into some proximity.

11 Christopher Bartlett and Sumantra Ghoshal produced an exhibit similar to Figure 13.4 in *Managing Across Borders*, p. 97. Our research has confirmed a conclusion of theirs with which we were initially most uncomfortable – namely that adjacent issues could be managed with different levels of co-ordination and differentiation.

12 Christopher Bartlett and Sumantra Ghoshal use the term 'administrative heritage', Chapter 3, *Managing Across Borders*, to describe a concept similar to our decentralization contract. We have found the latter term more useful because the idea of a contract leaves managers more aware of their power to change the contract so long as they can persuade the business unit managers to agree to the changes. The administrative heritage language is too passive because it implies that the past is a drag on the speed of change.

13 All the authors who have researched interrelationships acknowledge the existence of strong barriers to accepting know-how from other parts of the organization. Michael Porter summarizes the 'impediments of achieving interrelationships', pp. 385–93 of *Competitive Advantage*. The most interesting piece of direct research has been done by Tom Allen, an MIT professor, who studied the degree of technical know-how exchanged within laboratories. He found that technicians preferred to go outside for information and know-how, even though it was more readily available inside the laboratory, because of the perceived costs of working with colleagues – *Managing the Flow of Technology*, Thomas Allen.

Another reason for preferring the contract idea is that we identified situations where the contract changed when new managers from outside were appointed to the business units. These managers carried with them administrative heritage from the previous organizations that was just as strong as the administrative heritage of their new employer. The discussions that followed changed the previous decentralization contract as the centre managers adjusted to the desires of these new business unit managers.

Bartlett and Ghoshal refer to the work of Hannan and Freeman, 'Structural Inertia and Organisation Change', *American Sociological Review*, vol. 49,

1984. Hannan and Freeman talk about 'normative agreements' and explain why these agreements are resistant to change. The ideal of 'normative agreements' is, we believe, closer to the concept of a decentralization contract.

14 We collected all the case studies of major organization change for coordination and skill reasons produced by Harvard and Insead. Only one (Henkel) was a story of success. The others either documented failed efforts or described bold changes which, with the passage of time, proved not to work.

15 Recent work on mission and mission statements (*A Sense of Mission*, Campbell, A., Devine, M. and Young, D., Hutchinson, 1990) demonstrates that written statements are most powerful *after* the change has been achieved rather than beforehand. Because change is a political process clear statements of intention or vision can provide the ammunition needed for those managers determined to undermine the change.

We have observed that it is not unusual for the explanation to follow the action by months or even years.

Reproduced from Campbell, Andrew, 'Building Core Capabilities', unpublished paper.

Part IV

Synergy in practice

Chapter 14

Introduction to synergy in practice

Earlier chapters each focus on a particular aspect of synergy. Chapters in Part I examine how synergy enables a corporation to become more than the sum of its parts, and the pitfall of negative synergy. Part II identifies synergy opportunities and weighs costs and benefits. Part III looks at ways of ensuring that synergy benefits do materialize. The chapters in this part explore the experiences of different companies in identifying and achieving synergy benefits. These readings, therefore provide insights into how different companies have moved from the concept to the practice of synergy, and the challenges they confronted in doing so.

The first chapter, 'Diversification in the financial services industries', by Professor Robert Grant of Georgetown University, examines how different companies responded to the upheaval in the financial services industry brought about by deregulation, globalization of competition, and new customer needs. Grant's study focuses on six companies – Citicorp, BankAmerica, Merrill Lynch, American Express, Sears Roebuck and Prudential, who responded to the changing environment by diversifying broadly during the 1970s and 1980s. Whilst their core businesses ranged from banking to insurance to credit cards, Grant demonstrates how these companies each identified broadly similar opportunities in financial services, with their strategies converging around the concept of 'one-stop shopping', or providing corporate and individual customers with a range of financial products. Synergy goals underpinned their diversification strategies, with these companies aiming to combine businesses offering different services to gain benefits from shared activities and skill transfers. Merrill Lynch, for example, moved from brokerage into retail banking and real estate services, while Sears, which had long provided insurance services in its retail stores through Allstate Insurance, expanded into brokerage and real estate. The companies in Grant's study identified a variety of benefits from entering new areas of business, especially increased business through the cross-selling of products, economies of scale in the information technology required to support a variety of different financial services, and opportunities to capitalize on corporate image by promoting new financial products.

Grant's study is of particular interest because the changes in the financial services industry have been highly visible and the ambitious attempts of different companies to link businesses in the sector have been closely followed in the press and the management literature. To some observers, such as Michael Porter and Rosabeth Moss Kanter, American Express's strategy of becoming an integrated financial services company, and its high commitment to sharing activities and skills across its banking, credit card and insurance businesses, provided one of the most 'promising examples' of a diversification strategy based on inter-relationships across businesses. Porter, writing in 1985, said that it was too soon to judge the success of American Express's pioneering efforts,[1] but Grant's more recent study appraises the results of the synergy strategies of a sample of companies more fully.

Grant argues that the financial performance of the six diversified companies was weak, with none of them able to outperform their more specialized competitors consistently over the decade from 1977 to 1986. He also points to divestments, frequent reorganizations and internal crises as further evidence of the disappointing results of diversification. It was not lack of commitment that undermined the performance of the diversified financial services companies. American Express's efforts to identify synergy projects and create incentives for co-operation across its divisions are particularly noteworthy, but the other companies in Grant's sample also made concerted efforts to link common activities and to share skills. They gained some benefits from corporate branding and the transfer of know-how and skills, but these proved to be relatively modest and more than offset by the high costs incurred in co-ordinating activities across diverse businesses. Direct costs included extensive training of brokers and sales people to enable them to cope with a much broader range of financial products, and additional support and administration staff to provide the necessary links between those marketing the products and the financial specialists in different areas. High turnover in some newly acquired or restructured businesses, and low morale and performance also added to the costs.

One of the problems Grant identifies is that the very basis of these companies' diversification strategies – offering customers a range of financial services – proved to be of limited appeal to individual, corporate and institutional customers. These six companies invested considerable resources and managerial effort to gain synergies that, in retrospect, do not seem to have merited investment on such a scale; the strategies were, in Campbell's language, a mirage. This problem was exacerbated by the companies' failure to move as quickly, or as far, as they anticipated towards providing one-stop financial shopping. Both insurance agents and stockbrokers found it difficult to cope with a variety of products, and rivalries between investment and commercial bankers undermined efforts to generate new business through cross-referrals. It also proved difficult to allocate costs and revenues among businesses sharing resources and activities, and hard to monitor performance of the different businesses.

Whilst changes in the financial services industry did provide new opportunities, the companies in Grant's sample relied more on their overall vision of synergies than a comprehensive analysis of how they could gain specific benefits. And when they did attempt to gain synergies by exploiting common technology, cross-selling and using common sales forces to market a variety of products they discovered that the costs of creating these interrelationships outweighed the benefits. Grant concludes that the experience of these financial service companies suggests that diversification based on close interrelationships across diverse businesses demands an incremental approach. In trying to exploit many opportunities simultaneously, the companies he studied overreached their capabilities, leading to internal upheavals during a period when they also had to cope with a rapidly changing environment. Grant argues that companies need a much more targeted approach. It is not sufficient to recognize opportunities, or even to identify many common activities and skills across businesses; companies also need a thorough understanding of their own managerial capabilities to be able to make sound decisions on which opportunities to pursue. Grant's conclusion is supportive of the ideas developed in Campbell's article in the previous section. Both authors are arguing for a detailed, targeted approach to the management of synergy opportunities.

The second chapter, 'Rebuilding an Alliance', is by Varun Bery and Thomas A. Bowers of McKinsey. The authors discuss a problem all too familiar to managers: what to do when efforts to gain synergy stall? Their focus is on an alliance between an American and Japanese company, but the approach taken by managers in this case provides insights into how managers can overcome initial failures in their efforts to gain synergies.

In the case described here, the companies have been partners for two years, with the alliance based on the Japanese company acting as a subcontractor, distributing a new service for the American firm. Disagreements and mistrust between the partners became increasingly serious, with the Americans perceiving a lack of commitment to the product by the Japanese firm, and the Japanese managers resentful of their minor stake in the partnership and believing the Americans did not appreciate local market conditions. Clearly, the alliance was providing few benefits to either partner and would likely fall apart without restructuring.

In assessing its position, the American firm went back to the basics, undertaking a strategic review of the market and of the objectives of the alliance. The authors see this step as fundamental because efforts to restructure the alliance could not be worthwhile if it had no value. The American firm considered a range of alternatives to the alliance, such as acquiring a Japanese company or going it alone. Their analysis showed that the alliance with the Japanese firm remained the best option for achieving their marketing objectives, and this process helped in building a new commitment to making the alliance work.

The next step was to work out a new business proposition with the Japanese firm. The authors emphasize that the Americans did not simply propose new terms or offer to renegotiate the alliance. Instead, they worked with the Japanese firm to form a joint business plan. The focus was on generating options, not on arriving at a legal agreement. Although it took time to overcome past frustrations and distrust, the team formed by the two firms had a clear focus in designing a new business plan and this encouraged a co-operative effort. Also, managers on the team would be managing the new alliance, and this gave them a personal stake in making it work. Although it took fourteen months' work to restructure the alliance, this effort paid off in a much broader alliance with a more ambitious strategy than the previous agreement. Bery and Bowers argue that companies should regularly reassess both their objectives and approaches to synergy issues, and especially when their efforts to capture benefits fall short of expectations.

'Creating value in symbiotic acquisitions' is by Phillippe C. Haspeslagh of INSEAD and David B. Jemison of the University of Texas. This chapter, which focuses on how ICI managed the integration of an acquisition, is taken from their book, *Managing Acquisitions: Creating Value Through Corporate Renewal*. In their book Haspeslagh and Jemison argue that acquisitions are best understood as a means of renewing a firm's capabilities. They define these capabilities as a set of integrated managerial and technological skills that are gained mainly through experience, provide significant benefits to customers, and can be widely applied across the businesses of the corporation. Because capabilities are unique to a firm, transferring them is a complex process that has to be well thought out and well implemented. Haspeslagh and Jemison identify different approaches to transferring capabilities in acquisitions: in absorption acquisitions the aim is to integrate fully the resources and activities of two firms; in preservation acquisitions, the acquired firm remains autonomous but subject to the influence of its parent; and in symbiotic acquisitions the aim is to create interdependence between two firms to allow the transfer of capabilities between them.[2]

In the selection included here, Haspeslagh and Jemison describe the gradual but purposeful creation of interdependence between ICI and two of the businesses of Beatrice Chemicals – LNP and Fiberite. ICI acquired Beatrice Chemicals mainly for the anticipated synergies between these businesses and its own advanced materials division. Beatrice offered ICI access to US markets and an entrepreneurial, market-driven approach that contrasted with ICI's more technological focus. The challenge was to permit the Beatrice companies sufficient autonomy to preserve their capabilities, but also to ensure that both ICI and Beatrice benefited from the transfer of capabilities across the businesses. For a year after the acquisition ICI's managers refrained from establishing any direct linkages with Beatrice Chemicals, recognizing that it would be easy to undermine the company's entrepreneurial capabilities if Beatrice's managers were overwhelmed by expectations or demands. A manager acting as a gatekeeper suggested contacts within ICI to Beatrice managers, but left the initiative up to the individual businesses. Even when reporting relationships drew the companies closer together, it was largely the acquired company that set the pace for co-operation and co-ordination with its new parent, a process Haspeslagh and Jemison call 'reaching out rather than reaching in'. Eventually ICI reorganized its engineering plastics activities under one head, and LNP assumed responsibility for ICI's engineering plastics business in the United States. ICI's step-by-step approach paid off, with Beatrice managers coming to recognize the opportunities provided by being part of a larger corporation, and the contribution they could make to improving ICI's US businesses.

Haspeslagh's and Jemison's account of ICI's gradual integration of Beatrice's businesses shows that transferring capabilities from one firm to another requires both commitment and patience. The acquiring company has to be clear about its own objectives but also sensitive to the uncertainties and concerns of managers in the acquired firm. Learning has to occur on both sides before firms can share capabilities rooted in different organizational contexts.

The next chapter, 'Co-ordinating international manufacturing and technology', is by M. Therese Flaherty of Harvard Business School. Her research focuses on specific co-ordination projects undertaken by a group of US companies with manufacturing facilities in different countries. Flaherty observes that co-ordinating international manufacturing is a relatively neglected topic in the management literature, and her purpose is to describe the experiences of businesses that have gained synergies through specific co-ordination projects. Included in the study are two chemical businesses, two electronic businesses and a heavy equipment manufacturer. Whilst some of the companies Flaherty examined had rationalized their manufacturing facilities, or intended to do so, all of them planned to continue multisite international manufacturing. The aim of the projects was not, therefore, economies of scale in manufacturing but to gain benefits from sharing information and transferring know-how across different plants.

Local managers and their subordinates decided on projects they judged to be compatible with their circumstances and aims, and responsibility for the projects remained at unit level, with little involvement of corporate staff. The projects covered a wide range, from support services to manufacturing processes, and the benefits gained included improved negotiating power by procurement specialists through the sharing of expertise and information and better performance by a US plant from the sharing of know-how by its Japanese counterpart. Flaherty discovered that the success of some projects led to other, more complex, projects and that some units gained major unanticipated benefits through linkages with other units. A step-by-step approach seemed essential though, since managers often rejected projects that appeared too complex at the outset, or ones that did not provide direct benefits. For companies seeking better co-ordination of international manufacturing, Flaherty suggests that lower level employees in local facilities should be responsible for identifying and implementing specific co-ordinating projects, since they are most familiar with their unit circumstances and needs. An incremental approach may mean that companies forgo immediate opportunities – the managers in Flaherty's study rejected some projects because of their complexity and ICI held back on its expectations of the Beatrice acquisition. On the other hand, these count among the relatively few success stories in the literature.

In-depth studies like those in Part IV reveal what does – and does not – work in particular circumstances, and this may be one of the best ways of sorting out what the critical issues really are in seeking synergies. The authors in this part focus on different situations – diversification strategies, alliances, integration of an acquisition, co-ordination of international manufacturing – but their findings are surprisingly consistent. These authors argue in favour of the following:

1 Managers should focus on detailed analysis of the specific opportunities available and how they can be achieved rather than on the broad concept of synergy.
2 The details of what can be shared, and how it can be shared, are often best worked out by lower level employees in local facilities, since they are the people most familiar with the issues.
3 An incremental approach allows managers time to adjust to the changes and prevents overloading managers and corporate systems.
4 The centre must be clear about what it is trying to accomplish and sensitive to its own limitations as well as to the capabilities and concerns of managers in business units.

The readings in this chapter therefore provide managers with guidelines for a practical approach to synergy issues.

REFERENCES

1 Porter, M. E., *Competitive Advantage*, Free Press, New York, 1985, p. 410; Kanter, Rosabeth Moss, *When Giants Learn to Dance*, Simon & Schuster, London, 1989, p. 104.
2 Haspeslagh, P. C. and Jamison, D. B., *Managing Acquisitions*, The Free Press, 1991, pp. 23–32.

Chapter 15

Diversification in the financial services industries

Robert Grant

INTRODUCTION

During the past decade the financial services industries of the industria-
lized countries have been buffeted by deregulation, technological change,
changing customer demands, unprecedented economic and financial
turbulence, and the globalization of competition. In response to this
shattering of a formerly-benign business environment, financial service
companies have been forced to reformulate their strategies, restructure
their organizations and rethink their management systems and styles.

This paper reports on one aspect of this adjustment by financial
institutions: *diversification*. Between 1977 and 1986, in the United States
and in other advanced countries, regulatory change, innovation, market
evolution, and the quest for growth and profitability provided a specta-
cular impetus for diversification. Mainly by acquisition, but also by
internal growth, banks, insurance companies and securities companies
have increasingly invaded one another's markets. They have broadened
their market coverage and product scope to embrace commodity and
precious metal broking, credit cards, real estate broking, fund management, and a host of other finance-related activities previously undertaken mainly by specialist companies.

The rationale for diversification was impressive. The companies
pointed to customer preferences for one-stop shopping, cost savings
from the pooling of resources and activities, and the ability to transfer
skills and capabilities from one business to another. Yet, by-and-large,
the anticipated benefits have not been forthcoming. The leading diversifiers have, for the most part, shown poor profitability, strategic reversals
in several of their diversified businesses, and suspiciously-frequent
restructurings and senior management changes.

This report examines the diversification strategies, the performance,
and the management problems experienced by companies diversifying
within the financial services industry. The objectives of this report are:

- to identify the rationale for diversification by financial service companies and to appraise its validity;
- to establish why the presumed benefits failed to materialize;
- to identify the management problems which companies experienced in
managing diversification;
- to draw lessons for how diversifications can be better managed in the
future.

THE COMPANIES AND THEIR DIVERSIFICATION STRATEGIES

To select a research sample, I first identified all US financial service
corporations with assets of over $50 billion at the end of 1986 (see Figure
15.1). Sears Roebuck was added to the list. Although classified as a
retailer on the basis of sales revenue, Sears was a financial service
corporation in terms of the allocation of its assets (over 60 per cent of
which were within its insurance and securities businesses). The second
stage was to identify the most effective diversifiers during the previous
decade. Those firms which, during 1986, were engaged within North
America in at least three of the following fields: commercial banking,
insurance, investment banking, securities broking and real estate broking
were included within the sample of large, diversified financial service
corporations. The sample comprised six companies:

	Assets ($ billion)
Citicorp	196
BankAmerica Corp.	104
Prudential of America	103
Federal National Mortgage Association	100
American Express	99
Chase Manhattan	95
Salomon	78
J. P. Morgan & Co	76
Manufacturers Hanover Corporation	74
Aetna Life and Casualty	67
Sears Roebuck	66
Security Pacific Corporation	63
Chemical New York Corporation	61
Bankers Trust	56
First Interstate Bancorp	55
Merrill Lynch	53

Figure 15.1 US financial service corporations with assets in excess of $50
billion in 1986
Source: Fortune, 8 June 1987

- American Express;
- BankAmerica Corp;
- Citicorp;
- Merrill Lynch;
- Prudential;
- Sears Roebuck.

No clear distinction between 'diversified' and 'specialized' companies among the companies in Figure 15.1 was apparent. All the companies in the figure became more diverse over the period in terms of the range of financial services offered and geographical scope. Salomon Brothers merged with Phibro in 1985, which extended its activities from investment banking into commodity broking and new venture capital. Aetna Life's acquisition of Federated Investors and its partial interest in Samuel Montague has brought it much closer to retail and merchant banking. Several of the leading banks showed similar diversification patterns with a strong movement into investment banking by their overseas subsidiaries and a widening of their non-bank financial services both for retail and corporate customers. Both Bankers Trust and Security Pacific were highly diversified by 1986 but were excluded from my sample of diversified companies, first, because their diversification was more recent than that of the other companies so that it was too early to assess its consequences, and second, because their diversification was primarily overseas.

The management issues involved in international expansion raise another set of management issues. All the firms in the sample, with the exception of Sears, simultaneously pursued diversification and overseas expansion, while several US banking corporations diversified their overseas operations, particularly in London.

THE CONDUCT OF THE RESEARCH

Data was drawn from three sources:

1 *Financial statements,* including annual accounts and 10K reports were the primary source of information on financial performance.
2 *Annual reports, public statements by senior managers, and newspaper and periodical reports* were used to identify intended and emerging strategies, and as sources of information on the implementation and diversification strategies at the upper management levels.
3 *Interviews were conducted with sales personnel, account executives and office managers in local branches of the companies.* These interviews were the primary source of data on operational issues arising in relation to diversification. They also shed light upon some of the more senior-level management issues.

The pattern of diversification

Diversification by the six companies is summarized in Figure 15.2. The major feature of the figure is the increasing similarity in the activities of the companies between 1977 and 1986. The period was one of rapid diversification for all six of the companies. However, for all the companies, diversification had begun before our study period and, even by 1977, most of the companies in the sample were distinguished by the breadth of the activities:

- *Merrill Lynch*, even in 1977, was unusually diversified for a stock-broker. Its strategy – 'bringing Wall Street to Main Street' – was to tap what it believed to be a huge potential market for financial services among middle and upper-middle income households. It pioneered the 'financial supermarket' concept. Under the leadership of Donald Regan (CEO from 1971 to 1981), Merrill Lynch had acquired Family Life Insurance Company in 1974 and in 1976 established its Physical Commodities Trading Group and Merrill Lynch Asset Management (around the previously-acquired Lionel D. Edie and Co.).
- *American Express* was also atypical of financial institutions with its business based upon travellers cheques, credit cards and travel services. However, by 1977 it had taken steps towards the more mainstream financial institutions with its entry into international banking through the creation of AMEX Bank Ltd and American Express International Banking Corporation.
- *Citicorp*'s core business was its corporate and institutional lending. However, during the 1970s Citicorp began expanding the range of services it offered to its corporate and institutional customers, and extended its international operations. Because of regulatory restrictions, Citicorp diversification into investment banking and securities trading was primarily through its overseas operations. In 1975 Citicorp inaugurated its push into retail financial services because, declared Chairman Walter Wriston, 'The money is in people's pockets'.
- *BankAmerica*, like Citicorp, was also widely diversified, by the standards of US banking, in 1977. In addition to broad geographical diversity (in 1977 international earnings contributed more than half of net operating income), BankAmerica was active in credit cards, real estate investment, leasing and trust services.
- *Sears Roebuck* in 1977 was supplying a range of financial services including insurance (through Allstate Insurance Co. formed in 1931), and (through a number of businesses operated by Allstate Enterprises Inc.) mortgage finance, motor vehicle finance, mutual fund management and savings and loan operations in California.
- *Prudential* was also comparatively diversified for a mutual life insurance company with subsidiaries engaged in real estate development

Figure 5.2 The principal financial service activities of the companies, 1977 and 1986

	Banking services in US	Banking services overseas	Investment banking	Stock broking	Insurance	Credit cards	Commodity broking	Real estate broking
1977								
American Express						X	X	
BankAmerica	X	X						
Citicorp	X	X	X					
Merrill Lynch	X	X	X	X	X			
Prudential					X			
Sears Roebuck					X			
1986								
American Express	X	X	X	X	X	X		
BankAmerica	X	X	X	X		X		
Citicorp	X	X	X	X	X	X	X	
Merrill Lynch	X		X	X	X		X	
Prudential				X	X		X	X
Sears Roebuck	X		X	X	X	X	X	X

Figure 5.2 The principal financial service activities of the companies, 1977 and 1986
Source: Company annual reports, Moody's Reports

and management, health care, leasing, fund management and securities dealing.

Nevertheless, the key feature of the sample companies was their diversification during the decade 1977–86. With the exception of Merrill Lynch, which was basically a brokerage company, the primary direction of diversification for all the companies was into securities broking and investment banking. Prudential's acquisition of Bache Securities in 1981 was the first of a succession of incursions into Wall Street. American Express acquired Shearson, Loeb Rhoades Inc. (1981) and Lehman Brothers Kuhn Loeb Holding Co. Inc. (1984). Its takeover of E. F. Hutton (1988) established it as the largest US brokerage firm. Sears' purchased Dean Witter Reynolds Organization (1981). BankAmerica purchased discount broker Charles Schwab Corp. (1983). Citicorp created an investment bank operating in London, New York and Tokyo in mid-1982, established Newbridge Securities, a member of the NYSE, and acquired a string of other brokerage companies around the globe. Citicorp also offered discount brokerage services to its bank customers in association with Quick and Reilly (the second largest US discount broker).

The second major direction of diversification was the move by the four non-bank companies into retail banking services. For the most part this was achieved by the companies using their retail networks to distribute personal financial services that had previously been the preserve of banks. The key breakthrough was by Merrill Lynch which in 1978 began offering a checking account with credit facilities through its 'Cash Management Account'. This innovatory product was copied by several other companies, in the case of Sears, Prudential and American Express it was undertaken using their newly-acquired brokerage subsidiaries. American Express's movement into personal financial services was further widened by its purchase of IDS Financial Securities in 1985.

The two banks also increased their involvement in retail banking, mainly through acquisitions. Citicorp's move into personal financial services had begun in 1976. During the 1980s it expanded nationally through the purchase of failing saving and loans including: Fidelity Savings in California (1982), First Federal Savings in Illinois (1982), Biscayne Savings in Florida, First Federal Savings and Loan in California (1984). BankAmerica also focused more strongly upon retail banking. Its major domestic banking acquisition was of Seafirst Corp. of Seattle (1983).

Related to increased involvement in personal banking activities was entry into credit cards. Credit cards were regarded both as a profitable business in themselves and as a means of broadening the companies' customer bases for supplying a wider range of financial services.

BankAmerica had been a pioneer in credit cards; its BankAmerica Card was the launch for Visa, which was spun off as a separate company. During the post-1977 period the major development was the entry by non-bank institutions into credit cards: in 1979 Merrill Lynch offered a Visa card to holders of its Cash Management Account, and Sears launched its Discover card in 1985. Citicorp entered into travel and entertainment cards through the acquisition of Carte Blanche and Diners Club and began marketing its 'Choice' card in 1980.

Other directions of diversification were into real estate brokerage and insurance. In real estate, Merrill Lynch formed Merrill Lynch Realty Associates in 1978 and then proceeded to acquire a string of real estate brokerage companies, and Sears acquired Coldwell Banker and Company. All six of the companies increased their involvement in real estate investment and financing, in particular, American Express acquired Balcor, a leading real estate investment firm, and Citicorp, Merrill Lynch, Prudential and American Express substantially increased their mortgage financing activities.

All the companies identified life insurance as integral to their strategies of becoming diversified suppliers of personal financial services. However, there were comparatively few major acquisitions of insurance companies. American Express, Sears and Merrill Lynch started the period with large insurance subsidiaries, but the main enthusiasm of the companies was for selling insurance rather than writing policies. The principal acquisitions during the period were AMIC Corp. by Merrill Lynch and American Express's purchase of the Interstate Insurance Group (1981), Citicorp established an insurance subsidiary, AMBAC, and acquired British National Life Assurance (1986).

Many of the acquisitions and new ventures of the decade 1977–86 represented extensions of existing diversified activities rather than entry into new financial services: Prudential was already managing and selling mutual funds before the acquisition of Bache, Sears was engaged in real estate financing and brokerage before its acquisition of Coldwell Banker. Several of the acquisitions served mainly to strengthen the companies' position within a particular industry. For example, American Express's acquisition of Southern Guarantee Insurance Co. and Interstate Insurance Group was building on its existing Fireman's Fund insurance business; Citicorp's equity stakes in Vickers da Costa and Scrimgeour Kemp-Gee represented a strengthening of investment banking activities rather than diversification.

The motives for diversification

Why did this period see so many large financial institutions adopting such ambitious diversification strategies? To what extent did the convergence of the companies' range of activities reflect a 'shared vision' of the changes which were taking place in the environment, or of the 'key success factors' in the industry? What were the benefits diversification was expected to confer?

To investigate these issues, I drew upon two areas of evidence:

1 the companies' statements of their long-term strategic objectives;
2 the companies' descriptions of their rationale for diversification and the benefits they anticipated.

All six companies explicitly stated their goals of becoming broadly-based suppliers of financial services:

- American Express identified itself as supplying 'a diversified group of services';
- 'BankAmerica Corporation's overall strategic objective is to become the world's premier financial services institution', it announced in 1984 aiming to 'fill customers' financial needs fully';
- at Citicorp, chairman Walter Wriston defined the company's strategy in terms of the 'Five Is' – individual banking, institutional banking, investment banking, information, and insurance;
- as early as 1969 Merrill Lynch outlined its ambition of becoming, 'the firm the people turn to for all their investment needs';
- Prudential described itself as 'a full financial services organization', aiming to 'serve the needs of the broadest possible range of customers';
- Sears stated its ambition of becoming 'one of the largest financial service companies in the US'.

The firms' redefinitions of their businesses reflected an abandonment of conventional notions about the traditional types of product and service supplied by particular types of institutions, and the adoption of a more market-orientated approach. In most cases the companies defined their businesses in terms of supplying a full range of services to a particular customer group. In the case of Prudential, Sears, Merrill Lynch, and American Express, the primary customer base was US individuals, and it was serving the evolving needs of individuals that was the main driving force for diversification. The primary customer segments of the two banks were corporations, institutions and governments, and it was these customers with their increasingly sophisticated requirements that encouraged Citicorp and BankAmerica to diversify and globalize their operations. However, during the 1980s all these companies expanded the scope of their customer bases: Prudential, Merrill Lynch, American Express, and even Sears became increasingly committed to corporate clients, while Citicorp and BankAmerica strove to expand their retail activities.

The concept of meeting customers' financial needs as opposed to being suppliers of particular financial products was a dominant theme for all the companies. Merrill Lynch was the greatest enthusiast for the concept of the 'financial supermarket':

The new industries will be structured not along product lines but rather by customer groups – that is, small corporations, the affluent, the mass market, or other slices of the demographic pie. Also firms will no longer specialize in single product offerings, but instead will offer packages of products and services that can meet the needs of these segments . . . What is Merrill Lynch going to do about this? Our strategy is to become all things to some people. There are two important aspects of this strategy. First, we need to define 'some people'. Merrill Lynch intends to concentrate on those people with the financial resources to buy the products and services that we have to offer. Second, we must define 'all things'. Merrill Lynch will try to provide all of the important financial services that we think are necessary to maintain relationships in that market. We will service customers throughout their total financial life-cycle.[1]

At the same time, not all of the six companies accepted the necessity of supplying the full range of financial services. Citicorp, although one of the world's most diversified financial corporations in terms of its services and geographic market spread, described its strategy in terms of pursuing the opportunities made available by the changes in the banking industry rather than as diversification into new industries. In 1986, Citicorp broke down its activities into four groups, three of which were labelled as 'banking': individual banking, institutional banking, investment banking and 'information business and corporate items'. American Express, while recognizing the diversity of the services it offered, was fiercely resistant to the concept and the label of 'financial supermarket':

Despite the geographic scope of its operations and the breadth of its product line, American Express does not seek to become a 'financial supermarket'. We do not suffer from the illusion that we can provide all financial services to all people. We are not competing for the whole pie, just for certain slices.

(Annual Report, 1983)

What emerges, therefore, is that diversification was not driven by a shared perception of the type of organization that each of the firms wished to become. The common directions in diversity were more a consequence of individual responses to shared perceptions of the changes that were taking place in the industry. In all six companies, diversification was driven primarily by the desire to serve more fully existing customers' financial needs.

The anticipated benefits from diversification

An interesting feature of the diversification strategies of the companies was their clear and explicit analysis of the benefits which they expected diversification to yield. Figure 15.3 summarizes my findings concerning the major advantages which senior executives expected diversification to bring.

The statements show a surprising unanimity in the benefits that were anticipated from the diversification. The companies emphasized two main categories of benefit: economies of sharing resources and activities across different financial services, and the transfer of skills and competences from one business to another. Six areas of benefit are worthy of emphasis:

Sales and distribution advantages

In terms of the perceived benefits from the use of common resources, all six firms emphasized the advantages that would accrue from supplying a range of financial services through a common sales and distribution system. Following the acquisition of Shearson Loeb Rhoades in June 1981, the American Express chairman, James Robinson III, reported to shareholders:

In 1982 . . . Fireman's Fund Life insurance will be offered through the Shearson/American Express investment network in the United States.

	AMEX	BANKAM.	CITICORP	M.L.	PRUDENTIAL	SEARS
Changes in customer preferences	X					X
Economies of scope in sales and distribution	X	X	X	X	X	X
Economies of scope in finance	X					
Economies of scope in data processing and communication	X	X	X	X	X	
Competitive advantages of greater size	X					X
Increased capacity for innovation	X	X	X	X	X	
Ability to exploit distinctive competences in other markets	X		X	X	X	X
Benefits of risk spending		X	X			
To achieve increased sales growth			X		X	X

Figure 15.3 The reasons for diversification
Source: Company annual reports

Similarly, the new Shearson Financial Management Account will use the American Express Gold Card as a payment vehicle through which clients can access their accounts.

(Letter to shareholders, Annual Report, 1981)

Following their announcements of the acquisitions of stockbrokers Bache and Schwab, Prudential and BankAmerica emphasized the benefits of 'cross-selling'. Similarly, from the outset of its diversification into securities and real estate broking, Sears stated its ambition of combining the distribution channels for the various types of service.

Economies in information technology

Sales and distribution was not the only area where the companies anticipated economies of scope from common resources. Complementary to the distribution channels for financial services are the information and communication networks that supply market intelligence and operationalize transactions. A key distinguishing feature of the strategies of several of the companies in the sample was their commitment to technical leadership in information and communication networks. This was notably the case with American Express, Citicorp and BankAmerica. While BankAmerica (desperately seeking to remedy under-investment in technology during the 1970s) stressed the productivity-raising, cost-reducing merits of technology, Citicorp and American Express saw technology as primarily a means of gaining a differentiation advantage in supplying a range of services to individual customers. In its 1982 review of its business operations, a recurring theme in all three of Citicorp's divisions was the competitive edge conferred by technology:

Citicorp offers the only worldwide electronic financial network covering all commercial currencies and even today supplies the only on-line corporate banking services in many national markets.

(Annual Report, 1982)

American Express gave even greater weight to technology as the driving force behind diversification:

In the future, American Express will continue to use new technological tools to develop products that cross the traditional boundaries between businesses. We believe that success will go to companies providing products at the lowest cost while still maintaining standards of the highest quality. Thus, the Company's traditional emphasis on technology – coupled with its formidable marketing skills – is the foundation upon which we are building tomorrow's competitive advantage.

(Louis Gerstner, chairman and CEO, Travel Related Services, 1982).

The potential for cable networks to revolutionize the distribution of both goods and services to households was a potent vision for American Express at the beginning of the 1980s and was a major factor in its $500 million investment in Warner Amex Cable and its subsequent acquisition of Shearson:

Up to now, our slogan has been: 'Don't leave home without us.' In the future it could be: 'Don't stay home without us' as well. . . . This is the cable of tomorrow. The synergy is incredible.

(Chairman James Robinson quoted in *Forbes*, 25 May 1981, p. 100)

Economies in finance

A third common resource where potential for economies of scope were recognized was in finance. Commenting on the Shearson acquisition, Chairman Robinson observed:

The combination of the resources of the two companies offers another advantage as well. American Express Company is a net borrower of funds, while Shearson is a net lender. Therefore, the Shearson addition has reduced our exposure to the effects of short term interest rate fluctuations.

(Letter to shareholders, Annual Report, 1981)

The transfer of management skills

The benefits anticipated from economies of scope in common inputs and jointly-used facilities imply some measure of integration of the operations of the different financial service businesses. However, an equally important source of perceived benefit was the ability to transfer certain competitive advantages from one business to another. All the companies made reference to the benefits of diversification in permitting the company to apply certain 'distinctive competences' in the new business. Citicorp's analysis of its entry into investment banking placed considerable emphasis on its commitment to innovation, global coverage and the highest quality of personnel as the factors which would offer it competitive advantage in investment banking. Sears Roebuck stressed its expertise in managing large-scale, national distribution. Referring to the acquisition of Dean Witter Reynolds, Sears Chairman, Edward Telling, observed:

We believe this is a major opportunity for a company such as ours, which can apply the efficient distribution and the economies of scale on a national basis.

(Annual Report, 1981, p. 3)

American Express also gave weight to the management skills which it believed were applicable in other financial services:

Our leadership rests on the strength of our financial and management resources, our leading-edge use of sophisticated computer and telecommunications technologies and our traditional sensitivity to shifting consumer needs.

(Annual Report, 1982, p. 16)

Transfer of reputation

Both American Express and Sears also recognized the importance of their corporate reputations as an assurance to the customer. Irving Leveson of the Hudson Institute commented on the role of American Express in the new financial services industry as follows:

Added to these strengths are the intangible assets of the Company's 130 year history serving the financial and communications needs of consumers, companies and nations. They include our global brand recognitions and, most important, our reputation for integrity, reliability and quality.

(Annual Report, 1982, pp. 19)

Sears Roebuck offered similar comment:

These significant new business dimensions are in the best tradition of Sears Roebuck and Co. They are also a natural extension of our unique and long-standing relationship with the American consumer . . . Survey after survey has confirmed that Sears is one of the best known and most trusted commercial institutions in the nation.

(Annual Report, 1981, p. 7)

The advantages of size

Five of the companies, American Express, Citicorp, Merrill Lynch, Prudential and Sears, emphasized the benefits of size alone in generating benefits from diversification. The rationale here tended not to be explicit, but the key factor that the companies mentioned was the size and extent of their distribution networks. American Express and Citicorp focused on the global span of their operations and customer base; Prudential, Merrill Lynch and Sears emphasized their huge US distribution networks. The size of the network was seen as conferring competitive advantage in the entry of new financial services for two reasons: first, it made it possible to spread the fixed costs associated with new entry over a larger potential market; second, it offered advantages in dealing with geographically mobile customers (both American Express and

Citicorp targeted the international segment of very wealthy individuals) and multi-point corporate customers.

Apart from the synergistic benefits of combining different services within a single corporation, several of the firms saw diversification into other financial services as means of risk spreading (Citicorp and BankAmerica) and of increasing the growth potential of the corporation (Sears). The issue of growth is interesting; although mentioned only by Sears, it seems to have been an implicit motive of the others too. All six companies had grown rapidly in the past, establishing each as a leader in its own field with limited opportunities for substantial gains in market share. Each of the companies had strong, ambitious top management. Diversification provided an outlet for the growth ambitions of senior managers. It also provided an outlet for the profit earnings of the companies: as a group, the companies paid out less than a third of net income in dividends to stockholders during the late 1970s.

THE PERFORMANCE OF THE DIVERSIFIED FINANCIAL SERVICE COMPANIES

Method

The impact of diversification upon the performance of financial service companies was measured in three ways:

1 The profitability of each of the six diversified corporations was compared with the average profitability of specialized companies (weighted to reflect the spread across industries of each diversified corporation's assets).[2]
2 The performance of each business activity of the diversified corporations was compared to the average performance of specialized companies within the same financial service industry.
3 The diversifying acquisitions of each of the six diversified corporations were tracked over time to identify subsequent divestments. Such divestments were regarded as evidence of diversification having been unsuccessful.

Relative profitability

Figure 15.4 shows that the return on equity (ROE) and return on assets (ROA) earned by the five diversified companies was, overall, below that earned by comparable specialist companies. This poor performance was not uniform across the group: BankAmerica performed particularly poorly during the mid-1980s, and Sears Roebuck and Merrill Lynch turned in a consistently mediocre performance over the period.

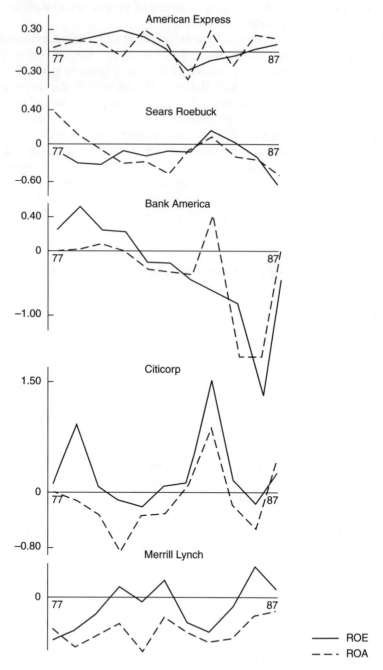

Figure 15.4 The profitability of each diversified company relative to that of specialized companies

However, not one of the diversified companies was able to outperform specialist companies on both ROE and ROA. Returns to shareholders over the period were also lower among the diversified companies than among the specialized companies.

It was clear that diversification failed to improve performance over time. The most intensive period of diversification for all the companies was 1981–82. Comparing relative profitability for the four years prior to this period (1977–80) with relative profitability in the four years after the diversification (1983–86), deterioration in both ROE and ROA is apparent (see Figure 15.5).

Divisional profitability

Comparing the performance of the divisions and subsidiaries of the diversified corporations with that of specialized competitors sheds

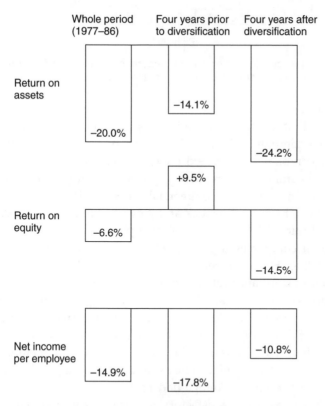

Figure 15.5 The average profitability of the diversified financial companies relative to that of specialized companies over the whole period, before diversification and after diversification

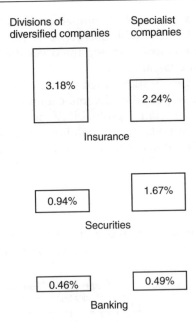

Figure 15.6 The divisional return on assets of the diversified companies compared with that of specialized companies

further light on the relative performance. Although the data on profitability by activity/subsidiary/division is incomplete and lacks consistency across companies, Figure 15.6 shows that, during the 1980s, the diversified companies performed relatively well (in terms of return on assets) in insurance, but relatively poorly in brokerage/investment banking and in retail and commercial banking. The long-established diversifications by Sears Roebuck and American Express into insurance through Allstate and Fireman's Fund, respectively, were highly profitable for both companies (although Fireman's Fund's profitability collapsed in 1984). However, the diversifications of the early 1980s have shown poor performance relative to more specialized competitors. The diversifications in broking and investment banking by Sears, Prudential, American Express and BankAmerica all earned returns below the average for the industry. Interestingly, the only company to enter investment banking by internal expansion, Citicorp, is also the only member of the sample to earn relatively high returns on assets and equity in this area. Entries into real estate brokerage had performed only modestly better. While Sears has earned a satisfactory return on its investment in Coldwell Banker, Merrill Lynch's real estate division was a continual drag on profitability and was divested in 1986.

	Number of acquisitions	Number of divestments
Horizontal[1]	24	5
Diversified[2]	36	12

Notes
1 'Horizontal' acquisitions and divestments are businesses in financial services where the company was already active at the beginning of 1977.
2 'Diversified' acquisitions and divestments are businesses in financial services where the company was not active at the beginning of 1977.

Figure 15.7 Divestments of diversified businesses among the diversified financial service companies 1977–86
Source: Company annual reports, Moody's Reports

Divestments

Evidence of the disappointing financial returns to diversification is supported by recent restructuring by several of the companies in the sample. Since 1985, a number of divestments of earlier diversifications occurred. The most prominent have been American Express's sale of its Fireman's Fund insurance subsidiary, Merrill Lynch's exit from real estate broking, BankAmerica's sale of Charles Schwab discount brokerage, and Sear's disposal of the Coldwell Bankers' commercial real estate business, Allstate's group life and health business, and other parts of its financial service businesses which served corporate and institutional customers. Figure 15.7 shows that the ratio of divestments to acquisitions among the six companies has been higher for diversified financial activities than for 'core' financial activities.

THE PROBLEMS OF MANAGING DIVERSIFICATION

In a recent article, Michael Porter of Harvard Business School argued that a successful diversification strategy is one which permits the sharing of activities and transfer of skills between businesses (see Figure 15.8 for a fuller outline of Porter's views). On this basis, one would expect that diversification in the financial services sector would have been outstandingly successful: the potential for transferring skills and sharing activities appeared tremendous. So what went awry?

Efforts of the companies to exploit shared activities and transfer of skills

One explanation for poor performance would be a failure by the companies to exploit potential synergies between the businesses. From the

'To understand how to formulate corporate strategy, it is necessary to specify the conditions under which diversification will truly create shareholder value. These conditions can be summarized in three essential tests:

1 The attractiveness test. The industries chosen for diversification must be structurally attractive or capable of being made attractive.
2 The cost-of-entry test. The cost of entry must not capitalize all the future profits.
3 The better-off test. Either the new unit must gain competitive advantage from its link with the corporation or vice-versa . . .

My study has helped me identify four concepts of corporate strategy that have been put into practice.

1 Portfolio management . . . is based primarily upon diversification through acquisition. The corporation acquires sound companies with competent managers who agree to stay on . . . In most countries the age when portfolio management was a valid concept of corporate strategy are past. In the case of increasingly well-developed capital markets, attractive companies with good managements show up on everyone's computer screen . . .
2 Restructuring strategy seeks out undeveloped, sick or threatened organizations or industries on the threshold of significant change. The parent intervenes, frequently changing unit management, shifting strategy, or infusing the company with new technology . . . The parent sells off the stronger unit once the results are clear . . .
3 Transferring skills leads to competitive advantage . . . if . . .
 - the activities involved in the business are similar enough that sharing experience is meaningful . . .
 - the transfer of skills involves activities important to competitive advantage . . .
 - the skills transferred represent a significant source of competitive advantage for the receiving unit . . .
4 Sharing activities . . . is a potent basis for corporate strategy because sharing often enhances competitive advantage by lowering cost or raising differentiation . . .

Both the strategic logic and the experience of the companies I studied over the last decade suggest that a company will create shareholder value through diversification to a greater and greater extent as its strategy moves from a portfolio management towards sharing activities. Because they do not rely upon superior insight or questionable assumptions about the company's capabilities, sharing activities and transferring skills offer the best values for value creation . . . '

Figure 15.8 Porter on diversification
Source: Porter, M. E., 'From Competitive Advantage to Corporate Strategy', *Harvard Business Review*, May–June 1987, pp. 48–59.

information available on the post-diversification management practices by the six companies, this was clearly not the case. Common to all six of the diversified financial service corporations was evidence of persistent efforts by top management to exploit economies of scope and transfer skills and expertise between the different financial service businesses.[3] The companies reported eight main areas where linkages between the businesses were exploited, these are listed in Figure 15.9. The evidence

Source of synergy	Action to exploit synergy	Companies reporting
Economies of scope in joint resources and activities		
In sales and distribution	Cross selling by staff Joint use of facilities Merging of distribution networks	All six companies Sears, BankAm., Merrill L., Citicorp None.
Data processing and communication systems	Sharing of facilities Creating single dp and communications unit	AMEX, Merrill L., Citicorp, Sears, BankAm
Finance	Reorganization to pool financial assets, centralize borrowing and cross-subsidize	AMEX, Citicorp
Research services	Sharing research services Centralizing into a single unit	Citicorp, BankAm., AMEX Merrill L
General management	Merging divisions or subsidiaries	All six companies
Transfer of skills and expertise		
Transfer of general management skills	Transfer of top managers between divisions/subsidiaries	All six companies
	Transferring systems used in one division/subsidiary to another	All six companies
Reputation transfer	Transfer of brand and company names	All six companies
Increased capacity for innovation	Introduction of new products, services of systems based upon the combination of resources from several financial services	All six companies

Figure 15.9 Managerial actions to exploit synergies in diversification
Source: Company annual reports

on the management actions in relation to each of these areas of synergy are described in Appendix 15.A at the end of the chapter.

The failure of diversification to yield significant performance benefits was primarily a reflection of the limited size of the benefits from sharing activities and transferring skills when placed against the difficulties that diversification presented to management. Careful examination of the experiences of the sample of companies revealed six major problems in managing diversified financial service corporations.

The limited appeal of 'one-stop shopping'

The rationale for the 'financial supermarket' rests primarily upon the logic of 'one-stop shopping'. By purchasing a range of financial services from a single supplier, economies are available both to the customer and to the supplier: the customer saves on transaction and search costs, while the supplier benefits from economies of scope in sales and distribution.

However, the appeal of one-stop shopping, both to individuals and corporate customers, proved to be more limited and slower to emerge than most of the companies envisaged. For all the companies, direct mail was a major vehicle for cross-selling to individuals, however, only Citicorp claimed much response in this area. Mass mailings by Dean Witter and Coldwell Banker to Sears customers produced a response rate of only 0.003 per cent, Shearson Lehman's mailing to American Express cardholders did better, but actual business generated was small.

The appeal of one-stop shopping to consumers was limited by three main factors. First, there are different markets for different financial products. Prudential's insurance customers and Sear's merchandise customers typically were not prime targets as customers for stock brokerage services. IDS's customers similarly offered limited potential for American Express credit cards or Shearson Lehman's investment products. Second, unlike supermarkets, different financial products are not usually purchased simultaneously. Hence, the willingness to purchase different products over time must be based upon a continuing loyalty by the customer. As marketing became more aggressive during the 1980s, so customer loyalty became increasingly fragile. The loyalty that did exist made it difficult for the diversified companies to wean customers away from their traditional suppliers of insurance, or IRAs, or banking services.

Among corporate and institutional customers, the diversified suppliers' attempts 'to serve all our clients' financial needs' met a similar lack of customer response. A notable case is the difficulty experienced by the commercial banks in using their banking relationships as a springboard for expansion into investment banking. The problems were almost identical to those experienced in trying to supply a broad range of financial services to individuals. First, the customers with which the banks had the closest relationships were primarily small and medium-sized firms, while the major issuers of securities were large companies and governments. Second, most issuers already had relationships with underwriters. Third, the loyalty of corporate customers for their investment bankers tended to be low. Citicorp, Merrill Lynch and Prudential-Bache bought substantial slices of underwriting business through a willingness to accept wafer-thin margins. But this price-sensitive business also tended to be highly mobile and failed to generate either loyalty or continuing business from corporate clients.

Difficulties in sharing sales and distribution systems

Limited customer enthusiasm was not the only reason for the failure of shared sales and distribution systems to yield the expected benefits. There were problems on the supply side too. Most evident was reluctance of sales personnel to adapt from being specialist sales executives to serving the broader customer needs. Despite the potential benefits of increased business and therefore bigger commission incomes, in all six companies diversification led to dissatisfaction among sales personnel. Some of the problems related to perceptions of status and are dealt with under the heading of 'culture clash'; other problems were tangible. At Merrill Lynch, brokers complained increasingly about information overload and the difficulty of selling over the telephone some of the more complex new products (such as tax shelters). As a result Merrill Lynch began to supplement its brokers with life insurance specialists in its larger offices, and with salaried employees to handle small transactions and routine customer enquiries.[4]

Some of the problems related to the different types of expertise and selling approaches required for selling different types of product. Prudential's insurance agents, used to selling products that protected against risk, had difficulty selling mutual funds that exposed the customer to risk. Insurance agents typically made two face-to-face sales a week, stockbrokers normally made around seven telephone sales a day over the telephone.[5] More experienced sales executives had preferences for dealing with particular types of customer. Dean Witter and Coldwell Banker employees were reluctant to staff the financial centres located in Sears stores.

The problems were not only in financial services for individuals. In the institutional and corporate markets, the ability to integrate sales and distribution networks and to achieve cross-selling also proved to be limited. This was particularly so in commercial and investment banking. Whilst there may be some potential relationship benefits between commercial banking and investment banking in obtaining underwriting business and engaging in mergers and acquisitions, there appeared to be few links when it came to the distribution of securities. Successful distribution of securities requires close, long-term relationships with portfolio holders such as insurance companies, mutual funds, pension funds and other institutions. This type of distribution network is quite different from that which the commercial banks have developed in their traditional businesses, and it partly explains the limited success of the US commercial banks in European investment banking.[6] Poor financial performance and high turnover of managers was evident at Citicorp's investment bank, and also in the London investment banks of Chase Manhattan and Security Pacific.[7]

Problems of reconciling specialized production with shared sales and support activities

Even where significant economies are present from sharing resources and common activities such as distribution and sales, research, information and communication systems, and various support services, management problems arise from reconciling economies of scope in certain activities, with economies of specialization in others. For example, in most production operations there are advantages in specialization on a product basis. Hence, efficiency suggests that production should be organized along conventional product lines (e.g. insurance, stockbroking, fund management, foreign exchange dealing, retail deposit taking). However, other activities are best organized along alternative bases, for example, distribution and sales by customer type, while certain common services such as research, communication, information can be centralized.

Attempts to organize distribution and sales on a customer basis, while production activities are organized on a product basis and other activities such as information or research are centralized, create problems of co-ordination that impose both transitional and continuing costs. The experiences of the six firm sample indicate a key transitional cost arising from the organizational change in retraining the salesforce to handle a broader array of financial services. All six of the companies emphasized their commitment to staff training and all introduced specific retraining programmes for their sales employees during the 1980s.

Managing co-ordination across different financial service businesses also imposed continuing costs. The introduction of 'relationship managers' and 'financial consultants' to market a range of financial services and interface between the diversified corporation and the customer necessitates communication and co-ordination between the salesman/adviser and the financial specialists in each of the product market areas. A consequence for several firms was that rather than offering economies of scope in distribution and sales such arrangements led to increasing costs of administration and support services.

If economies of scope exist in downstream activities (sales and distribution), while economies of specialization exist in upstream activities, this may imply less vertical integration within financial service corporations. William Gregor, senior vice president of Management Analysis Center, Cambridge, Mass., asks:

Where do companies want to participate in the distribution system? Do they want to be a manufacturer or a distributor? In the past, the financial services industry has been heavily vertically integrated. For many institutions such integration is not going to be easy in the future. More people are going to have to decide whether they want to manufacture – whether they have the economies of scale to do that well – or whether their real value added is in their distribution capability.[8]

Culture clash

Probably the most visible problem of diversification was the frictions generated by organizational and operational changes that were involved in the integration and co-ordination of different financial service businesses within a single corporation. The resistance of sales personnel to offering a wider range of financial products was only partly a problem of retraining and information overload. Many of the problems appear to have resulted from the challenge that the diversified financial corporations presented to the rigidities and expectations associated with the organizational cultures particular to different types of financial institution. Merrill Lynch was one of the first to experience resistance from its brokers to the widening product range that they were expected to market. Whilst complaints focused upon the pressures of keeping informed about new product offerings and meeting increased commission targets, the critical underlying issue appeared to be the adjustment in role and status from stockbroker to that of a general financial adviser and sales person. An estimated 16 per cent of Merrill Lynch's account executives left the firm in 1983 (*Fortune*, 6 August 1984, p. 47).

Some of the most resounding 'culture clashes' within the diversified corporations have been between investment banking and other activities. This primarily reflected the elitist, glamour image associated with the investment banks backed by the generous remuneration of their senior employees. As a result, attempts to bring investment banking within the ambit of other financial services sparked serious interpersonal rivalries and organizational problems. Citicorp led the way in integrating its investment bank within a broader framework of institutional financial services. Tom Theobald's leading role in forging a global investment bank from Citicorp's investment banks in New York, London and Tokyo, merging Citicorp's treasury department into the investment bank, and then establishing close co-operation between investment banking and commercial banking resulted in deflated morale and a stream of departures of key employees from Citi's investment bank (*Business Week*, 28 July 1986, pp. 56–8; *Euromoney*, December, 1986, pp. 78–92). Similar transitional problems were experienced in the integration of the long-established Lehman investment bank into Shearson-American Express.

Interviews with branch managers and sales executives among the sample companies confirmed the resentments, frictions and fears that were aroused by absorption within diversified financial service corporations. At Sears it was interesting that whilst Allstate agents identified closely with the image and values of Sears, brokers at Dean Witter did their utmost to minimize their association with Sears and resented Sear's attempts to impose its 'mass merchandising' approach upon them.

Conflicts between different financial service businesses within the same enterprise represent a diversion of time and energy and impose mediation costs on top management. At American Express, Shearson Lehman conflicted with American Express Bank over which of them would run merchant banking operations in Japan, while a project to sell insurance to IDS clients was stalled for two years because of disagreement over whether the insurance would be sold by direct mail or through IDS financial planners (*Fortune*, 16 February 1987, p. 80).

Providing incentives for co-operation

One of the key difficulties in making co-operation work across different financial services was in providing incentives to exploit the potential for economies of scope and transfer of skills. The great merit of the conglomerate as an organizational structure is that operational responsibilities can be decentralized and each business can operate as an independent profit centre. Managing linkages between business necessitates either increased head office intervention which inevitably undermines divisional autonomy, or the introduction of incentives to promote the desired co-operation. Implementing such incentives is no easy matter. At the sales level providing commission incentives for cross-selling and cross-referral is in principle easy. In practice complex commission structures give rise to dissatisfaction and the propensity for sales executives to push those products offering the highest return per unit of time.

In areas other than sales, incentives for co-operation are more difficult and gaining the necessary momentum may necessitate a concerted organization-wide drive. American Express has gone further than any other of the six sample companies to create such incentives in the form of top-down exhortation and individual rewards. Under the banner of 'one enterprise', chairman James Robinson made the quest for synergies a primary theme of corporate strategy. The requirement for senior executives to identify two or three 'one enterprise' projects in their annual strategic plans was reinforced by a system of extra bonuses to be awarded to each manager on the basis of contribution to the 'one enterprise' theme. In 1985 AMEX Bank chairman Robert F. Smith received $80,000 in recognition of the bank's introducing Shearson to its overseas clients and selling $240 million of money orders and travellers' cheques for the Card Division (*Fortune*, 19 February 1987, p. 80). A key responsibility of corporate strategy manager Ursula Burke is a monthly report on the status of each 'one enterprise' project circulated to the company's top 100 executives.

Problems of control

Part of the increased operating costs experienced by the diversified corporations reflects the increased difficulty of setting and monitoring performance targets and auditing efficiency in companies with interrelated businesses. Where sales and distribution systems, promotional activities, research services and information networks are being shared between businesses, cost and revenue allocation becomes difficult, and profit and efficiency targets are difficult to set and monitor. The frequency of reoganizations at Merrill Lynch, American Express, Citicorp and Prudential during the period 1982–86 is indicative of the difficulties in establishing appropriate structures for managing corporate–divisional relationships and interdivisional relations.

These reorganizations have lacked any common direction across the companies. At Merrill Lynch the primary emphasis of the reorganization between 1984 and 1986 was decentralization, pushing profit responsibility down from the three operating divisions to 15 newly created business units. The decentralization was accompanied by a centralization of support functions into a separate headquarters support division. New financial control systems were installed in 1986 including a performance measurement system 'enabling us to realistically allocate overhead costs to provide a clearer picture of the true profitability of our diverse businesses' (Annual Report, 1986, pp. 2–3).

Prudential's reorganization was also driven primarily by the desire for greater decentralizaation and business unit accountability. In addition to decentralizing its insurance operations, primarily by geographic dispersal, Prudential-Bache went through two major restructurings. In 1982 it was reorganized into eight major operating groups 'structured around its various sales forces and lines of business' (Annual Report, 1982, p. 10). In October 1985 it was again restructured to realign domestic and international branch systems and form a new Capital Markets Group and a Merchant Banking Group (Annual Report, 1985, pp. 2–3).

Among all the companies it appeared that, rather than diversification yielding economies, the major consequence was increasing costs. The low overall profitability of the diversified companies was a result of cost growth outstripping revenue expansion. Some of these costs were transitional costs arising from growth. In particular, a number of firms incurred increased costs due to increased write-offs of bad debts. These were normally a direct result of taking on new business in order to increase market share. For example, Citicorp's desire to expand its Diners Club credit card business resulted in heavy losses due to the high proportion of new card holders who defaulted on their accounts. The other major cause of rising cost was increased operating cost. Escalating administrative and support costs were a particular problem for Merrill Lynch. In the five years to 1986, costs of compensation and benefits rose 168 per cent compared to total revenue which rose 138 per cent. CEO, William Schreyer, acknowledged overstaffing in the tier of middle managers, especially in support functions such as planning, marketing, internal controls and communication (*Wall Street Journal*, 12 August 1986, p. 2).

Cost increases were also driven by the propensity for high remuneration business areas to generate demands for pay increases in other businesses. This pressure was strongest among the banks, reflecting the higher unionization of their employees. At Citibank a key source of friction between commercial and investment bankers was the higher salaries and bonuses received by the investment bankers. In other companies similar jealousies constrained co-operation between stockbrokers and insurance agents in cross-referral and cross-selling – brokers tended to earn higher incomes than insurance agents.

In general, however, the problem was one of corporate managements' overeagerness to throw money at their newly acquired subsidiaries, and inability to monitor and control costs closely. Merrill Lynch has found getting to grips with cost control especially difficult: between 1982 and 1985 total employment grew from 37,900 to 44,000; by October 1987 it was up to 47,000 – growth of costs had consistently dwarfed that of revenue.[9]

Lack of adequate control over operations was also evident in an apparently increasing propensity for major blunders among the companies. Because of the size of individual market transactions, the intense competition of financial markets, and the volume of transactions for which a single employee may be responsible, effective monitoring and control systems are an essential requirement for success in financial markets. During the 1980s several instances of misjudgment and ineffective controls occurred among the six diversified companies. Examples are listed in Figure 15.10. While isolated examples cannot be regarded as

BankAmerica	Losses in the mid-1980s from excessive lending to the farm sector, to resource-based companies and to Latin America.
	Unauthorized trading by employees at Schwab of customers' shares between 1985 and 1988.
American Express/ Shearson-Lehman	Collapse of profitability at Fireman's Fund.
	Potential $100 m+ losses from investment in MCorp, a near-bankrupt Texas bank.
	Adverse publicity arising from poorly-managed involvement in the hostile takeover of Koppers in 1988.
Merrill Lynch	$350 m+ lost by a single trader in mortgage-backed securities during Spring 1987.
	Losses of up to $100 m in the London investment banking operation as a result of poor management, uncontrolled costs, and lack of market penetration.
Citicorp	$40 m lost by a poorly-monitored Dublin stock trader (1987).

Figure 15.10 Examples of losses incurred by the diversified companies as a result of poor judgment and inadequate control

a consequence of diversity, they do point to the difficulty that such large and complex organizations encounter in reconciling the corporate management functions of resource allocation and strategic planning with the close attention to detail that is so important in the financial sector. The problem has been succinctly stated by Henry Kaufman:

How does the management of a financial institution – whether an insurance company, a securities firm, or a commercial bank – that becomes more diverse adequately control all its new and different profit centers? It is a difficult task to understand the risks and rewards and to stay within the outer limits of risk-taking to avoid a Penn Square disaster. It not only requires setting goals; it requires hands-on management. I doubt very much whether decentralization succeeds in that kind of environment . . . Managing financial conglomeration will be an exceptional challenge and poses great risk. I am not convinced that financial institutions today have the management skills at the most senior level to perceive and understand the developments in the five or six or seven different areas of their business.[10]

CONCLUSIONS

The rationale for diversification: is it valid?

The fact that diversification had not proved successful in financial terms does not necessarily invalidate the arguments upon which the diversification moves were based. Clearly many of the realized benefits were much smaller than anticipated. In particular, the appeal of one-stop shopping proved to be limited to both individual and corporate customers. Furthermore, it appears that there are few benefits from diversification in terms of cost economies. Not one of the companies was able to lower costs or reduce employment through sharing activities between different diversified businesses.

Yet in some areas it appears that diversification did enhance the companies' competitive capabilities. Transfer of reputation worked well for American Express and Citicorp, and to some extent for Prudential-Bache. Diversification also seems to enhance the innovative capacities of the companies. During the period Merrill Lynch, American Express/Shearson, Lehman, and Citicorp were leaders in the introduction of new products and in developing new areas of business.

If companies are to exploit the advantages of sharing resources and transferring skills and competences more effectively, a much more closely targeted approach is called for. The identification of potential synergies in broad terms is not enough. Detailed examination of the specific benefits and how they are to be attained is needed. Sears's entry into diversified financial services could not be justified simply by the strength of the Sears's franchise and evidence of the penetration of Sears's in-store credit cards into upper-income households. Similarly the commercial bank's entry into investment banking needed a much more searching analysis of how their particular strengths and expertise could be used to yield competitive advantage against already-established investment banks.

Intercompany co-operation as alternative to diversification

A key issue that must be addressed in analysing the synergies that diversification can yield is whether diversification is necessary to exploit these benefits. The theoretical literature has long recognized that economies of scope do not necessitate diversification if they can be exploited through co-operation by specialist companies. For example, to exploit the benefits of cross-selling does not require that the suppliers of the different services are under common ownership. Similarly, in the case of research services and communication and data processing networks, it may be possible for the suppliers of different financial services simply to co-operate.

While most of the companies in the sample accepted the imperative of diversification in order to supply the customer with a broad range of financial services, American Express recognized that this is not the only route and points to the potential for financial service firms to co-operate through networking arrangements:

The industry will perforce range from single product boutiques – such as small bond houses – to large, broad-based companies . . . Some may be linked together in varying degrees by a network made possible by vast data processing and telecommunication systems. The most important feature of these 'networking' arrangements is that they are co-operative but do not reduce the benefits of competition. Networking relationships are based on the principle of mutual benefit – realizing economies of scale, creating synergy between products and organizations and allowing each partner to do what he does best.

Networking is by no means a new concept in financial services. Correspondence banking and investment banker syndication of securities underwritings are examples of long-standing co-operative ventures . . .

What is new, however, is that the explosive growth and diversity of networking among US financial service institutions that formerly avoided co-operative ventures . . . Firms are increasingly buying from, selling to, and co-venturing with other companies to reach new markets, create new products or broaden their geographic reach . . .

The ultimate implication of networking is that there is room for both large and small institutions. The new services, service combinations and delivery systems will make it easier for smaller institutions to compete.

(Annual Report, 1982, p. 15)

There are many examples of co-operation by independent companies to exploit linkages between different areas of business. Citicorp, for example, introduced 'personal insurance centers' into some of its retail banks. These insurance centres were staffed and serviced by American International Group (Annual Report, 1984, p. 17). A number of banks and savings and loan institutions introduced discount brokerage services in association with brokerage companies. In real estate brokerage, Coldwell Banker used discounts on home furnishings at Sears as an incentive to home buyers. Long and Foster, a Washington, DC real estate broker, signed up a local department store to offer a similar scheme (*Forbes*, 3 November 1986, p. 123).

The extent to which co-operative arrangements between independent companies capture the benefits of economies of scope depends upon the costs and effectiveness of such arrangements compared with organization within a single company. The growth of co-operative arrangements between different types of financial institution suggests that many economies of joint resources can be exploited through contractual agreements, without the co-ordination costs and inflexibilities that arise in the diversified corporation. However, some of the other benefits from diversification, such as exploiting brand and company reputation, knowledge of international financial markets, expertise in the design of new financial instruments, and other firm-specific intangible assets, cannot be effectively captured through arrangements between independent companies.

Understanding the business

It is clear from the experiences of several of the companies in our sample that a major source of errors and poor performance was a misunderstanding of the business entered. Diversification decisions need to be based upon careful analysis of the attractiveness of the business to be entered, and a profound understanding of the factors responsible for success within that business. In many cases diversification decisions appear to have been wanting on both counts. The rush of companies into investment banking was based upon the notion that this area of business offered fabulous returns to participants compared with traditional banking and securities broking. Such expectations failed to take account of the highly competitive nature of the underwriting business, the high risks involved (which became all too apparent after the British Government's BP flotation), and the fact that the entry of so many well-financed participants into a comparatively small market would inevitably drive down margins.

The disappointing performance of several of the entrants into investment banking also underlines the need for a careful understanding of the determinants of success in a new industry. In commercial banking superior profitability is achieved through careful assessment of credit risk, effective management of the loan portfolio, and efficiency in transactions processing. Key success factors in investment banking are orientated much more around effective deal making and razor-sharp judgment of the market. Many of the problems the commercial banks experienced in their securities businesses arose through the imposition of strategies and management systems which were not consistent with the key success factors in the securities business.

The strategic management problem

Managing diversified business corporations calls for the highest order of management expertise. In the manufacturing industry companies have struggled with the problems of managing diversity for most of this century. The first major breakthrough was the introduction by Du Pont and General Motors of divisionalized corporate structures in the early 1920s. The second was the innovations made by General Electric during the early 1970s. These included the introduction of the strategic business unit as the basic unit of strategy formulation, the development of portfolio planning matrices for strategy formulation and resource allocation, and the formation of the strategic data base which later broadened into the PIMS (Profit Impact of Market Strategy) programme.

The experiences of the six large, diversified financial corporations in the sample point to the problems that arise when managements' imagination in conceiving and launching potentially successful strategic initiatives extends beyond their ability to implement those initiatives effectively. One problem of managing diversity in the financial services industry is that the tools that have been developed for strategic planning within diversified firms have been developed by and for manufacturing companies primarily. Take, for example, the use of the 'strategic business unit' concept. Proposed by McKinsey and Company to General Electric and subsequently adopted by most large diversified corporations, SBUs have greatly facilitated strategy formulation, resource allocation and performance control. The essential requirements for using SBUs is that the company can be separated into clearly delineated businesses, that separate financial statements can be produced for each unit, that these statements can be adjusted for inflation to reveal the real performance of the business, and proformas can be drawn up selecting different assumptions about the environment and different strategic options.[11]

Identifying SBUs within large financial service corporations is no easy task: deciding whether to identify business units on the basis of customer groups, geographical areas or products can be exceptionally difficult; the closeness of relationships between different business areas often means that each business unit is far from independent strategically, financially or operationally, while the greater complexity of profit and loss accounting in financial service companies means that meaningful statements of financial performance at business unit level are difficult to obtain. Merrill Lynch's problems of establishing effective cost control and mapping out a clear strategic direction owe much to the difficulties of determining an organizational structure that permits efficient operation, effective strategic decision making, and allows costs and revenues to be allocated sufficiently precisely for the performance of each unit to be tracked.

Organization structure: integration or autonomy

A key issue in the strategic management of diversified financial service corporations concerns the relationships between the different businesses. How far should corporate headquarters seek to integrate and co-ordinate the different business areas?

The evidence is mixed. Co-ordination and integration are needed if the benefits of shared activities and transfer of capabilities is to be achieved, however, such co-ordination has frequently given rise to more costs than benefits. On the evidence of past experience it would appear that, in the short to medium term at least, the safest bet is to permit acquired businesses to operate as autonomous subsidiaries. Such a policy is particularly attractive where the different businesses require different strategies and organization. For example, commercial banks and investment banks not only need to compete in different ways, commercial banks require hierarchical structures with clear decision rules, while investment banks require flat organizational structures with individual autonomy and few rules. In the European securities markets, commercial banks that have operated their securities firms semi-autonomously (e.g. Barclays and DZW, and First Boston Credit Suisse) have performed better than those that have maintained much closer management links.

The problem, however, is that since most of those who acquire (particularly those who acquire financial service companies) pay hefty acquisition premiums in relation to book value and previous market price, then such hands-off management cannot easily be justified on financial grounds. A second problem concerns the need for effective control. In manufacturing industry, conglomerates such as Hanson Trust and General Electric can control their subsidiaries simply through monthly, quarterly and annual financial targets. In financial markets the risks of losses and damaged reputation that can arise from misconduct by a single employee means that top management cannot completely decentralize operational control. (The problems of General Electric with its subsidiary Kidder Peabody is a case in point.)

Ultimately, therefore, if diversification in the financial services industry is to be successful firms must seek methods of co-ordinating and integrating their businesses that avoid the managerial problems identified in this report. The evidence points to the importance of moving slowly and carefully. Almost all ambitious attempts at sharing resources and activities failed. The greatest gains appeared to come from transferring reputation, marketing expertise, technological know-how and top management skills. If companies move cautiously and progressively in exploiting these opportunities for co-operation they stand a good chance of avoiding the traumas, resentments and uncertainties that have characterized post-acquisition management in most of the industry.

An incrementalist approach can also avoid top management becoming overburdened by the demands of internal administrative affairs. When the external environment is in a state of flux, the primary responsibility of management is to ensure that strategies are consistent with the environment, that opportunities are being identified and exploited, and that major threats are guarded against. If internal reorganization and restructuring impose too heavy a burden on management time, the costs in terms of operating performance can be high.

APPENDIX 15.A ACTIONS TO EXPLOIT SHARED ACTIVITIES AND TRANSFER SKILLS IN THE DIVERSIFIED FINANCIAL CORPORATIONS

Sales and distribution

In all six companies the primary source of synergy sought was in distribution and sales. By channelling a range of services through a single point of contact the companies sought to achieve cost economies as well as to serve better the needs of customers. The lead was taken by Merrill Lynch, which has used its national network of account executives to sell a steadily increasing product range. By 1984 it was encouraging its account executives to become licensed real estate brokers and in some locations replaced its commissioned account executives with salaried 'financial advisers'. Similar approaches were followed by Prudential-Bache, which 'launched a major training programme to prepare its account executives to serve as total financial planners' (Annual Report, 1983, p. 8), and American Express, which redesignated its 4,500 Shearson 'investment executives' as 'financial consultants' (Annual Report, 1982, p. 36). By 1985 Prudential reported that: ' . . . average gross production of account executives increased to $226,000, a gain of more than 50%. This lifted Prudential-Bache to second place among nine full line securities firms . . . up from ninth of nine as recently as 1981' (Annual Report, 1985, p. 8). There was little actual integration of sales and distribution systems; the closest was Sears which established in-store financial centres which featured Dean Witter, Allstate and Coldwell Banker desks. 'Cross-selling' was the principal means used of increasing each sales person's sales volume. For example, Prudential insurance agents began selling seven mutual funds developed by Prudential-Bache Securities; at Sears, the Dean Witter Financial Services Group provided mortgages for some 15 per cent of the residential properties sold by Coldwell Banker; Schwab brokerage centres were introduced into Bank of America branches; by 1985, 308 Sears Financial Network Centers were operating within Sears stores.

Research

Both Merrill Lynch and American Express emphasized the benefits of centralized research serving a range of financial services: Merrill Lynch's team of over 120 highly qualified equities analysts and technical analysts was backed by a highly sophisticated equity data base with continuously up-dated corporate financial projections. American Express emphasized the competitive edge it gained through its sophisticated market research carried out internally and externally through organizations such as the Hudson Institute and SRI International (Annual Reports, 1982 and 1983). It identified its expertise in identifying and understanding consumer financial behaviour and preferences as a key factor in revitalizing the performance of its acquisitions.

Data processing and communication systems

American Express formed a new Financial Institutions Services division which comprised its Money Order division and its newly acquired First Data Resources Inc. and Payment Systems Inc. Citicorp established an 'Information Business' as a separate corporate business area; Prudential formed a Long Range Computer Planning Task Force to plan use of electronic technology. Several sample members internalized computer and communication services rather than relying on external suppliers; Prudential set up an internal computer time sharing service and acquired Gifford Fong Associates, an investment technology consulting firm and Tesseract Corporation, which develops computer systems for managing personnel, employee benefits and payroll; Merrill Lynch formed International MarketNet a joint venture with IBM to provide market information to its own and to external brokers, invested in Teleport Communications, a satellite communications company, and acquired Broadcort Capital Corporation which provided clearance and execution functions both internally and for other brokerage firms.

Transfer of reputation

Benefits from reputation transfer were achieved primarily by stamping corporate identity on to the new financial activities by changes in the names of new subsidiaries and divisions: Bache became Prudential-Bache; Merrill Lynch prefixed its name to all its financial service subsidiaries with the exception of Family Life Insurance Co.; Citicorp identified its subsidiaries by a 'Citi' prefix; American Express added its name to most of its acquisitions during the 1980s (e.g. IDS became IDS/American Express); Sears Roebuck, on the other hand, has maintained the names of its acquired financial service companies, but emphasized the Sears connection through the names of new financial products (e.g. Sears/Dean Witter money funds and IRAs and Sears Home Mortgages).

While the benefits of reputation transfer relate primarily to customers, reputation transfer has also enhanced the companies' ability to attract high-quality employees. American Express observed that a sharp increase in job applications to IDS following its acquisition in 1983.

Exploiting economies of scope in finance

Diversification provided potential gains both through the pooling of financial resources and from balancing positive and negative cash flow businesses. Explicit recognition of economies of pooling financing and economies of avoiding the money markets was given by American Express:

Corporate and subsidiary senior financial executives world-wide, for example, participate in a daily 'cash call' to discuss the Company's cash flow requirements, thus enabling us to reduce daily borrowing costs by co-ordinating use of available short-term funds.

(Annual Report, 1982, p. 20)

In addition, most of the companies offered evidence of attempts to channel funds internally – for example Prudential and Sears used the funds generated in their insurance business to finance loans and investments in their other businesses, such as mortgages and corporate finance; also, Citibank, Merrill Lynch and Prudential pointed to the strength that their capital market activities and investment banking operations derived from the overall size of their financial bases.

Exploiting economies in management

Merging divisions and subsidiaries into one another in principle permits economies to be gained from eliminating the duplication of management structures and support activities. In practice, evidence of this was limited. The major examples of organizational changes which merged separate financial service businesses were mainly associated with changes from a traditional product-based structure (e.g. securities broking, insurance, mortgage financing services) to a customer-based structure (e.g. institutions, small business customers, corporations and individuals). Several companies (including Merrill Lynch, BankAmerica and Citicorp) introduced divisions specifically tailored to the requirements of high net worth customers. The banks (Citicorp and BankAmerica) also merged a number of financial services into their newly formed retail divisions. While some companies reported substantial efficiency gains from restructuring (Citicorp reduced staff in its Institutional Bank by 15 per cent in 1986), it was not apparent that these gains were a consequence of opportunities made available by diversification rather than the simple elimination of slack.

Transfer of management skills

Generally speaking, financial corporations have not pioneered innovation in general management methods. Hence, a distinguishing feature of the diversified companies is that they were among the leading companies in the application of modern management methods to the financial services industry. To the extent that general management technology is general rather than industry specific, this established a basis for transferable competitive advantage. All six of the diversified companies in the sample took steps to transfer management practices from established to new businesses. Merrill Lynch gave particular emphasis to its corporate management strengths as a basis for leading successful entry into new markets. In addresses to securities analysts, the chairman and president of Merrill Lynch pointed to the company's ability to adapt to new customer needs, the leadership and vision provided by top management, the strong and flexible management-by-objectives planning system, and the strength and sophistication of the sales organization. The main emphasis in American Express's transfer of expertise to its acquired businesses has been the company's commitment to and expertise in marketing and customer service:

The combination of American Express's marketing savvy and commitment to service is a potent force in reaching America and the world. 'We are a dynamic, hard-driving group of people', Mr Robinson says. 'We have big ideas and we know how to follow through on them.'

(Annual Report 1983, p. 20)

In integrating diversifying acquisitions, the diversified companies typically replaced the top management of the acquired companies, often by internal transfer. American Express's strategy for Lehman was to transfer some of Shearman's drive and hunger for business to the conventionally staid Investment bank. At Prudential-Bache, George Hall from E. F. Hutton wasted little time in clearing out the ranks of top management and reorganizing the reporting structure after his appointment in July 1982. Management transfer was not always one way – American Express's acquisition of Shearson was accompanied by Shearson's CEO, Sandy Weill, becoming president of American Express, a move aimed at injecting increased flexibility and opportunism into American Express.

Increasing innovatory capabilities

It was clear from the evidence of the companies' experiences that innovation had a close, two-way relationship with diversification. All six of the companies were leaders in the new financial service industry in introducing new products, new services and new approaches to business. Diversification was to some extent a consequence of such innovations: in developing new financial products and services the firms were constantly pushing at the boundaries of traditional markets. At the same time, diversity also provided the combinations of skills and experience and the corporate infrastructures that facilitated innovation and gave the diversified companies an advantage over more specialized competitors in developing new areas of business.

The main objective evidence of diversity facilitating innovation was the flow of new financial instruments and services that resulted from the companies combining and rearranging financial products and services into new packages. The most startling example of this was Merrill Lynch's 'Cash Management Account' which allowed account holders to deposit money in a Merrill Lynch money market fund, to draw on these funds by means of cheques or a Visa card (issued by City National Bank of Columbus, Ohio in co-operation with Merrill Lynch) and borrow on their accounts up to 50 per cent of the value of securities owned by the account holder and deposited with Merrill Lynch. In one step, Merrill Lynch had moved from investment services into personal banking offering a product, an interest-bearing checking account, that the retail banks could not match. In the following five years Merrill Lynch's lead was followed by other companies offering variants of investment accounts linked with banking services: Shearson American Express introduced its 'Financial Management Account' (1982), Dean Witter Group introduced its 'Active Assets Account' (1981), BankAmerica launched 'Cash Maximizer' and 'Investors Checking Service' accounts (1983), Citicorp introduced its 'Citibank Financial Account' and 'Focus' account (1984), and Prudential-Bache introduced its 'Command Account' (1982). This was followed by the introduction of 'home equity accounts' – all six companies introduced accounts through which individuals could borrow against the value of their homes.

As the financial services revolution gathered pace during the 1980s, so the diversified companies sought new ways of developing products that combined elements from different financial services. Between 1984 and 1986, a substantial proportion of the growth in Prudential's life insurance business was generated by new investment-oriented insurance products that built upon Prudential's diversified investment services. Diversification into real estate by American Express, Prudential, Merrill Lynch and Sears encouraged the launching of real estate based investment funds. In serving corporate and institutional customers, Citicorp's commitment to meeting the full range of financial needs encouraged it to take a leading role in developing 'swaps', Euronotes, and new financial vehicles for leveraged buy-outs.

REFERENCES

1 John L. Steffins (Senior Vice President, Merrill Lynch, Pierce, Fenner and Smith Inc.) 'The demand for financial products', p. 57. In Arnold W. Sametz (ed.) *The Emerging Financial Industry,* Lexington Books, D.C. Heath and Company, Lexington, Mass., 1985.
2 Relative profitability was calculated as follows:

$$\frac{\pi_i - \bar{\pi}_i}{\pi_i}$$

where, π_i is the profitability of diversified firm i;
$\bar{\pi}_i$ is the average profitability of specialized firms, weighted to correspond to the same spread of activities as firm i, that is:

$$\pi_i = \Sigma_j \frac{(\pi_j \cdot X_{ij})}{X_i}$$

where, π_j is the average profitability of specialist firms in industry j;
X_{ij} is the sales (or assets), of firm i in industry j;
X_i is the total sales (or assets) of firm i.
3 An indication of top management's emphasis of the need to exploit these sources of synergy is that the frequency with which mention in the chairman's letters to shareholders during the years 1982–86 was made of the need to manage integration. The following table indicates such references for the six sample corporations:

	1982	1983	1984	1985	1986
American Express	X	X	X	X	
BankAmerica	X	X	X		
Citicorp		X	X	X	X
Merrill Lynch		X	X	X	
Prudential	X	X	X	X	
Sears Roebuck	X	X	X	X	X

(*Note:* for Prudential, the CEO's 'Year in Review' statement was the basis of information.)
Source: Company annual reports

4 Pankaj Ghemawat, *The Retail Financial Services Industry in 1984,* Harvard Case Services, No. 9–384–246, 1984.
5 *Ibid,* p. 10.
6 See Brian Scott Quinn 'Commercial Bank Strategy in Global Securities Markets versus Creating Shareholder Value', paper presented at the Strategic Management Society Conference, Amsterdam, 18 October 1988.
7 'London is Proving to be a School of Hard Knocks', *Business Week,* 11 April 1988, pp. 94–5.
8 William Gregor, 'Strategic Planning of Consumer Financial Services', in Sametz, A. W. (ed.) *The Emerging Financial Industry,* Lexington Books, D. C. Heath and Company, Lexington, Mass., 1985, p. 120.
9 'Merrill Lynch, the Stumbling Herd', *Fortune,* 20 June 1988, pp. 43–50.
10 Henry Kaufman, 'Financial Institutions and the Fragile, Volatile Financial Markets', in Sametz, A. W. (ed.) *The Emerging Financial Industry,* Lexington Books, D. C. Heath and Company, Lexington, Mass., 1985, pp. 26–7.

11 Robert A. Howell, 'Strategic Planning in a Volatile Economy', in Arnold W. Sametz (ed.) *The Emerging Financial Industry*, Lexington Books, D. C. Heath and Company, Lexington, Mass., 1985.

Chapter 16

Rebuilding an alliance

Varun Bery and Thomas A. Bowers

If an alliance is to survive and bring profits to both partners, it must be able to manage change and to accept change in itself. Effective rebuilding can strengthen an alliance's underlying business proposition as well as the relationship between the partners (see overleaf). We found this to be true in the case of the US and Japanese transportation companies with which we worked for a period of two years. We also found that a commitment to rebuilding can help companies avoid the sustained period of stagnation or decline that many alliances suffer.

Managing the basic parameters of such a relationship must be a conscious, ongoing process. Keeping an alliance alive requires a flexible structure that permits continuous evolution of products, technology, scope and ownership. In fact, although companies entering alliances often focus on developing the right contract, the hallmark of successful alliances is that the partners develop a strong co-operative spirit and rarely, if ever, need to refer to the contract.

THE PARTNERSHIP SOURS

A cross-border alliance is much more volatile than many executives realize. Given the increasing rate of change in the international business arena, an alliance designed to meet today's needs is unlikely to be appropriate for the medium to long term. A recent McKinsey study of 49 major alliances in the Triad – the United States, Europe, and Japan – showed that more than 30 had problems in the first three years, 19 of which dealt with their problems by broadening their scope.

Volatility, of course, is a natural part of living with alliances. If it is ignored, however, it can create difficulties, as it did between the US and Japanese partners noted here. The two companies had been working together for two years and there was a growing mistrust and lack of commitment in the relationship. Both had misgivings, but these were not being adequately communicated because of flawed reporting structures and linkages.

Structural Flaws

The Japanese partner's misgivings stemmed from the fact that it was a subcontractor, not a true partner. It was compensated on a cost-plus basis for distribution in Japan. All revenues accrued to the US partner. Ultimate authority for service design rested there as well. In order to centralize planning for a global product line, the US company had been making many of the product and pricing decisions for the Japanese market. This approach had worked in other Asian markets, yet it was failing in sophisticated Japan.

Worse, the Japanese partner was faced with a conflict of interest. The distribution agreement dealt with a substitute for a significant existing service. Although the Japanese partner saw this substitution as an opportunity and as inevitable over time, the flaws in the agreement and in the relationship made them reluctant to lead the shift to the new service.

The US company was increasingly frustrated with its Japanese partner's resistance to agreeing to product and pricing changes that had already been implemented in other markets. This frustration blossomed into mistrust when the results of the service agreement were poor and there were signs that the Japanese partner had reverted to promoting its existing services rather than the new service. As a result, the US partner's level of commitment to the alliance started to tail off.

Communications failures

The poor communications links between the companies exacerbated the problem. The alliance reported through the US company's Far Eastern organization to the US headquarters. Since much of the central product planning was done there, the Far Eastern organization had limited flexibility to accommodate the changes requested by the Japanese. Although some of these requests were passed on to headquarters, little action was taken against them, since there was no precedent for country-specific service offerings.

Managerial exchanges around these product line debates grew increasingly heated and were complicated by language barriers. The situation had deteriorated to the point at which the US side began to view the Japanese as uncooperative, and the Japanese felt the US company was inflexible and not fully in touch with conditions in Japan.

Restructuring successes

There are a myriad reasons why alliances reach a crisis. Once there, they can frequently be difficult to rebuild. However, a growing number have been successfully revitalized through the determined action of one or both parents and have then gone on to new levels of success.

One example is the 50–50 joint venture formed by Caterpillar and Mitsubishi Heavy Industries back in 1963 to serve as a distribution channel for Caterpillar bulldozers and wheel loaders in Japan. After an initial period of high growth, the alliance became ineffective because Mitsubishi's small specialty equipment group (including tunnelling machines and excavators) had not been included in the alliance. An unexpected shift in demand away from bulldozers and toward hydraulic excavators eroded the joint venture's competitive position. Both Mitsubishi and the joint venture were losing out by selling incomplete product lines in the extremely competitive Japanese market.

Once management realized that the 20–year-old structure had become a major handicap, the joint venture was completely restructured in 1987. Mitsubishi's hydraulic excavator division was merged with the alliance, removing competitive conflicts and roughly doubling the alliance's size. It has since emerged as a much stronger competitor and is a key element in Caterpillar's global strategy to compete with Komatsu by applying pressure in its home market.

Another example, the restructuring of a 38-year-old alliance between Monsanto and Mitsubishi Kaisei, shows that finding focus is not a one-time event, but a continuing process. This alliance was originally set up to leverage the parents' technologies for various market opportunities. Over the course of its life, it entered a wide range of businesses, including gallium-arsenide chips, thermoplastic elastomers, rubber additives, engineering plastics, and even artificial turf.

In part because of its expansion, the alliance experienced increasing marketing and product conflicts with its parents. After a long-overdue review by a joint team, Monsanto and Mitsubishi Kaisei agreed to shrink the alliance to less than half its previous size and focus on engineering plastics, an area in which there are technology and skill synergies between the parents. The best of the remaining businesses were spun back to the parents.

Problems with alliances are often solved only when the situation has deteriorated into a crisis. In 1963, Hewlett-Packard (HP) and Yokogawa Hokushin Electric set up Yokogawa Hewlett-Packard (YHP), a 49–51 joint venture, to sell scientific instruments in Japan. At the outset the objectives of the venture were unclear. HP's expectation was to grow at a gradual pace that would allow the venture to reach break-even quickly. HP assigned only one person to the venture and gave management control to Yokogawa, which they believed had the required skills to develop the venture. Yokogawa's primary goal was to build a market presence; profits were of secondary concern.

Problems arose when Yokogawa used its management autonomy to build its market position aggressively without adequate regard for profits. They assigned a large staff complement to the venture, set up a large new plant, and purchased substantial amounts of new equipment. Things came to a head when the venture incurred large losses in the first two years, falling far below HP's expectations and pushing the venture close to insolvency.

This provided the trigger for HP to renegotiate the venture and take control. They appointed a co-president and, under his guidance, transferred operating skills to the venture. At the same time they reduced the headcount and sold excess equipment. HP also created training programmes for Yokogawa in order to fill gaps in management skills. On this new platform of superior expertise and management skills, YHP became profitable in a year and has been one of the most successful joint ventures to date.

TAKING STOCK

The souring of the alliance led the US company, which clearly held the dominant position, to review its overall strategy for the Japanese market – and even its need for a partner (see Table 16.1). This was the first

Table 16.1 Steps in rebuilding an alliance

Evaluate alliance	Develop redesign options	Define new alliance
• Decide whether existing alliance is best vehicle to achieve objectives	• Gain agreement of partner to restructure alliance and jointly develop general nature and scope of new relationship	• Develop business objectives and plans for new alliance
• What internal or external changes are making the alliance ineffective? • What are your current objectives? • Is an alliance still necessary? • Is the current partner still the right partner? • Can the alliance be fixed?	• Does the partner want to restructure the alliance? • What is the ideal business proposition that combines the strengths of both parents and makes the alliance a viable standalone entity? • What changes are needed to rebuild trust?	• What are the objectives and strategy for the alliance? • What are the detailed plans including products, technology, organization, etc.? • What are the parent company contributions?
US parent company decides to restructure alliance →	Nonbinding letter of intent signed by both parent companies →	Contracts signed to form new joint venture

strategic review of the Japanese market that the company had conducted since the original alliance had been set up. At that time, the US company's objective had been to establish a foothold in Japan. Since then, aggressive initiatives by other leading foreign competitors had made the Japanese market a strategic priority in establishing a global business.

The review was conducted, with our assistance, by a team from the US company consisting of managers representing key functions. It was led by a manager from the Far Eastern headquarters through which the alliance reported, but the rest of the staff were sent over from the United States. Although the Japanese company was not involved in the review process, the US company had made them aware that it was going on and invited them to join in the assessment of the problems with the existing alliance.

The team's first task was to interview major customers and industry experts to assess their needs and to ascertain their perspectives on market evolution and on the service offerings of key providers in the market. We then helped them to carry out an economic analysis to evaluate trade-offs among the US company's build, buy and alliance options.

The build option

The market analysis showed that the 'go-it-alone' strategy would take too long to show real benefits in a rapidly evolving competitive situation. Breaking into the high-volume corporate segment of the market would require several years of building relationships and credibility among corporate buyers. Further, although the company had world-class operational skills, it had little experience in providing the high level of customer service required in the Japanese market. Until the company could build credibility, it would be difficult to hire and keep the high quality Japanese talent needed to bring customer-service skills in-house. A further drawback of the build option was that real estate was an important element of the cost structure of the business. Any new entrant would be at a considerable disadvantage to established providers that had significantly lower-cost facilities.

The buy option

Buying a Japanese company was an expensive option and likely to be fraught with difficulty. The list of candidates consisted of larger companies: the only players of adequate size to have the required corporate relationships were generally part of larger conglomerates. For a foreign company to acquire a Japanese company of such size was unprecedented.

A decision to buy would be expensive and difficult to execute because of the large portion of equity in friendly hands.

The alliance option

Although it was not the perfect solution, an alliance was still the best course to follow. However, the business proposition of the original alliance was seriously flawed. As already noted, the alliance covered a fledgling service that was an offshoot of a much larger existing service. To build credibility with customers and to ensure that the new service was successful, the alliance had to offer both the existing and the new services.

A review also indicated that the current partner was clearly the best choice – even under a revised business proposition. It had a dominant position in the local market for the new service, and a significant position in the cross-border market for the existing service. Given the right structure, the US company and its current Japanese partner were well positioned to become the leading overall player in the business.

This objective view of the market-place, coupled with a clearer understanding of each party's misgivings, rejuvenated both partners' desire to work together. As the true nature of the Japanese market and its specific requirements became apparent to the US partner, they became willing to consider a product line tailored specifically for Japan-originated services.

Because this strategic review gained visibility at the highest levels of the two companies, both could see that defining the right business proposition was even more crucial in the new competitive environment. They also realized that, with the right structure, a more comprehensive alliance could not only win in the market-place, but also be a vehicle for skill transfer between them.

REBUILDING BEGINS

The challenge that the two companies faced was how to redesign the alliance to capture the opportunities that had been identified and, at the same time, to rebuild mutual trust. Starting by renegotiating the contract did not make sense. Three years' worth of frustrations would get funnelled into the negotiations. The chances that such an approach would lead to a broader, more equal structure were very low.

The alternative was for the companies to begin to work together as partners to define the best business proposition. Once a winning plan had been agreed to, they could then negotiate the specific terms of the new alliance and of the parent company contributions to it. By focusing from the outset on co-operation, rather than negotiation, the objective was to arrive at a solution that captured potential synergies and helped build the working relationship needed to make the alliance work.

Given the state of the relationship, trying to co-operate on a joint business plan without such a new demonstration of commitment would have been impossible. There were major complaints on both sides. As a prelude to actually rethinking the alliance, the partners needed an agreement that addressed and alleviated these complaints, thereby leaving managers free to sit down and discuss how they should work together.

A basis for commitment

The solution was a joint effort by the two companies to develop a 'letter of intent' that addressed all major concerns. A key element for the letter of intent was that it should not be legally binding. This allowed the senior management of each side to demonstrate the commitment needed for the two sides to start working together, but it kept the alliance design process open-ended enough to allow for adjustment and restructuring as new ideas emerged.

A small working team of key managers from the two parent companies was charged with developing options for redesigning the relationship. The first few weeks of this effort became an exercise in venting frustration. Communications between the parents had been so inadequate that neither side understood the other's position. Even simple facts about the business, such as historical volumes, were hotly disputed.

Once through this initial phase, in which understanding was strengthened and trust established, the working team began to brainstorm possible options for tapping the strengths of both parents. Although this process was difficult at first, the new focus of a common objective gradually led to ideas for significantly broadening the scope of the relationship. Options emerged, for example, for co-operation in totally unrelated geographic areas, such as Europe. By focusing on 'win–win' business propositions the team was gradually freed from the 'tit-for-tat' negotiating mode that had hitherto characterized the relationship. This was the break-through that allowed the two companies to begin working together to capture the potential synergies in the alliance.

Top-level option generation

The next critical step used a series of discussions at the chief executive officer (CEO) level. Options developed by the working team were taken separately to the steering committees of the two parent companies. The senior management of each could react to the ideas on the basis of their perceived business merit, without having to commit to a particular mode of participation. Clearly unacceptable options were eliminated and feed-back on the remaining possibilities was communicated to the other side. These went back to the working team for further development. This mechanism allowed the two CEOs to work out a meeting of the minds on the long-term positioning of the alliance without having to take adversary positions often required in a direct negotiation process.

This whole process took six months and resulted in a simple, four-page letter of intent to create a totally new alliance. For the Japanese company, it promised that the new alliance would be a 50–50 joint venture in which they would become a completely equal partner. For the US company, it promised that conflicts of interest would be eliminated by having the Japanese partner fold their competitive business into the alliance.

Beyond this, the letter of intent included few details. The specifics of new alliance structure, parent company contribution, product offerings, and marketing strategies were all to be worked out during the next six months. Joint venture contracts were to be signed only after the CEOs of both parent companies had agreed that the business proposition of the new alliance was 'optimal'.

A NEW BUSINESS PLAN

Following the success of the effort to draft a letter of intent, a new working team was established to develop the optimal business plan and work out the details of the scope and structure of the alliance. This team reported to two steering committees: one for the US parent company (consisting of the chairman, the head of international, and the head of sales and marketing), and the other for the Japanese parent (consisting of the chairman, the president, and the head of international).

The role of this team was to generate ideas and plans for the new alliance which would then be taken to the respective parent company steering committees for reaction and further direction. This team became, in effect, the advocate for the new business. It was structured with marketing, sales, and operations subteams to sharpen the focus on the key business issues that needed to be resolved.

Motivating for success

Several factors contributed to make this phase of the process work, even given the history of mistrust that existed between the two companies. First, the managers selected to lead the joint team were destined to be – and became – the top managers of the new alliance. They were put on the project full-time and knew that their futures depended on properly structuring the alliance. Most other team members were also selected because they were ultimately to become employees of the new company. As a result, the team gradually became much more concerned with developing a viable business than, for example, with whether the US or Japanese parent was going to pay for the software development of key information systems.

Second, although the senior managers of each parent company were closely involved in directing the formation of the alliance, they did not negotiate face-to-face with their counterparts in the other. This allowed them to react directly to the joint team's ideas and plans and to concentrate on arriving at practical business solutions, rather than having to respond to positions adopted by the other side. The integrated business plans, by definition, incorporated both costs and benefits for each parent company, which put a premium on all team members taking a business, rather than a transaction, perspective on their work.

As in developing the letter of intent, the alliance redesign process was smoothed by having a neutral third party act as facilitator at both the steering committees and joint working team levels. The key issues of geographic scope and parent company business contributions were resolved by iterative indirect discussions between the steering committees, which focused on how best to build the business. At each stage ideas from the working team were reviewed by each steering committee. This senior-level feedback was communicated to the other company and to the working team which then began its next iteration. An indication of the success of this process is that both companies agreed to expand the business significantly beyond what had been agreed to in the letter of intent.

Resolving detailed arrangements

Both steering committees felt that the parents' contributions should be balanced, yet they were convinced that building the best business was more important than the initial financial arrangements. To ensure co-ordination with alliance scope and business plans, the joint working team became the vehicle for resolving issues of parent company contribution and transfer price. These were the final difficulties that needed to be resolved before contracts could be signed to launch the new alliance.

For these discussions, senior finance managers from each parent company temporarily joined the team. A conscious decision was made not to set up a separate negotiation process for these issues. We wanted to ensure that the spirit of co-operation would not be replaced by one of negotiation.

Although resolving the financial arrangements added two extra months to the original six-month schedule, the co-operative nature of the effort was maintained. As a result, the joint venture contract captured both the business and the financial agreements and required very little final negotiation. All major issues had been resolved through the joint working team process.

THE ALLIANCE REBUILT

The process used to revitalize the alliance succeeded in creating a more equal and viable entity and in helping to repair a damaged relationship. The new 50–50 joint venture made the Japanese company a full partner in the business. It also created an integrated product line – consisting of current, new, and hybrid services – that was unmatched by any existing competitor.

By combining American and Japanese sales forces, gaining broader access to the parents' customer bases, and developing a more integrated business with better economics, this approach created a solid base for new growth. At the same time, management teams and organizations had been developed in the United States and Japan that were able to launch the restructured business two months after the contracts – and less than a year after the letter of intent – were signed.

Looking back, there were several keys to the successful restructuring of this alliance.

- The entire process was designed to develop and maintain a spirit of co-operation and equality. The focus was on idea generation and building a better business, rather than on negotiation.
- The top management of both parent companies recognized that the overall business proposition was compelling. They were committed to building a strong long-term alliance and were not overly focused on the short-term balance between the two sides.
- Joint working team members were very committed to the alliance because of their personal stakes in its future.
- The process was kept focused and moving by having a neutral third party as a facilitator and communications link at both the senior management and the working-team levels.
- There was a recognition from the outset that time and patience would be required to develop the business plan, structure the deal, and do a large part of the initial implementation before the contracts were signed. Thus, both partners were prepared to maintain their enthusiasm throughout the 14 months it took to restructure the alliance.

Although this process may not work for all alliances facing difficulty, there are many situations in which a co-operative restructuring process can be effective. The experience reported here indicates that companies need to think creatively about means as well as ends as they try to tap the full benefits of their relationships with other current or potential partners.

Reproduced from Bery, Varun and Bowers, Thomas A., *Rebuilding an Alliance*, in Bleeke, Joel and Ernst, David, eds., *Collaborating to Compete*, John Wiley & Sons, New York, 1993. Pages 67–78.

Chapter 17

Creating value in symbiotic acquisitions

Phillippe C. Haspeslagh and David B. Jemison

Symbiotic acquisitions present the most substantial challenges to managers, who find themselves torn between the twin needs of preserving the acquired company's culture and encouraging interdependence to fulfill the acquisition's purpose. As a member of the ICI-Beatrice gatekeeping team commented: 'We knew from day one that they had to retain their entrepreneurial, market-oriented culture and be run at arm's length. Yet at the same time, we had to find ways to get the synergy.'

In our research, the companies that succeeded in this unnatural act were those whose interface managers were able to shepherd a carefully evolving pattern of interactions (see Figure 17.1).

The pattern *began with preservation* of the acquired company (as we discussed above), while the acquiring company made changes in its own

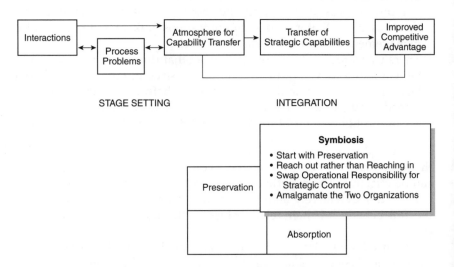

Figure 17.1 Key integration tasks by integration approach

organization so it could be better juxtaposed to the acquisition. Next, the acquiring company gradually encouraged interactions between the two organizations, preferably at the initiative of the acquired company's managers, a process we will call *reaching out rather than reaching in*.

After that, strategic control over the acquired firm was gradually affirmed, while operating responsibilities of the managers of the acquired firm were increased, a process we *call swapping operating responsibility for strategic control*. This process set the stage for a gradual *amalgamation* of the organizations, which is the essence of symbiotic acquisitions.

A good illustration of effective management of a symbiotic acquisition is ICI's movement of two Beatrice businesses (LNP and Fiberite) into its Advanced Composites business.

AMALGAMATING BEATRICE CHEMICAL COMPANIES AND ICI ADVANCED MATERIALS[1]

Starting with preservation

For subsidiaries like LNP and Fiberite, the first year of the Beatrice acquisition represented a situation of de facto preservation. They were kept completely at arm's length from ICI and run by Ben Lochtenberg through the buffer of their own former small headquarters organization, Wilmington North.

Original objectives had been re-emphasized. Any operational contact with ICI was clearly initiated by LNP or Fiberite people, even though ICI managers like Rex Palmer and his colleagues, with whom they discussed strategic and operating issues, continued to suggest people in ICI who might be useful to talk to.

Juxtaposing the organizations

At the end of the first year, formal reporting responsibilities changed. The former Beatrice Polyvinyl operations began to report to ICI Resins and Coatings; LNP and Fiberite reported to ICI Advanced Materials; and the remaining six into ICI Speciality Chemicals. The composite materials businesses (LNP and Fiberite) were headed by Dick Bucher and juxtaposed to ICI's own operations in the advanced materials field under Hal Logan, with whom they shared a common boss in the person of Hugh Miller, PEO Advanced Materials and Electronics.

With the original gatekeeping gone, initiative for co-operation increasingly came from the ICI side. Commented a wary Robert Schultz, the general manager of LNP:

ICI should recognize that the accidental bullet kills just as surely as the intended one – they say they want to leave us alone, but at the same time they want to collaborate on this and then on that. They do try not to smother us however, and we try to live this day by day.

At the same time, Schultz clearly was optimistic about the outcome of such collaborations:

ICI has the answers, but not the questions; LNP has the questions. Merging has given us access to world-class technology. In the UK we now interface not only within Advanced Materials but also with the New Sciences group. We have spent the whole year working out what we can use from them. One result is a fiber that combines the properties of stiffness and toughness, which used to be mutually exclusive. We are comparing formulae with the advanced materials group (Logan's operation) and have found that some of their grades are better and some of ours are better.

LNP people felt a strong commitment from ICI in several ways. 'There is a lot more interest in the company and a lot more opportunities', commented one manager. Operationally they were being asked to take over the marketing of Victrex, an ICI product that had not been doing well in the United States. Also, all capital investment projects were approved very promptly. Commented Bucher: 'ICI resources have allowed us to continue growing; we could have plateaued otherwise.'

No pressures were exerted to have LNP buy from ICI, even when the mother company had the equivalent new materials. At the same time, LNP of its own volition began to experiment with using the ICI sales forces in some countries where their distributors were not working out well.

Throughout, ICI's expectations of performance results seemed balanced, with some managers complaining: 'ICI has the right strategic vision, only it expects it a bit too fast for reality,' whereas others noted: 'For the next year, budget expectations have been slowed, something which was unheard of under Beatrice. It is understood that emphasis will be on the progress towards long-term objectives.'

As time went by, Logan had more frequent direct discussions with Schultz and Bucher spent more of his time on Fiberite. Whilst LNP slowly developed a practice of working with its ICI counterpart, its sense of identity remained unchanged: 'LNP is a very special company and will continue to be so under ICI, if it is handled right.'

Another manager commented: 'We would like to continue the growth of the past year with the same choice over use of the ICI infrastructure and very little if any integration or loss of identity. Were we to become part of Advanced Materials, it would severely affect people in the organization.'

The Amalgamation Stage

In February 1987, LNP was formally shifted from Composite Materials (Bucher) to Engineering Plastics (Logan), and all engineering plastics activities were consolidated under one individual. While this could be construed as putting LNP under the control of ICI, LNP people like Schultz spoke of it differently:

ICI was not doing well in plastics in the US before the acquisition. The business was badly managed and the technical calibre not very high. As a result, LNP has been given stewardship for what ICI already had in the US. We are trying to upgrade their quality with the least upheaval possible.

My task has been to make LNP, Victrex, and other ICI products combine into a cohesive engineering plastics organization and to give ICI enhanced visibility without losing the previously separate images. The view in the US is that ICI looks to LNP to help the other pieces over here. We have the influence, not them.

In September 1987, a geographic organization was set up with three general managers (Europe, Far East, and the United States). Appointed US general manager, Bob Schultz assumed responsibility for selling all product lines in the United States. Hal Logan stated:

We are trying to bring LNP into ICI Advanced Materials. The US organization for Engineering Plastics is LNP. So we are trying to change the name affiliation to ICI Engineering Plastics, but retain the market responsiveness.

Bob Schultz commented on this change;

With the shift in businesses (and some others which were lifted from other parts of ICI), there was a doubling in the size of this part of Advanced Materials, which everybody realized led to a need for restructuring.

So we met in Long Island in June to decide how we would structure and how we would call ourselves. By involving me, they cleverly involved LNP. Engineering Plastics was born at this meeting – with three regional general managers, with all products under their aegis for their territory, and four business managers with responsibility for the world-wide strategy drive. After much debate it was decided that these business managers would be made subordinate to the territorial managers so that the local market flavor would never be overriden.

Schultz's comments illustrate ICI's success in helping people adjust to new realities:[2]

At the time of the Long Island meeting, it was assumed that if I took the US position, I'd relinquish my LNP presidency (the title should be

International Business Manager – it's just a legacy). I had an emotional reaction – it was like cutting the cord; I didn't want to lose my baby. It was probably an immature reaction, but after all, I had grown LNP from $3 million to $100 million. Anyway, I created an impromptu logic to keep it, and they let me. But in August, at the time of preparation for announcement, I started thinking maybe I should not be wearing both hats. Maybe both are full-time jobs. My boss said, 'No, we agreed; let's try it.' But last week I told him it was time we started looking seriously at a timetable for me to relinquish LNP, as I'm not doing justice to either position.

By that time (January 1988), Schultz clearly saw himself in the middle, contributing to protecting what was productive in LNP and helping ICI to be more successful in this kind of business:

I have been trying to keep ICI out of LNP in this sense (in the sense of not taking on big-company habits). You have to be wary; it's like slicing a baloney; each slice is so thin it does not matter, but in the end you are left with nothing. Someone like me is needed to bridge the gap, run ICI and LNP. I can ease things, build confidence, create less fear.

I hope we can manage a middle ground. There is a preservation need: we have a dedication, almost an obsession, to giving the customer what he wants. The market interface skills of LNP are vital. ICI's plastics culture would have been a disaster. For example, their salesmen have no expense budget; they do not make their own sales forecast. Where is the pride of ownership in that?

On the other hand, if the ICI pieces start to take over this culture and get successful, maybe they need less independence. If there has been any surprise, it is that LNP has so soon been driving the ICI plastics business.

In the meantime, the amalgamation was proceeding step by step. ICI committed resources for a modern headquarters for the engineering plastics business in the United States about twenty miles from LNP's Malvern, Massachusetts site. Talking about the new building, an LNP manager commented:

It will really be an LNP building up there; we will have 110 LNP people for a couple of dozen Victrex and Fluor people only. LNP Malvern will be closed down. It is bursting at the seams anyway; we have people in rented trailers and rented offices on the other side of town.

The move was expected to usher in further changes:

We are still on the LNP incentive plan. In 1988 we will have to bring LNP/ICI plans closer. We will be in the same building, and it would be difficult to have different systems.

Despite this increasing amalgamation of the two organizations it would be misleading to say that by 1988 LNP had been absorbed into ICI. Indeed, the company had retained all its original qualities, which ICI had been (relatively) lacking: customer orientation and entrepreneurial drive. It was, in fact, largely ICI's Advanced Materials organization that had become more differentiated from ICI's core business mentality. Less discussed, but equally important, this facet of the integration allowed the two acquisitions to come together without destroying LNP's original capability.

STAGES IN SYMBIOTIC INTEGRATION

The slow evolution of LNP's integration into ICI illustrates the challenges present in symbiotic acquisitions. The pattern begins with preservation steps and then moves through an intensive process of amalgamating the two organizations. As can be read between the lines in the example, the texture of the relationship between the acquired and acquiring company; the atmosphere created; the respect for differences and for the acquisition's purpose alike; the continuous evolution towards the future vision; and the continuous concern to bring people along define more than any specific actions what a symbiotic integration is all about. Four stages can be recognized in this evolving process:

1 starting with preservation;
2 reaching out rather than reaching in;
3 trading operating responsibility for strategic control;
4 amalgamating the organizations (see Figure 17.1).

Starting with preservation

The initial steps in a symbiotic acquisition are the same as in preservation. At first, all contacts need to be channelled through a formal gate-keeping structure that emphasizes the capabilities for which the company was acquired in the first place and keeps managers focused on achieving their original operating objectives. In the Beatrice example, that was literally the case, as the LNP and Fiberite companies were initially kept together with those Specialty Chemicals companies that would remain in a preservation mode.

There are some differences in this stage from a pure preservation situation, however. Expectations for symbiotic acquisitions tend to be higher. More attention needs to be paid to managers' reactions in the acquirer in symbiotic acquisitions and to the organizational reporting of the new unit.

Premiums paid and patience needed

It is difficult to begin a symbiotic integration with a clear preservation orientation because the premiums paid for the kind of acquisitions that require a symbiotic integration tend to be substantial. For example, in ICI's acquisition of the Beatrice companies, a price of $750 million was necessary to top competing offers from competitors like Akzo, BASF, AMOCO, and others. Most of the synergy such a figure implied had been imputed to LNP and Fiberite, the two businesses that provided the potential to reinforce the newly created Advanced Composites business. This created pressure within ICI to pursue those synergies. It also created initial fear among managers in the acquired firm that they would be stretched to make up for the price that had been paid for their company.

ICI was able to allay those fears, first by holding them to their own budgets and later by focusing on long-term progress. Increasing resource commitments in the absence of financial results put high demands on the corporate system. Some of the same qualities we discussed in Chapter 5 [of Haspeslagh: *Managing Acquisitions*] as key to acquisition decision making carry over in the integration phase. In this phase the quality of the strategic vision and the degree to which it is shared in the acquirer become important. There has to be a clear understanding between the corporate level and the interface managers about the strategic objective, the kind of time horizon that will be needed, and the organizational path that should be followed.

Turning the tables on one's own troops

We noted earlier that in symbiotic acquisitions the legitimate claims for involvement by the acquirer's operating units are much stronger. They have been asked to help support the justification by identifying the synergies that could be expected with their own area of business. We described in Chapter 9 [of Haspeslagh: *Managing Acquisitions*] how the ICI Advanced Composites people (just like their colleagues from the Mond division) argued against the acquisition team and wanted to split up the Beatrice companies immediately. The acquiring managers will have to agree not only to a delay, but also to go one step farther – to prepare their own organization for the fact that if it is on the receiving end of a new capability, it may have to change its own way to become a good 'receptor'.

Side by side

In addition to preserving the acquired company from uncontrolled interactions, the gatekeeping structure is typically set up so that the acquired unit and the operating units with which it interfaces become adjacent, reporting to a single executive. In the Beatrice example this change came in two steps. First, ICI and the Beatrice Advanced Composites businesses were put under the same senior executive; subsequently they were put side by side under one operating manager (Logan). The role of that single senior executive is to develop and push the strategic vision and also to start reformulating the purpose on both sides, especially on the side of the host organization. The heads of both operations, in this case, Bucher and Logan, should offer assistance. The senior executive will have to be a statesman, providing the required overall vision and pressuring both organizations for awareness and change.

Reaching out rather than reaching in

After an initial emphasis on setting the stage properly on both sides and controlling any urge for headquarters staff or operating unit involvement, it is time to pursue the real purpose of the acquisition: achieving a rich capability transfer between both sides. The boundary between the two firms must be transformed into a semipermeable membrane. The key to this in the situations we studied was in the style and the direction of initial and subsequent contacts. The initial substantive interactions between the firms were originated by the managers in the acquired firm as much as possible. As already discussed, to facilitate this, the acquiring firm put a few experienced people at the disposal of the acquired units to point to resources in its organization that could help solve some of their problems. In this way, the acquired company could perceive benefits accruing to it from early interactions. As one acquiring manager commented: 'The idea is that we open our hands and let them walk in the candy store and refrain from pushing anything in particular on them.' If the complementarity of resources and problems is really there, the time lost in exercising such restraint will be small.

Trading operating responsibility for strategic control

Voluntary interactions, even if nudged along, will go only so far. Over time, as some of the early contacts and interactions began to bring results, symbiotic acquisitions required a gradual stepping-up of the influence over the acquired company. This involved the managers steering a middle road, between the expectations of the mother company and the reluctance of the acquired organization. The earlier comment of Schultz, who acknowledged the benefits of the collaboration and his concern for the preservation of LNP, illustrates the ambiguity of this process, an ambiguity that reaches deep in the organization. One of the LNP managers, after discussing a number of positive developments, returned to his fear: 'They must realize we are a company, not a business.

If they ever were to change our name, it would not be the same place anymore.'

The ability to exert increasing influence over the acquired company, and to avoid getting hung up on 'symbiotic' issues such as names and logos, was typically a function of the degree to which managers in the acquired firm felt that the capability transfer was operating in both directions.

Handing over significant responsibility for part of the acquirer's own business to the acquired organization, as ICI did by making LNP responsible for marketing its Victrex and other product lines in the United States, is often the most effective way to start pulling the strategy and priorities together. More operating responsibility is entrusted to the managers in the acquired firm, while the acquiring firm begins to take firmer control of strategy. At the operating levels both organizations remain distinct. The managers in the acquired firm still identify largely with their own company, yet a few people and resources have moved to the other side.

Amalgamating the organizations

Ultimately, the whole process must lead to a true amalgamation in which the two organizations combine to become a new, unique entity. This combination must be accomplished without losing the character that underlies the capabilities of the acquired company, and superfluous differences must be reconciled. The Beatrice example illustrates a number of mechanisms that can accelerate such a gradual evolution. Senior managers in the acquired unit can be assigned double roles: one is to act as the traditional guardian for their units, and the other is to take an overall perspective that involves them in the broader strategic outlook.

Another mechanism is physically or geographically to regroup the individuals, if not the organizations, for example, by investing in new buildings, such as a headquarters or R&D labs.[3] Our research suggests that the increased understanding bred by geographic proximity lessens demands for maintaining other differences, such as retaining separate benefit structures.

Whether an acquired company succeeds in transforming itself without losing its intrinsic characteristics depends on the calibre and ability of business managers, who can make the transition from a small- to a large-company setting. Not everyone combines the entrepreneurial ability to grow a $3 million operation into a $100 million one and the managerial ability to adjust to operating within a complex multinational with a matrix organization structure. Such managers must continue to care deeply for their own organization, yet become realistic and careful never to obstruct the purpose of the acquiring company.

Successful transformation also depends greatly on the long-term perspective of the acquiring company, which must be willing to add the required resources and adopt the time horizon that will be most productive. Above all, the quality of the integration process in symbiotic acquisitions, as in absorptions or preservations, depends on the quality of interface management.

MANAGING THE INTERFACE

Irrespective of whether an acquisition is an absorption, preservation, or symbiotic, integration is a highly complex process. The difficulties in bringing two organizations together are legion. The people in one company, by virtue of their acquisition, are often set to claim their ownership rights, whereas the people in the other company are frequently alienated and defensive. The ensuing problems affect capability transfer both directly and indirectly through their impact on the atmosphere. The balance between pushing for capability transfer and protecting the acquired organization's identity is a delicate trade-off among the demands of the situation, the intended evolution, and the dynamic at a given time. Because of the complex and dynamic nature of this process, the essence of value creation is really assured by the group of managers who manage the interface and perform the gatekeeping role.

We suggested in Chapter 10 [of Haspeslagh: *Managing Acquisitions*] that it is better to think not of one individual, but of a number of people who jointly fulfil a constellation of roles. Three types of individuals are an integral part of the gatekeeping unit: the head of the host structure, the head of the acquired unit, and a small number of resource people. Managers who head the host structure like Leif Johansson at Electrolux, Eddy Brouwer in BP, and Ben Lochtenberg and Hugh Miller in ICI, successfully steered the integration process, relying upon their own skills and the support of their top management in dealing with corporate colleagues. Others, like Stefan Wilcke in Eurochem, had neither the foresight nor, more importantly, the support to mobilize the necessary forces in the situation.

The success of these individuals at managing the acquisition process upwards, downwards, and laterally hinges a great deal on their credibility within both organizations and (except in absorption acquisitions) their ability to be mavericks who can set their own rules (and have them tolerated). Interestingly, many of the successful gatekeepers we studied were bicultural. For example, Brouwer was the only Dutchman managing a BP subsidiary, and Lochtenberg was an Australian working for a British company in the United States. Others were bicultural in the sense that they had not, like most of their colleagues, spent their entire career in the firm. They were sensitive to the reality of life in the smaller organization, even while working for the huge one, and to differences among national cultures. They could perceive, for example, that what to an American ear seems a small suggestion may be interpreted by a British manager as an order from his boss.

A second key player in the gatekeeping team was the head of the acquired unit. Sometimes the existing manager was kept on, as were Schultz at LNP, Lodders at Hendrix, and Chiswell in Dymo. In other situations, a manager was brought in from the parent firm, such as Wibault in Francoplast and Walker in Trouw, or from the outside, such as Verri in Zanussi. The decision whether to confirm the existing manager or to recruit the new one is crucial. It depends on the relative importance of preserving continuity of management in the acquirer, providing industry know-how to the acquired and acquirer alike, and being trusted and experienced in one's own organization. In all cases the managerial burden imposed by the acquisition requires an individual of a character and calibre well above that required to run a similar business independently or within one's own company.

The third set of players in the gatekeeping team comprised the resource people, experienced managers from the acquirer's organization, who are recruited into the acquired company or generally made available to it. These are the people who, like Palmer in Beatrice, or Pritchard in Hendrix, and many others we interviewed, are assigned to positions that are often subordinate to the rank they would have in their own organizations.

In many ways their real role is not the one reflected in the lowly formal position they occupy. Seeking to allay the mistrust of the acquired company, they must build credibility by being helpful and by sharing their expertise. It takes a certain modesty and much interpersonal skill to play this vital role, as they must constantly walk a fine line between the positions of the two companies. As one of them commented:

It is a great challenge to balance affiliation. I try to tell myself and others that my affiliation is neither with the acquired unit nor with the division of our company that it interfaces with. My affiliation is with our Board and its goals.

The delicate balance is between what is perceived by the managers in the acquired firm, and what is perceived by our managers. At first, in this job, you seek credibility with the acquiree. Later on, it is with corporate that you must assure credibility. It is then that the declared support and authority that you have been told you are given become important.

Another manager described his gatekeeping task in very similar terms, at the same time reflecting its intrinsic orientation:

Our first job was to establish credibility, both with the managers in the acquired firm and with corporate. Our next task was to get their people to see what our company had to offer. Our third task was to get our organization to learn from them.

The qualities required of the members of the gatekeeping team and their crucial impact place a great premium on the way in which acquisition staffing decisions are made. The de facto criterion seemed to be (as in Eurochem) the normal internal job market of who is up for a new assignment. Other companies in which such staffing decisions are a matter for executive committee consideration are likely to make better choices.

Beyond the choices, these situations also make heavy demands on the leadership of top management. Having appointed these managers, they must be willing to back them up and provide them with the resources needed to bring in long-term results.

SUMMARY

We discussed how the integration process in different types of acquisitions takes on a very different character, each requiring from the acquiring organization a different repertoire of skills in interaction management. We also described how the process can be managed. Although for each type of acquisition there are some clear steps, the real quality of the integration process lies in the subtleties required to respond to the different needs for interdependence and autonomy.

Regardless of the type of acquisition, the overriding image deriving from the successful integration efforts we observed is one of corporate-level managers, interface managers, and acquired company managers engaging in a continuous process of adaptation and learning. They have substantial responsibilities, and while immersed in a constant stream of action, they must keep their eyes fixed on the strategic mission of the acquisition and the firm itself.

REFERENCES

1 For an extensive description, see 'ICI: the Beatrice Acquisition', written by Alison Farquhar under the supervision of Associate Professor Phillippe Haspeslagh, INSEAD/CEDEP, 1988.
2 See Goffman, E., 'On Cooling the Mark Out: Some Aspects of Adaptation to Failure', *Psychiatry*, 15, 1952, pp. 451–63 for the classic treatment of adjusting to a new reality.
3 See Allen, T., *Managing the Flow of Technology*, Cambridge, MIT Press 1977.

Chapter 18

Co-ordinating international manufacturing and technology

M. Therese Flaherty

For many managers the term 'global manufacturing' conjures up visions of consumers the world over driving identical, black Model Ts, eating the same cereal, and using computer keyboards with the same alphabets. In this vision one gigantic factory, with huge economies of scale, manufactures sufficient volume to supply the world market with a single design at low cost.

But in some technology-intensive business units global manufacturing also means something else: co-ordinating a number of plants internationally that may or may not make similar products. Proper co-ordination of these plants has the potential of reducing costs and enhancing the effectiveness of multiple manufacturing operations while preserving some diversity in final products and in location of manufacturing. For example:

- A US heavy equipment manufacturer offered many options on its basic product line, which was manufactured at two plants in the United States and Europe. The business unit was able to ship interchangeable products from both plants. This meant that the two-plant system could fill orders more quickly, shift some orders between plants in response to exchange rate fluctuations, and assure a steadily rising production rate for a third plant as it began operation.
- A US chemical manufacturer acquired a plant in Europe that had been losing money for its original owner. As expected, specialists from the corporate technical group improved the operations of the new plant. But they also improved the manufacturing process of a plant in the United States by using knowledge gained at the European plant. The improved process enhanced the characteristics of the US plant's product so as to appeal to a large and growing market in the United States.
- Two US electronics manufacturers started systematic programmes to purchase from vendors in several countries. As a result they saved up

to 30 per cent of the costs of purchased parts and materials for certain products.

The issue of co-ordinating international manufacturing has been given little attention by academics.[1] Until the 1970s most companies that had manufacturing facilities in several countries ran their manufacturing operations independently. To be sure, there had long been important exceptions: the major petroleum companies co-ordinated supply lines from the Middle East to their customers, and early in the twentieth century the Ford Motor Company supplied its European assembly plants with some parts from the United States.[2]

Co-ordinating international manufacturing is likely to become more important as companies adopt global strategies. Two academic developments would assist managers in designing and implementing global manufacturing strategies. One is a framework for thinking about co-ordination. The other is an understanding of the experiences of companies that seem to be good at it. These developments would help managers identify opportunities for co-ordination, evaluate the potential of particular co-ordination programmes, and overcome problems likely to be encountered during implementation.

In this chapter I present such a framework and illustrate its use with examples of international manufacturing co-ordination from the experience of five US companies. Two are primarily in chemicals, two in electronics, and one in heavy equipment. They are all reputedly well-managed, Fortune 500 manufacturing companies. They all serve industrial, rather than retail, customers. Each company has over 30 per cent of its sales and assets outside the United States. Managers in all of them have devoted considerable attention to co-ordinating their international manufacturing operations. Within each company, I selected for study one technology-based business unit that was world-wide in its customer and manufacturing base. In discussing the experiences of these business units, I refer to them as Chemicals A and B, Electronics A and B, and Heavy Equipment.

Many issues that arise in the co-ordination of international manufacturing are, of course, similar to issues that arise in the co-ordination of multi-site manufacturing operations located within one country. To the extent that the two sets of issues are the same, this chapter contributes to the management of multisite operations in general. But some of these issues are of much greater significance in the international than in a single-country context. For example, geographic distance, divergence in customer requirements, and differences in company culture can all be much greater in international than in single-country manufacturing. Finally, other issues arise in international manufacturing that are simply not encountered in domestic manufacturing. For example, exchange rate fluctuations and national trade policies can be critical considerations in managing an international manufacturing system.

MANUFACTURING STRATEGY OF TECHNOLOGY-INTENSIVE BUSINESS UNITS

Multinational manufacturers in research-intensive industries, which include the five companies considered here, steadily accounted for most of the large and growing exports and foreign direct investment by US manufacturing companies during the post-war period. Specifically, between 1962 and 1977, US companies in the five most research-intensive industries accounted for over two-thirds of the exports and foreign direct investment made by US manufacturing companies, but less than 40 per cent of the total shipments from US factories. Furthermore, between 1966 and 1978 the nominal stock of foreign direct investment in fixed assets by US manufacturing companies, which had been accumulating since the nineteenth century, approximately doubled.[3] As Table 18.1 shows, companies in those industries – with the exception of the air transport sector of the transport industry – held at least 30 per cent of their sales and fixed assets dispersed over several countries outside the United States.

Such companies, which base their competitive advantage largely on technology, depend on manufacturing in important ways. They earn profits on their technology largely by selling their products. The amount by which they profit from their technology depends on various factors; for example, on the time at which they introduce their products relative to the time that their rivals introduce their competing products, the availability of the products to customers in many locations, the conformance of the delivered products to specifications, and the design of the product.[4]

As these US companies encountered more internationally competitive customers, rivals, and vendors during the 1970s and early 1980s, they were particularly dependent on their international manufacturing. Many of these internationally competitive companies based outside the United States focused on different manufacturing tasks and used different manufacturing approaches than did their US counterparts. The US companies needed to learn about these approaches as part of their response to these new rivals. The US companies also found that some of their most technologically sophisticated customers were for the first time located outside the United States. This meant that US companies whose manufacturing and design employees interacted closely with customers had to work with companies outside the United States. And some US firms found that the operations of their long-time US customers had become international; those customers were demanding international service

Table 18.1 Distribution of Sales and Assets of the Five Research-Intensive US Industries over Different Geographic Areas, 1981

	US	Canada	Western Europe	South America	Middle East	Asia	Total Non-US
Chemicals SIC(28)							
Sales	63	8.6	16	3.3	4.7	0.0	37
Assets	68	8.9	15	3.4	0.0	3.6	32
Non-electrical SIC(35)							
Sales	61	9.2	19	1.5	0.1	0.5	39
Assets	67	9.7	21	1.5	0.1	0.6	33
Electrical SIC(36)							
Sales	63	3.2	18	5.2	0.0	3.0	37
Assets	69	2.9	17	6.2	0.0	4.0	31
Transport SIC(37)							
Air transport							
Sales	50	7.8	4.6	0.0	0.0	0.5	50
Assets	79	12	7.7	0.1	0.0	0.8	21
Non-air transport							
Sales	68	7.6	14	7.5	0.4	0.2	32
Assets	64	9.3	17	8.3	0.2	0.2	36
Instruments SIC(38)							
Sales	63	8.6	20	1.0	0.0	2.5	37
Assets	70	7.8	20	0.6	0.1	2.1	30

Source: Data in Compustat II, Geographic Segments File

and products that could be used interchangeably regardless of where the products were manufactured. In meeting all these international challenges, US managers had to devise new international manufacturing strategies.

In this Chapter I define *manufacturing strategy* as the broad plan by which a company or business unit develops, introduces and manufactures products in order to satisfy customers' needs better than competitors. Such strategies generally specify the decisions that will have long-lasting effects on the business and that usually require large financial commitments. Manufacturing strategies typically include:

- number, size, and location of plants;
- technology and equipment choice;
- assignment of materials, components, and products to be made by specific manufacturing facilities;
- vertical span of the manufacturing process;
- policies for manufacturing support activities;
- policies for technology support activities.[5]

The first four are decisions that require large lump-sum investments and that relate to the equipment and buildings that comprise the company's or the business unit's factories. Taken together, they define the set of plants and their manufacturing facilities abroad.

In contrast, the last two categories of manufacturing strategy are policies that guide the daily activities of manufacturing and other technical employees located at geographically dispersed facilities.

Policies for manufacturing support activities encompass the daily activities that ensure the desired production is accomplished at the right time in the right place in the right way. These policies relate to procurement, production planning, and other activities listed in Table 18.2. Hayes and Wheelright call these the 'infrastructure categories' and include them in manufacturing strategy because they can be as expensive and time-consuming to change as the first four categories.[6] I include them here for an additional reason. In globally competitive business units the strategic use of geographically dispersed facilities can be enhanced by the interaction of manufacturing support activities at one location with those at another.

For technology-intensive business units there is another category in the list of manufacturing strategy components: policies for technology support activities. These are also listed in Table 18.2 and refer to the design of new manufacturing processes and products and their introduction into manufacturing. One example is a policy requiring the use of common parts and processes in new product designs. Another is a policy requiring research on the basic manufacturing technologies used by a business. Such policies are the guides within

Table 18.2 Support activities

Manufacturing support activities

- procurement
- aggregate production planning
- daily production planning and expediting
- quality assurance
- employee management and development
- manufacturing engineering

Technology support activities

- product design and improvement
- process design and improvement
- new product and process introduction

which employees in technology and manufacturing develop the future manufacturing capabilities of the business unit. These policies require that the activities of employees in engineering and technical development be directed in part by manufacturing strategy. Manufacturing policies dealing with technology support activities typically require interactions among technology and manufacturing employees, customers, and vendors that are located in widely dispersed facilities.

REASONS FOR THE GEOGRAPHIC DISPERSION OF MANUFACTURING FACILITIES

Each of the five business units I studied had developed a manufacturing strategy entailing plants in several countries. In several cases the managers intended to do further rationalization of the plants and reassignment of the products among plants within the following five years. But in all cases the managers intended to continue manufacturing in plants in several different countries. These strategies sacrificed some economies of scale and ease of management that would have been available had there been fewer plants for the same volume. They were designed to take advantage of major opportunities available to companies with internationally dispersed manufacturing facilities.

The key economic model of multinational expansion rests on two ideas. The first is that technology-intensive companies possess competitive advantages based on intangible (technology) assets that can be transferred within a company with ease, but outside a company only with more difficulty. The second is that using one's own technology in foreign manufacturing allows a company to earn a larger return on its technology than would be possible through an arm's-length sale of the technology.[7]

Business scholars, while recognizing the opportunities associated with establishing foreign manufacturing facilities, also emphasize the costs and risks involved. Their research suggests that US managers prefer to locate manufacturing in the United States to avoid the cost and risk associated with the management of foreign manufacturing. Actions of competitors, however, which threaten their home market or foreign markets, are frequently sufficient stimuli to overcome managers' risk aversion.[8]

The benefits of foreign manufacturing for the five business units largely fell into five general categories, which relate closely to the general reasons for dispersion discussed in Chapter 1 [see Chapter 1 in Porter: *Competition in Global Industries*]. First, managers could enhance their long-term business relations outside the United States by manufacturing abroad. For example, when Electronics A and B established manufacturing facilities in Europe, their managers found that they had made a believable commitment to serve local customers well over the long term. Furthermore, in all five business units local manufacturing allowed manufacturing and other technical employees to work closely with customers in order to better design customers' products and to identify problems after both had begun production.[9] This provided enhanced service and responsiveness to local customers' needs. Finally, managers in all five business units learned valuable lessons by operating manufacturing facilities abroad. They found, for example, that managing facilities in Japan allowed them to learn more effectively than they otherwise could have about Japanese manufacturing practices, the requirements of Japanese business customers, and the Japanese distribution system.

Second, managers could gain access to local, immobile factors of production by locating manufacturing outside the United States.[10] Electronics A and B, for instance, located their high-volume, labour-intensive operations in areas with low labour costs such as the Far East, Mexico, or the Caribbean. For other operations, they and the Heavy Equipment managers were attracted to locations with abundant, high-quality engineers or good industrial infrastructures. The relative costs of production and the pools of desirable immobile resources in different geographic areas were changing. For example, one manager of a new Electronics B plant located in the United States with participative work systems said that in 1984 his costs were competitive with those of offshore assembly plants.

Third, managers could reduce transport costs significantly by locating close to customers those manufacturing facilities that add bulk and weight. For instance, in part to avoid international shipment, Chemicals

A had six geographically dispersed plants that manufactured products from locally available materials. Not surprisingly, transport costs were less of an issue for Electronics A and B than for the other business units I studied.[11]

Safety problems involved in transporting some chemicals also made multiple foreign manufacturing locations attractive for Chemicals A and B. In some cases, regulations explicitly restricted the movement of each particular materials across national boundaries.

Fourth, managers could satisfy some demands of and gain benefits from local governments by locating manufacturing plants in their country. Some businesses received subsidies to locate in particular areas; others received protection from imports. In trying to respond to the demands of individual countries while preserving some economies of scale, Heavy Equipment and Chemicals A and B had adopted the strategy of building plants in one country and exporting from there to other countries in the region.

Fifth, managers could hedge against a number of location-specific risks by locating manufacturing facilities in several countries. Among these risks were local government instability and exchange rate fluctuations. Managers in Electronics A considered political stability when locating facilities in Asia. When the pound sterling appreciated relative to the US dollar, Chemicals A closed a UK plant and transferred production to the United States. Later, partially in response to the strong US dollar, Heavy Equipment increased production from a Latin American plant for export to the United States. All of these examples entail long-term adjustment of capacity to demand. None of the business units had moved production among countries in response to short-term exchange rate fluctuations, although managers in Chemicals B and Heavy Equipment were considering the possibility.

THE STRUCTURE OF GEOGRAPHICALLY DISPERSED MANUFACTURING

A business unit's manufacturing configuration is designed to capture specific benefits of internationally dispersed locations and it conditions the requirements and the opportunities for managing synergies among facilities.

Figure 18.1 illustrates the manufacturing configurations of the five business units. They have three to nine manufacturing plants (denoted by circles) and one to five warehouses (denoted by rectangles). The material flows are denoted by arrows. The circles are labelled with numbers to indicate the manufacturing process and products of the plant. Circles in one business unit labelled with the same number are plants that have similar products and more or less similar manufacturing

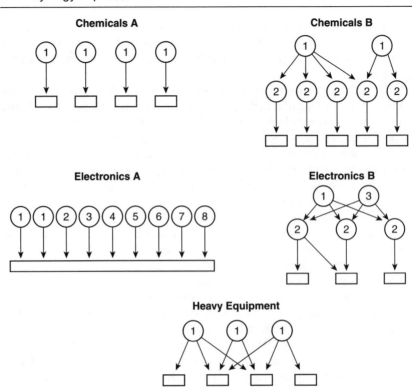

Note: Circles represent manufacturing plants; rectangles represent warehouses. The numbers in the circles indicate the kinds of manufacturing process and the products processed: if these are more or less similar in two plants in a business unit, then the plants are labelled with the same number; if not, then the plants are labelled with different numbers.

Figure 18.1 Actual material flow configurations

processes. Warehouses are included in these configurations to indicate the flows between manufacturing plants and customers.

Three general characteristics of manufacturing configurations in global business units are suggested by these examples. The first characteristic is that in each business unit several plants have manufacturing processes that are more or less similar. This feature gives rise to opportunities for managing interactions among manufacturing plants. For example, improvements made at one plant can be used by another, and a given product can be made at more than one plant.

The second characteristic is that the pattern of material flows in each business unit is simple relative to the theoretical possibilities. In measuring simplicity it is difficult to be mathematically precise while being faithful to the managerial issues. But in this case there are two partially acceptable measures, both of which indicate simplicity.

Table 18.3 Comparison of Actual with Possible Numbers of One-Way Material Flows between Plants in the Five Business Units

	Number of plants plus warehouses	Possible number of one-way material flows	Actual number of one-way material flows	Actual as a percentage of possible
Chemicals A	8	56	4	7
Chemicals B	12	132	15	11
Electronics A	10	90	9	10
Electronics B	8	56	11	20
Heavy equipment	7	42	8	19

The first indicates that there are few inter-plant shipments relative to the theoretical possibilities. There could, in theory, be two one-way material flows between any two facilities – plants as well as warehouses. The number of possible one-way flows of material and products among n facilities in one business unit is $n(n - 1)$. Electronics A, for instance, had nine manufacturing plants; theoretically it was possible for there to be 72 one-way material flows among them. Yet there were no material flows at all between the manufacturing plants in that business unit! Including Electronics A's single warehouse, 90 one-way materials flows were possible, but there were only nine. Similar calculations made for all the business units show that they used only 7 to 20 per cent of the possible one-way material flows (Table 18.3). The simplicity of the material flows in the configurations is also indicated by a second measure. At most two manufacturing plants processed any particular material or subassembly before it reached a warehouse.

The third characteristic is closely related to the second. As managers developed global manufacturing strategies, they simplified their manufacturing configurations in order to make them more manageable. Managers at Electronics A, for example, introduced modular product designs and eliminated one assembly plant, and Electronics B decreased the number of plants that processed any given shipment.

THE NATURE OF CO-ORDINATION

The managers of the business units I studied had, during two or more decades of international operations, benefited from many of the advantages of internationally dispersed manufacturing discussed previously. But they had also forfeited economies of scale in plant and equipment and encountered considerable difficulty in managing their many manufacturing facilities to achieve synergies. They had managed their manufacturing plants located in different countries fairly independently of each other and of related technology support activities.

But, during the 1970s and early 1980s the managers responded to business crises by beginning a number of projects to capture synergies among manufacturing facilities. The projects reduced many of the problems, and suggest that the potential benefits of managing internationally dispersed plants interdependently could be significant. These projects involved various forms of co-ordination among dispersed plants. In discussing these projects, I use the term *co-ordination* to mean the sharing and use, by different facilities, of information about manufacturing and technology support activities. Most of the co-ordination projects, regardless of which activity was involved, shared several management characteristics. Their goals were set in terms of performance of manufacturing support activities, as opposed to advice for later action. They typically were performed by employees who were also responsible for the support activity, with minimal involvement from corporate staff. They required significant and new ongoing communication links among internationally dispersed sites. They were designed to fit and take advantage of the special circumstances of the business unit. Some projects directly supported material flows among plants and warehouses, but many were not associated with inter-site material flow at all.

As managers gained more experience with co-ordination projects, they found that projects and their effects interacted. Some projects were necessary before others could be undertaken. Some groups of projects had effects that, when taken together, made the operation much more effective than the sum of direct effects of the individual projects. Several projects, begun individually, seemed in retrospect to fit together as a programme.

The co-ordination projects in these business units differed tremendously in their details, and the business units differed in the projects they undertook. But in all the business units, projects that focused on the same manufacturing or technology support activity fell into two or three well-defined categories. Within each such category the projects provided similar benefits and management challenges.

PROJECTS TO CO-ORDINATE MANUFACTURING SUPPORT ACTIVITIES

Managers in the five business units considered here found significant opportunities for co-ordination projects in three of the six manufacturing support activities listed in Table 18.2: procurement, production planning, and manufacturing engineering.

Procurement is the obtaining of material, subassemblies, components, and equipment needed for manufacturing from outside vendors. In Heavy Equipment and Electronics A and B, international co-ordination projects in procurement seemed to provide significant benefits to the business, while there were fewer significant co-ordination projects in the international procurement in Chemicals A and B.

Three categories of projects to co-ordinate procurement internationally appeared to lower cost and improve quality. First, procurement specialists at a plant in one country helped their counterparts at other, not necessarily similar, plants in other countries identify and negotiate with vendors in the first country. Electronics A and B and Heavy Equipment, for example, all saved up to 30 per cent of the local costs of the products (ranging from machined metal parts to printed materials) they purchased internationally, without sacrificing performance or conformance to specifications. Second, procurement specialists from similar plants in different countries brought the costs and reliability of their local vendors into line with those in other countries by quoting the contracts similar plants in the same business unit had made with vendors in other countries. This was especially effective if the similar plants had almost identical requirements and if the foreign vendors could supply all the plants. Indeed, one US vendor to Heavy Equipment that used such information in a broad-based programme improved methods and reduced manufacturing costs by one-third in one year. Third, in four of the five business units, procurement specialists at plants in Japan during the early 1980s arranged for a number of professionals from various plants in other countries to visit local vendors and learn about technical and management practice. During the early 1980s, this access to the managers of effective Japanese manufacturing operations was a major asset to the managers of US-based manufacturing who were seeking rapid and far-reaching improvements in their own manufacturing practice.

Several considerations restricted the use of such international procurement projects. Managers felt they could only source high-volume parts with stable designs internationally. It was difficult, time-consuming and not always feasible for distant, low-cost vendors to incorporate engineering or volume changes quickly. This appeared to be due in part to vendors being located so far from designers that rapid and broad-based communication relating to engineering specifications was difficult; in part to less extensive engineering support at remote vendors; in part to the vendors' production processes which, though labour-intensive, were best suited to long runs; and in part to the longer inventory pipeline required to source reliably at a distance. Furthermore, a local manufacturing plant appeared to be a major asset for a foreign plant in identifying and working effectively with local vendors. For example, Heavy Equipment and Electronics A and B all sourced from vendors located close to their international plants. Furthermore, Electronics B had found a corporate international purchasing group to be inadequate to facilitate local procurement on a continent where the business had no manufacturing plant. Even lead plants (responsible for engineering specifications of products for their own and several foreign plants) in the United States tended to focus on US vendors and to ignore foreign vendors. Managers' personal experience in foreign manufacturing management seemed to increase the likelihood that a plant would procure outside its immediate locale. Finally, plants that were not themselves 'in control', that is did not perform according to expectations on a daily basis, had difficulty using foreign vendors unless they built large buffering inventories.

While international co-ordination in procurement appeared promising for only three of the five business units, all five business units had begun international co-ordination projects related to aggregate production planning, as opposed to planning for shorter horizons. *Aggregate production planning* is the specification – usually monthly – of approximately what volume of which products will be manufactured at what date in the plant for the following period, usually a year.

The first type of international co-operation project arose in direct support of material flows between related plants in manufacturing configurations in which one plant or warehouse processed the material or components made by others, as was the case with Chemicals B and Electronics A and B. Until the early 1980s, these flows had been managed at arm's-length with large inventories serving to decouple the plants' production schedules. But during the early 1980s, these technology-intensive business units encountered more competition, smaller manufacturing margins, higher interest rates, rising material costs, more rapid product changes and pressure to reduce the inventory held between plants. This required closer co-ordination between the aggregate plans of the related plants, and it was managed differently by the business units. Electronics A began planning production of key products centrally at the business unit level with each plant receiving an order of precisely how much to deliver monthly; Chemicals B used a headquarters staff group in negotiation with plant planners to ensure that the monthly plans drawn up by the various plants were consistent; and Electronics B relied entirely on negotiations among independent plant schedulers who were under pressure to reduce inventories.

International sourcing from the business unit's own plants seemed to be limited by the same flexibility, cost, control and responsiveness issues that restricted international procurement from independent vendors. It was more difficult and slower to introduce design changes to products assembled in offshore plants than to products manufactured in the United States. This was in part because of difficulties in rapid, complete, long-distance communication; in part because these factories (like many outside vendors in those geographic areas) found product changeovers and engineering changes difficult; and in part because the business units maintained ten weeks or more of extra inventory between the US plants and related offshore plants. Unanticipated volume changes could also be difficult for remote plants to accommodate quickly, particularly if the plants were not 'in control'; extra inventory costs, shortages, and delays in response at least the length of the inventory pipeline could ensue. Furthermore, the attention of distant management could be difficult to claim. In Electronics B, for example, offshore plants serviced several onshore business units; thus, they were faced with conflicting service requirements, all of which were impossible to meet. In contrast, Chemicals B plants' requirements of intermediate materials had unchanging specifications. For that business unit, inter-plant conflicts related to volume adjustments, and those conflicts had been largely eliminated after the source (which had been a joint venture) became a wholly owned subsidiary with the same incentive and administrative systems as the plants to which it shipped.

The second type of international aggregate planning arose in planning production schedules for one plant to ship products to customers of similar plants in other countries. Managers in all five business units did this to a significant extent, and they argued that the capability to transship products from international plants to customers in other countries could be very valuable. They could, for example, guarantee a smoothly rising output rate to a new plant during its start-up years; they could shift orders among plants internationally to hedge exchange rate fluctuations; and they could meet peak requirements in one plant with capacity elsewhere and conserve capacity in the long term.

The requirement that products made by different plants be interchangeable to customers severely limited this sort of transshipment for Chemicals A and B and Heavy Equipment. Engineers at similar plants had, for example, improved the process, used local vendors, customized product options for their customers, and changed packaging without complete documentation. So plants that had been established to make interchangeable products could not do so after several years. Indeed, engineers at corporate headquarters at Heavy Equipment, where custom products were important, designed an information and telecommunications system that would allow complete documentation of all existing parts, products, and their material content, as well as accommodate new parts and products. In contrast, managers at Chemicals A noted that between plants in different countries some product and process differences had arisen that resulted in product attributes that were not essential to customers, but that customers had accommodated in their manufacturing processes. Chemicals A gradually substituted a new, improved product line for the old one; the new process would be controlled at all plants to ensure that most customers could use products from all plants. Introducing the new, uniform product line required different operating procedures for each plant because the plants used basic equipment that had been built at different times for different volumes and that had useful economic lives of over 30 years.

The problems of maintaining the interchangeability of products with the same specifications that were manufactured at different plants without prohibiting improvements was difficult for the chemicals and electronics business units. Chemicals A was working to control the process in each similar plant within a very narrow range, or 'window'; but this raised the prospect of stifling experiments that might lead to valuable innovations. Heavy Equipment controlled the process for making each part and product configuration within a very narrow window; but many product configurations could be designated by each plant, so each plant offered extended product variety. Projects to achieve the required similarity were undertaken by business unit-level engineering groups in all three business units.

I use the term 'manufacturing engineering' here to include all the engineering activities located in a plant. These activities provide support for the manufacturing process and improve it. The three types of international co-ordination projects focusing on manufacturing engineering related to incremental changes in the process or products. They were:

1 transferring technological improvements developed at one plant to other similar plants;
2 transferring manufacturing responsibility and capability for one product from one plant to another;
3 fixing problems that arise in one plant by changing the process at a related plant that processed the same product or material.

The opportunities for transferring technological improvements among similar plants located in different countries appear to be large. For example, Chemicals A found that for one product its European plant had improved costs by over 20 per cent; its manufacturing specialist responsible for the improvements was able during several trips to institute comparable cost savings in two other plants. Electronics A and Heavy Equipment found regular meetings among engineers and managers at similar but geographically dispersed plants useful in initiating transfers of improvements. One impediment to these transfers was area managers' reluctance to invest their resources for the benefit of another area; in Chemicals A this reluctance was overcome by pressure from top business unit managers who knew all the people involved from their own earlier work experience in Europe. Another major impediment to the transfers was the reluctance of manufacturing managers to admit that they could learn from other plants.

The second type of co-ordination project arose in the two electronics businesses: transferring products and processes from production facilities focused on new, low-volume products in the United States to similar plants focused on high-volume products in the Far East or other low-labour cost regions. Manufacturing engineers in US plants at Electronics A and B 'stabilized' the process (to the point where there were few engineering changes each month in the United States). If the product turned out to sell in high volume, processes that were more efficient for high-volume production were developed; the products were then transferred to similar plants in the Far East. Engineers in the 'lead plant' in the United States in one case in Electronics A developed a new assembly process that included some automation for a high-volume product and then moved with the process to the Far East for six months to ensure effective transfer. In contrast, Electronics B engineers from the Far East typically lived in the US lead plants for six months before accepting a new product responsibility. Both groups 'debugged' all equipment in the US lead plant, and both were satisfied with the effectiveness of their project.

The major limitations on the effectiveness of these transfers appeared to lie in the difficulty each offshore plant had in responding to the conflicting demands of several US plants or businesses and in the choice of products to be manufactured offshore. For example, one difficulty would occur when management of an offshore assembly plant needed to choose which of several products for different businesses to manufacture. Another would occur when the offshore facility was capacity-constrained and managers needed to choose between an old, high-volume product and a newer, potentially high-volume product whose price might be lowered and demand increased as a result of the transfer. The management of the shared offshore assembly plant by several plants and/or businesses inevitably was fraught with conflict and the possibility that suboptimal decisions would be made.

The third type of international co-ordination project in engineering was fixing technical problems that arose in one factory by making changes in another factory. Electronics B, for example, encountered this possibility as it introduced new products to production in the United States. In Electronics A similar possibilities arose in designing new products. In both businesses the main impediment to co-operation across plants was a formal management evaluation system in which the plant managers were judged independently as cost or profit centres. In both businesses top managers overcame the problem temporarily – but not permanently – by suspending the formal evaluation and incentive systems. I conjecture that these issues would arise more frequently in businesses with frequent new product introductions and in plants related by systems technology than in other businesses.

PROJECTS TO CO-ORDINATE TECHNOLOGY SUPPORT ACTIVITIES WITH MANUFACTURING

Technology support activities located outside manufacturing contribute to the development of a business unit's future products and its future manufacturing capabilities. To be effective they require some co-ordination with manufacturing. Managers in the business units I studied were working to enhance the performance of their ongoing co-ordination projects in product and process design and improvement.

Many of these projects addressed the same issues addressed by single-site or single-nation manufacturing business units. For example, Chemicals A and Electronics B had discovered that some process technologies, which were being developed by competitors, had been ignored by their own technology support groups; they had no mechanisms to review systematically and regularly current process technologies for possible opportunities. Both established formal processes to review process technology opportunities at the business unit level. Another issue, which was not confined to business units doing international manufacturing, was increasing the speed and improving the quality of the new product design-to-market process. Electronics A and B and Heavy Equipment were all addressing this issue by introducing manufacturing considerations into the design process earlier and by extending the responsibility of design into manufacturing. Like many other business units, in their first efforts they saw decreases in design-to-market periods from, for example, seven years to three, and improvements in their new products that were better designed for manufacturability than earlier products. Like many single-nation business units, they found sophisticated telecommunications systems to be a major asset in introducing new products.

Each business unit I studied, however, was also beginning co-ordination projects between technology support activities and manufacturing that were aimed at several related issues not encountered by single-site or single-nation business units in anything like the same form. These managers had decided that they would maintain multiple similar plants making the same products rather than consolidate their manufacturing operations into one 'world plant'. They continually confronted the problem of 'how similar' to make and maintain the plants, products, and processes.

I previously defined similar plants loosely as those that manufactured the same products with more or less the same technology. Here it is worthwhile to be more specific. 'Similar' covers a broad range. At one extreme similar plants in a business unit produce overlapping parts of the same product line with different processes for different business missions. For example, among three plants of Electronics B, one was focused on low cost, another on establishing a foreign market presence, and the third on new product introductions and technical leadership of the similar plants. In Heavy Equipment and Chemicals A and B, similar plants focused both on serving their geographic areas with some products based on the same designs and processes but somewhat customized for each area, and on some products that served the world and were identical throughout. In all the business units similar plants produced products that had the same specifications, but the plants used processes that differed by virtue of having, for instance, different vintages, different de-bottlenecking and improvement efforts by local engineering, and different vendors.

Increasing similarity seemed to make a larger degree of co-ordination possible. For example, similar plants in Heavy Equipment that had different volume and parts requirements could work together to identify vendors internationally, but only when they had virtually identical vendor requirements could they use their contracts to help make vendors in the United States more competitive with those located in other regions. Chemical products that were more alike could be used by a wider group of customers, in this case increasing similarity of products increased the potential extent and benefits of plants' shipping to the customers of other similar plants. In Chemicals A, the more similar plants' processes were, the more process improvements discovered at one plant could be easily transferred to others.

The degree of similarity in product and process among a business's internationally dispersed plants also seemed to condition the extent and types of manufacturing co-ordination and technical support that were possible. In Heavy Equipment the similarity required to make international procurement projects worthwhile was considerably less than that required to make it possible for several plants to ship interchangeable products to customers. Similarly, transferring the technological improvements among plants required more similarity of process and product in Heavy Equipment and Electronics A than the procurement projects, and in Chemicals A and Heavy Equipment shipping interchangeable products required still more similarity than many process transfers.

It also seems that business units based on different technologies and in different markets would require and benefit from different amounts of similarity of product and process. The Electronics business units, for example, shipped interchangeable products world-wide with apparently little concern for controlling for more similar processes. But Heavy Equipment required close control of specifications for parts and product options to do that, and the Chemicals business units required close process control. For these three business units, the technology support problem of how similar to make the processes and products among plants was particularly difficult.

The new product and process design and introduction processes also appeared to be easier if the plants had similar products and processes, and if new products used parts and processes in common with existing ones. For example, in the Chemicals business units introducing a new product that would be made using each plant's existing equipment required that central engineering define different operating procedures for each plant; and the more divergent the process equipment the more involved the process of defining new operating procedures. Likewise in Electronics A if a new product used many of the same parts as existing products, then introducing it to manufacturing required less purchasing effort than if it used few common parts. Furthermore, if several plants manufactured the same products using common parts, then a new product required only one design and much less incremental purchasing, inventory, management, training and equipment design. Common processes and parts also meant less confusion during manufacturing for any given product mix. It meant less changeover time between different products, less inventory, less new equipment, and better reactions to volume and mix changes.

Similar processes also meant that it was easier to communicate about new processes. This was particularly noticeable for business units using advanced communications systems. In Heavy Equipment, for example, employees in the European plant routinely at the end of their workday on Monday submitted a technical question via computer mail to their US counterparts, had the US employees process it during their workday, and received an answer at the beginning of the European workday on Tuesday. The managers attributed the speed of answer to both the communications system and the common technical contexts of the two plants.

There are, of course, potential disadvantages to close similarity in processes and products across plants. The first is the possibility that commonality would lead to excessive product homogeneity for customers. For Chemicals A and B, some product homogeneity across similar plants was acceptable to customers, and that was the business unit's goal. For Electronics A, products used in different countries had to accommodate different power supplies and had to have lengthy documentation in the local language. Modularizing manufacturing maximized the parts of the product that did not require customization and made clean interfaces with the parts of the products that did not achieve high process commonality while preserving the required heterogeneity for the customer. Heavy Equipment's customers required significant customization, on each order. There central engineering designed an information and communication system that required all similar plants to document their project, part, and material specifications for all to access so that any plant with a specification usable at one plant could make a product acceptable to the customer. In this case the information system – at a cost – gave the similar plants broad and identical potential product sets; but similar plants rarely manufactured the same products. These approaches suggest that some technologies allow plants to have process commonality with considerable product variety.

A second potential disadvantage to closely similar plants would be important if the control required to maintain close similarity would stifle innovation in plants. Individual plant improvements in process and product had been significant in all the business units. For example, Chemicals A's plant in Europe had co-operated with the local applications engineering group and with local customers to refine their process, enhance product properties, and lower costs considerably relative to other plants in the business unit making the same product. In some regimes under consideration with common processes and control at all plants, the experiments that were formerly done quickly and informally would require the permission of central engineering; the bureaucracy and the difficulty of formally conducting the valuable experiments would be much greater. Managers in Heavy Equipment were also concerned that their comparatively much more permissive cross-plant process control through their information system would hinder local engineers in providing customers with custom designs.

Managers in all the business units encountered problems in implementing their plans for making processes and products more similar. The first was generally in getting central engineers' attention and effort. As in initiating co-ordination activities in manufacturing, crises and comparisons among plants were useful in this. Another problem was that the required engineering effort itself was large in business units like Chemicals A where many products and much capital equipment in several plants were redesigned. (The manufacturers also appointed a manufacturing manager at one plant to keep track of process performance monthly at all plants.) A third problem was particularly evident in the Electronics business units where engineering and manufacturing managers would have liked to co-ordinate across facility boundaries, but the formal incentive and evaluation systems discouraged them; in both cases the managers involved suspended the formal system and evaluated their subordinates with much more close attention and with, at least temporary, good effect. Electronics A managers, for example, mandated a change in engineering requirements and measurement of the number of new parts in a product; on the first new product, designers drastically reduced the number of new parts per product. A major difficulty in increasing the commonality of parts and processes is giving designers quick and easy access to parts and processes already in use. Group technology and computer aids to design were helpful in doing that for Electronics A and for Heavy Equipment. Finally, with the major technology support organizations for all five business units located in the United States, non-US plants in several business units had different access to technology support than US plants. This appears to have been an advantage for one plant, which as a consequence worked more closely with its local applications engineering group and made major process and product improvements. For the Electronics business units this, coupled with relatively low engineering support at low-cost/high-volume assembly plants, may have been responsible for the stop in cost-reductions related to 'learning' when products were transferred from US plants to those in the Far East.

MANAGING CO-ORDINATION IN INTERNATIONAL MANUFACTURING

In all five business units individual co-ordination projects were undertaken in anticipation of their direct benefits. However, by 1984, managers in each business unit had also realized major indirect benefits of many of the successful projects. Indeed, in retrospect, in each business unit several projects seemed to form a coherent history as a programme. The following brief histories describe several such interrelating projects in each of the three business units.

- Between 1975 and 1982 central engineering in Heavy Equipment developed a common product classification system in which each product design and customizing change could be specified. Second, a different staff group independently developed a computer communications system to link all plants in one network. During the early 1980s, as both of these developments were put in use, a control system administered by central engineering was implemented. It required that plants could only institute a change in or an addition to the common product definition with central approval and that all changes would be instituted at all plants on the same day. For the first time this ensured that products made at one plant were, from customers' standpoints, interchangeable with those made at other plants and that customers' spare parts could be defined accurately. The computer communication system that linked all the plants allowed engineering changes to be processed rapidly enough to ensure that customer service was not sacrificed and that plants could proceed quickly without awkward delays in their designs of new product options.
- After this, Heavy Equipment introduced a monthly central aggregate planning function for the European, US, and Latin American plants. In this context, managers considered shifting production among the plants in response to different patterns of capacity requirements, plant development, and even such other phenomenon as exchange rate

fluctuations. Further, introducing a new product to manufacturing in Europe proceeded much more smoothly and quickly in 1984 than it ever had before.

- In 1980 Chemicals A acquired a plant with a process related to processes the business unit had already established at other plants. Subsequently central engineering improved that process and made the acquired plant much more productive than it had been before. Central engineering then took some ideas from the acquired plant's process and introduced them to a US plant. Managers at the US plant were assisted in their efforts by the employees at the acquired plant. In the United States product attributes improved so much that demand increased substantially. This, in turn, justified developing a new, improved product line for all the plants world-wide.

- In 1983 a manager at a US plant in Electronics A – who had previously worked at the Far Eastern plant – suggested that purchasing experts at the Far Eastern plant help identify local vendors. After the vendors were identified and contracts placed, the US plant had saved 30 per cent on the delivered costs of those internationally sourced items. Those particular items were also used – and consequently sourced from the Far East – by the business's European plant, whose engineering for that product was done by the US plant. After that, the European plant began to use Far Eastern sources for products it had developed itself.

Clearly, in all three cases individual projects, which had been undertaken in anticipation of their direct benefits, turned out to have major additional and unanticipated benefits through interactions with other projects. The independent projects in Heavy Equipment, for example, turned out to allow central management to shift production orders among plants internationally at the notice of the aggregate plan rather than at the timing of strategy changes. In Chemicals A central engineering had improved the process at the acquired plant with no expectation of also improving the US plant's process and ultimately developing a successful world product. In Electronics A the manager who began the Far Eastern plant did not expect to aid the business unit's international sourcing programme so much. What began as isolated projects turned out to be the beginnings of longer-term programmes to co-ordinate international manufacturing.

Certainly a limited a preliminary study such as this can make no pretence to presenting solidly grounded recommendations to managers of co-ordination projects. The applicability of my observations and their refinement are clearly areas for future research. But they do suggest several considerations for managing the co-ordination of international manufacturing. I explore those implications here.

The fact that in these instances groups of projects appear to be *inter-related* seems to have several implications for managing such co-ordination projects. It suggests that such groups of related projects should be managed centrally as programmes. Evaluation of some projects that are not justifiable on the basis of their direct benefits – for example, projects to use common parts in design or to establish a telecommunications network for the business unit – should take into account their indirect effects in, among other areas, making new product introductions easier. Also, top management should overcome the inevitable organizational impediments.

In addition, in these instances some projects were more effective if certain other projects had prepared for them. Managers of such co-ordination projects should note that some projects should *naturally precede* others. Similarity of plants' processes and products, in particular, appeared to be a natural precedent to many types of co-ordination projects. Similarity, as discussed previously, seemed to make more co-ordination possible in terms of both co-ordination focused on different support activities and higher degrees of co-ordination focused on one activity. For example, plants needed the capability to make interchangeable products before they could ship to each others' customers. Like similarity, business unit-specific international communication systems seemed to facilitate many other co-ordination projects. In evaluating projects that 'naturally precede' others, managers should take into account the indirect benefits that result from the co-ordination projects for which they prepare.

Furthermore, many of these co-ordination projects seemed to have *major unanticipated consequences* that themselves led to later projects and benefits. This property, in contrast to the first two, seems to imply that such projects should be managed in a decentralized, *ad hoc* manner. This would allow those lower-level employees, who are located in internationally dispersed manufacturing and technology support facilities and who are most likely to recognize new opportunities, to act on them without extensive bureaucratic justification.

Finally, it appears that in these business units technology support projects were critical to obtaining the benefits of co-ordination. This was because the usual activities of technology support in designing and improving products and processes determined – within some limits determined by customers – the similarity and relatedness of products and processes among internationally dispersed plants. In turn the degree of product and process similarity among plants determined many of the opportunities for co-ordinating international manufacturing. Finally, in technology-intensive business units technology support and the effects of co-ordination on the speed and effectiveness of new product and process introduction and improvements can be critical to competitive success.

These observations suggest at least a two-pronged approach to managing the co-ordination of international manufacturing. Such an approach would assign responsibility for proposing and carrying out most co-ordination projects to independent, geographically dispersed manufacturing and technology support employees. It would also assign responsibility to top business unit managers for initiating the programme, assuring that it has direction and scope appropriate to the manufacturing strategy and configuration of the business unit, and provide some aid in overcoming organizational impediments to co-ordination. A regular review of co-ordination projects would allow top business unit managers to capture the benefits of unanticipated opportunities identified by support employees, enabling them to take advantage of important interrelations among projects. Few additional staff employees should be required.

In this scheme lower-level manufacturing and technology support employees would propose, design, and execute co-ordination projects. They would need authority and resources to execute co-ordination projects involving several sites. These are the employees most likely to identify new, unanticipated follow-on co-ordination projects because they know their own projects, problems and resources best. If they were also aware of what improvements similar plants were making, what co-ordination programmes were being undertaken, and what resources other plants had, they could identify new opportunities even better.

Top business unit managers could facilitate such lower-level activities by, for example, increasing employee familiarity with projects and their counterparts at other sites, improving inter-facility communication facilities, and increasing the similarity of the products and processes among plants. For the first purpose several managers of these business units had instituted regular meetings (typically three or four times a year) among manufacturing support employees at similar plants. At the meetings support employees discussed their recent inter-and intra-plant projects and proposals; follow-up visits among manufacturing sites were usual if opportunities were identified. While meetings improved awareness, sophisticated communication systems seemed to help geographically dispersed employees to keep in touch throughout the year and carry out the co-ordination projects themselves. Finally (as discussed previously), to the extent that plants had similar projects and processes, support employees would find more opportunities for co-ordination projects among them.

Business unit or company managers themselves would be facilitators, protectors, and reviewers. They identified the crises that spurred the

co-ordination projects, suspended formal incentive and evaluation systems when they contradicted the requirements of co-ordination, and
overcame the impediments of top area managers. They also reviewed
the progress of projects whose size might not ordinarily have brought
them to the attention of the top management.

The regular reviews should serve to address difficult and broad issues
like establishing a degree of familiarity among plants, improving the
inter-plant communications system, considering the previous relations
between projects, identifying large organizational impediments to co-
ordination, or providing adequate technical support to manufacturing or
manufacturing co-ordination. They should also be receptive forums to
review and communicate unanticipated opportunities for co-ordination
projects.

CONCLUSION

The managers of the five business units I studied each co-ordinated
manufacturing and technology support activities to increase the effectiveness of their internationally dispersed operations. The particular
support activities they co-ordinated and the extent of the co-ordination,
as well as the benefits they derived from them, varied considerably from
business unit to business unit. They ranged from sharing information
about vendors located world-wide, to controlling production processes
so that products with the same specifications would be interchangeable
in customers' applications to improving the processes for manufacturing
products by incorporating improvements made in several locations.

These observations suggest that companies derive greater value from
co-ordinating manufacturing and technology support activities at different sites if the operations located at different sites are more similar. This
follows first, because opportunities for co-ordinating support activities
between two sites increase as the processes at the sites become more
similar and second, because it is easier and cheaper to co-ordinate
operations which have more in common. For example, two operations
with very different products and processes could share vendors. But
operations with processes which are tightly controlled so they are identical could manufacture products which would be interchangeable in
users' applications, and share vendors. In particular, projects to make
geographically dispersed operations more similar appear to have been
prerequisites to some of the most valuable projects co-ordinating manufacturing and technology support activities.

Increasing the similarity of geographically dispersed operations was
expensive and difficult, however, because each operation was unique
because of its history and customers. Furthermore, the constituency
served by each on-going operation had to be served continually by the

business while the co-ordination in manufacturing and technology support was underway. Neither the ultimate expense nor the extent of such projects were known with certainty to the managers at the start. Consequently, even though some co-ordination projects proved surprisingly valuable, managers in most of these business units chose to eschew many types of co-ordination projects because the costs were perceived to outweigh the benefits.

Managers of the more extensive and successful co-ordination programmes generally began with a group of apparently unrelated projects, each of which could improve the manufacturing or technology support activities located at at least one site. One of the basic projects typically addressed the similarity of several geographically dispersed operations. Over time, the managers found that some projects were in fact interrelated and provided extra benefits. They found that other projects needed to be abandoned or redirected. In general, it appears that the most successful approach to taking advantage of co-ordination possibilities is to set out in the general direction of co-ordination with a number of parallel projects in manufacturing and technology support, monitor them closely, and be willing to make mid-course corrections.

REFERENCES

1 There are a few notable exceptions that deal mostly with the frequency of cross-shipments rather than with the management of interactions among manufacturing plants located in different regions. Pomper, C., *International Investment Planning: Integrated Approach*, New York: North Holland, 1976 presents a plan for a United States based chemical company's plant world-wide in which plants in Latin America regularly ship products to customers in Europe near another plant. Curhan, J., Davidson, W. H. and Suri, R., *Tracing the Multinationals*, Cambridge, Mass.: Ballinger, 1977, p. 397, present tabulations of data on multinationals that reveal that in 1975 less than one-fifth of all the subsidiaries in their sample cross-shipped more than 10 per cent of subsidiary sales. In 'Influence in the Multinational Enterprise: The Case of Manufacturing' in Stobaugh, R. and Wells, Jr., L. T., *Technology Crossing Borders* Boston: Harvard Business School Press, 1984, p. 265–92, H. de Bodinat presents evidence that fewer than one-quarter of the 33 multinationals he studied had cross-shipments greater than 10 per cent of subsidiary sales. He also addresses the question of how these flows would be managed by investigating the influence of headquarters in managing the flows. His investigations relate to the level of influence of the headquarters rather than the problem addressed here. Scherer, F. M. *et al.*, in *The Economics of Multi-Plant Operation*, Cambridge, Mass.: Harvard University Press, 1975, pp. 397–8 conclude that there is little ongoing administrative co-ordination among the many multisite manufacturing operations he studied, but they expect such co-ordination to increase.
2 A. Chandler, in a private communication in April 1984, supplied these early examples of co-ordinating international manufacturing operations. But he agreed that such co-ordination was rare until the 1970s. Duerr, M. G. and

Roach, J. M. *Organization and Control of International Operations*, New York: The Conference Board, 1973 also support this observation.

3 For the period until 1962 see Gruber, W., Mehta, D., and Vernon, R., 'The R&D Factor in International Trade and Investment of United States Industries', *Journal of Political Economy* 75 (1967). For later periods see Flaherty, M. T., Ghoshal, S., and Stobaugh, R., 'Comparative Advantage versus Global Competition', manuscript, 1984. Of course, inflation during that period would tend to overstate the growth rate, and exchange rate fluctuations would distort it. But the general conclusion that foreign direct investment by US manufacturers grew significantly seems warranted.

4 See Flaherty, M. T., 'Market Share, Technology Leadership, and Competition in International Semiconductor Markets', in Rosenbloom, R. S. (ed.), *Research on Technological Innovation, Management and Policy* Volume 1, Greenwich, Conn.: JAI Press, 1983 for evidence on this point from the semiconductor industry.

5 In 'Manufacturing – Missing Link in Corporate Strategy', *Harvard Business Review*, May–June 1969, W. Skinner's early enunciation of manufacturing strategy differs from this one largely in that (1) it mentions management systems, but does not emphasize policies for manufacturing support; and (2) it classifies technology support activities as part of the business's resources, rather than as part of manufacturing strategy.

6 Hayes, R. H. and Wheelright, S. C., *Restoring the Competitive Edge*, New York: Wiley, 1984.

7 Caves, R. E., *Multinational Enterprise and Economic Analysis*, New York: Cambridge University Press, 1982 provides a thorough statement of this argument and a survey of the relevant economics and business literature.

8 Vernon, R., *Sovereignty at Bay*, New York: Basic Books, 1971 p. 75, discusses the motives of manufacturing companies to establish foreign manufacturing subsidiaries in these terms. Stobaugh, R., *Nine Investments Abroad and Their Impact at Home*, Boston: Division of Research Harvard Business School, 1976, chap. 8, pp. 187–91 reaches a similar conclusion about the companies he studied. Knickerbocker, F. T., *Oligopolistic Reaction and Multinational Enterprise*, Boston: Division of Research, Harvard Business School, 1973 reaches a similar conclusion in studying a number of foreign investments in a given industry. Moxon, R. W., 'Off-shore Production in the Less Developed Countries – A Case Study of Multinationality in the Electronics Industry', *The Bulletin* (1974) pp. 98–9, provides positive statistical evidence on this point.

9 Stobaugh, R., 'Creating a Monopoly: Product Innovation in Petrochemicals', in Rosenbloom, R. S. (ed.), *Research on Technological Innovation, Management and Policy*, Volume 2, 1985 presents evidence that for petrochemical businesses, manufacturing in large markets fosters close contact with customers and facilitates innovation.

10 This is a well-researched phenomenon. Moxon, 'Offshore Production', presents evidence that in the electronics industry going offshore for low-cost labour was necessary for many companies to meet competition.

11 Stobaugh, R., 'Where in the World Should We put That Plant?', *Harvard Business Review*, January–February, 1969 presents evidence that petrochemical products whose transportation costs relative to product value were higher were manufactured outside the United States earlier than those with lower relative transportation costs. Scherer *et al.*, *Economics of Multi-Plant Operation*, also presents empirical evidence on the importance of relative transport costs for the location of production.

12 Skinner, W., 'The Focused Factory', *Harvard Business Review*, May–June 1974, identifies many of the problems a manufacturing plant would be likely to encounter if it served several businesses that had different requirements.

ACKNOWLEDGEMENTS

I am indebted to managers in five US-based manufacturing companies who generously shared with me many of their concerns and innovations in managing their international manufacturing operations. I am also indebted to Michael Porter for his support through the colloquium and his comments which helped me to focus my research. Robert Stobaugh's comment helped to clarify my thought as well as my expression. Also very helpful were comments on drafts of this chapter by Robert Hayes, Richard Rosenbloom, Steven Wheelright, and Earl Sasser. Finally, I am indebted to the Division of Research of the Harvard Business School for financial support of this research. Of course, the responsibility for remaining errors, omissions, and misstatements is mine.

Index